W[...]
S‌HE T[...]

WHO DOES SHE THINK SHE IS?

My Autobiography

Martine McCutcheon

with

Matthew Wright

ARROW

First published in the United Kingdom in 2000 by Century

Arrow Books Limited
The Random House Group Limited
20 Vauxhall Bridge Road, London SW1V 2SA

Random House Australia (Pty) Limited
20 Alfred Street, Milsons Point, Sydney
New South Wales 2061, Australia

Random House New Zealand Limited
18 Poland Road, Glenfield
Auckland 10, New Zealand

Random House South Africa (Pty) Limited
Endulini, 5A Jubilee Road
Parktown 2193, South Africa

The Random House Group Limited Reg. No. 954009

www.randomhouse.co.uk

A CIP catalogue record for this book
is available from the British Library

MIX
Paper from
responsible sources
FSC® C018072

Typeset in Garamond by MATS, Southend-on-Sea, Essex

Printed and bound in Great Britain by Clays Ltd, St Ives PLC

ISBN 0 09 941598 4

The Random House Group Limited supports The Forest Stewardship
Council (FSC®), the leading international forest certification organisation.
Our books carrying the FSC label are printed on FSC® certified paper.
FSC is the only forest certification scheme endorsed by the leading
environmental organisations, including Greenpeace. Our
paper procurement policy can be found at
www.randomhouse.co.uk/environment

ACKNOWLEDGEMENTS

First of all I would like to thank my fans. At all times you have been very loyal, and very kind. Thanks for all your support and helping make many of my dreams a reality. To all at the BBC, thanks for giving me a wonderful opportunity to play such a wonderful character. The end of her gave me a new beginning – one I have always dreamed of. To all at Virgin, thank you for taking my music seriously and showing everyone that, as a team, we could do it. My lawyers, Schilling & Lom, thank you for all the advice. A big thanks to all at Random House, and to Matthew Wright. To all my close friends, especially Alex, William, Anthony and Dee, I love you all madly. Thank you for loving me and putting me first – who needs hangers on when I have you. To my Nanny Hemmings, Auntie Sandra and Yasmin, I don't see you as often as I'd like to, but always know I am here for you and love you. To my Auntie Kim and Carrine, thank you for your unconditional love. To my Jonathan, I love you like no-one before. Thank you for always thinking I'm the best girl in the world. You have given me a new-found confidence, I love you so much.

To my little brother LJ, and Alan, the most reliable men around – I love you. To my Mum, everyone knows I love you so much and now they will see why. To everyone else in the book, thanks for the good times and/or the bad, it all just makes me stronger. I thank you all . . . Martine.

CHAPTER 1

A Star Is Born

MY MUM ALWAYS said I was special. I know all mums say that but my Mum, Jenny, insists something happened on Friday 14 May 1976, the day I was born, that really made her believe it.

She was in the dingy delivery room at the Salvation Army Mothers' Hospital in Clapton, in the heart of the East End of London. She'd been in labour for 36 hours and she'd just about had enough. It was a hot spring that year with the warm mornings building up to scorching days. From what I'm told about the day that I made my first big entrance, it was particularly claustrophobic and muggy in the delivery room. Outside the sky became quite overcast. In fact, as Mum recalls, it was dark as dusk. And so, after days of driving her round the bend by refusing to come out of her womb – I had been due on 22 April – I finally ventured into the world, a scrap weighing seven pounds, three and a quarter ounces. At the very moment the midwife prepared to cut my umbilical cord, the sun

I

suddenly broke through the humid cloud outside and beamed right on me. Mum says the room was completely dark except for this ray of light. She still sees it as a special sign.

Cradling me in her arms as she was taken back to a ward, Mum began to wonder what she would call me. She'd had lots of boys' names in mind because she'd been sure she was going to have a boy. She'd been reading a book of names and their derivations. It said that the planet Mars ruled at this particular time of the month, so she'd thought she might call her baby son Martin.

But I turned out to be a girl, and so Mum thought of Martine instead. It was a very unusual name back then and, thinking about it, it is still not common now. There really aren't that many of us around. Mum chose Kimberley as a second name, after her sister, and Sherrie as a third, after her close friend Sherrie Jeffrey. So I was named Martine Kimberley Sherrie.

Now I'm not blowing my own trumpet but my birth was just about the best thing that happened to my Mum that year. In fact, for Jenny Ponting – that's Ponting not Pontin, like the holiday-camp people, thank you very much – it's hard to imagine how times could have been worse.

Mum was born on 15 March 1956 at the City of London Hospital. That's within the sound of the Bow Bells, which makes her a true Cockney. Her mother was a housewife and her father a bakery worker. Well, he *had* been at the time of her birth, but throughout her childhood he went from job to job with long periods of unemployment in between. Mum says she knows that her mother's parents were really disappointed by her own mother's choice of husband.

Anyway, within a year of marriage, my Gran gave birth to a son, my Uncle Laurence, and later, to my Mum. Two more children followed soon after, my Aunts Kim and Carol, and then another, my Uncle Chrissy.

The way Mum remembers it, her father wasn't the most pleasant of characters and her childhood was far from idyllic. Mum thinks that her parents took on far more than they could cope with both financially and emotionally. I know it sounds hard, but my Mum was actually quite pleased when her father died a couple of years ago. He'd never really worked and had at times behaved like a tyrant towards Gran who was a slight, Irish-looking woman. He'd shown no inclination to help bring their five children up as a proper family. They'd get whacked for this and whacked for that, more often than not with a leather strap, and would sometimes go to bed hungry. They would often have to go to school with no socks or decent clothes at a time when kids were ridiculed for such things. Anyway, my Mum's upbringing made her determined to give me the very best chances in life. She felt she had missed out with her own childhood and she would never let that happen to me.

Mum had happier times, though, when she, Laurence and Kim went to stay with their great-aunt, Margaret. Auntie Margaret had raised my Gran after her mother had died in childbirth. She didn't have much money, but she lavished her young charges with love and kindness, and she taught them some of the fundamentals of life, such as how to brush their teeth, knowing right from wrong, having self-respect and having no shame about where they hailed from. She lived in a pre-World War Two flat in Highbury, north London, which seemed old to my Mum at the time. It had only one bedroom, which the three kids and Margaret shared, but

Mum says it was blissful, and she never liked going back to stay at her Mum and Dad's after those visits.

Mum left home at sixteen and rented a flat in Islington – behind Camden Passage where there's a yuppie antiques market today – with a friend, Sylvia Wales. The pair of them had – excuse the pun – a whale of a time and Mum, who was enjoying work at the Alfred Marks employment agency, was earning good money too. She became engaged to twenty-six-year-old John Faulkner, whom she'd met when she was fifteen. He was her first love and Mum says he was a wonderful man. He wanted to marry her and look after her, but she was so young when he asked and there were many things she wanted to do with her life. Settling down was not yet one of them. She needed to spread her wings after years of living with her family, having to look after her younger brother and sister. So she and John split up and she went off to work as a waitress at Butlin's in Minehead. Later she had second thoughts about breaking up with John and came back to London, but he'd moved on.

My Mum had first met my father, Thomas Hemmings, when she was thirteen. He was a flash so-and-so and a bit of a Jack the Lad, but she wasn't interested, which only made him keener. He had dark hair and eyes, just like a male version of me. They didn't meet again until 1973, when Mum was seventeen.

She had gone out one afternoon with her sister Kim, who'd just had a baby, and they were having a coffee in a bookshop-cum-snack-bar. In those days, as now, Mum was a feisty sort. She was very determined at times, yet full of contradictions like most women, masking a very soft and sensitive side to her nature with a façade of bravado.

Physically, she was very popular with men, despite wearing those awful seventies outfits featuring tank tops and crushed-velvet flares. She always had painted nails and glossy red lips when she went out in the evening, and had a fabulously curvy figure. Blue-eyed, big-bosomed and long-legged she was a real looker, and these days often blames me and my younger half-brother Laurence, or LJ, for ruining her figure. 'Have kids,' she jokes, 'and everything in your body moves south.'

Thomas wandered over and perhaps did recognise Jenny from when she was much younger. Anyway, he made his approach using that corniest of chat-up lines: 'Don't I know you from somewhere?' But it worked: they chatted, he asked her out and they went off to the Dragon Arms, a pub nearby for their first proper date.

He was about five foot eleven, handsome and two years older than Mum – and she was smitten by him. She was vulnerable, I suppose, because she was still on the rebound from John; and Thomas, or Keith, as he was known then, was considered to be quite a catch – as she quickly realised. He never went far without a woman chasing after him. Anyway, she really fell for him . . .

The relationship progressed steadily until, a few months later, the seemingly happy couple moved into a bedsit in Muswell Hill. Jenny was still working for Alfred Marks, where her job involved interviewing candidates who were looking for clerical and secretarial jobs, and she was very good at it by all accounts. It wasn't long before she was promoted to their branch at the Strand, where she was made an assistant manager. She always got on well with her boss, Sue Nelson.

Of course, as at the start of any new relationship, things looked rosy and when they had first begun stepping out Mum seemed to be everything Keith had ever wanted.

Outwardly, Keith appeared smart and streetwise. He loved his music and introduced Mum to the world of the West Indian Hackney scene. They listened to records by the Average White Band, John Holt and Bob Marley. Keith seemed to offer Mum independence as well as security. Their sexual relationship was wonderful, and through Keith she met a wide new circle of friends. They were regulars at Hackney's flourishing illegal party scene. Gatherings known as boogie parties were held at private addresses and run by West Indians. Musicians would turn up and play, while people smoked pot and brought beers. Most guests would have to pay an admission charge, but, when Jenny was with Keith, they always got in for nothing.

In those heady, early days of their romance, the pair were smitten with each other, but Keith's passion soon showed itself in a more ugly form. His love rapidly became an obsession. Mum reckons he was the most insanely jealous man she's ever met. If they went to a pub, Mum soon learned to keep her eyes glued to the floor in case Keith should think she was scouting the bar for other men. If he suspected she was looking at someone, he would simply grab her, whip her out of her chair and drag her home. So much for the independence he'd seemed to encourage in their earlier days . . . Mum was too terrified to say a word. A slap in those days put women in their place, but it wasn't just these increasingly frequent episodes of domestic violence that worried Mum: it was also the incessant jealous interrogations.

Keith needed constant reassurance that Jenny was 'his girl' and was not looking for anyone else. He had to know where she was at all times and would forever check on her. A friend innocently saying, 'I saw your woman Jenny a little while ago,' would send Keith completely spare. As a result, Mum felt she couldn't go anywhere without the fear that somebody would spot her. She had nothing to hide. It wasn't as if she was off out with another man – but that wasn't what Keith thought. Neither logic nor reason ever got through to that twisted mind of his. By now my Mum was often confiding to Sue at work about her wretched home life.

It was in the autumn of 1975 that Mum discovered she was pregnant with me. She still maintains my father was excited at first when she told him, but she thinks that, when the news sank in, his feelings changed. He was almost jealous of the fact that somebody else was going to come into their lives. Even before I was born it seemed he had begrudged the thought that Jenny would have a child to care for, someone else to think about. She says he changed completely as the nine months rolled by until he did not seem interested in the baby. She believed that it was when Keith realised he would have more responsibilities – that it would be a struggle and he'd have to get a proper job – that he went off the idea of having a baby. Her whole pregnancy was like being on a roller-coaster ride. One minute Keith would be supportive and the next he'd be in a terrible mood. He began to drink heavily and smoke more dope.

Dad's mood swings became so extreme, even during the early stages of the pregnancy, that Jenny began to wonder if they could cope with a baby and she even thought about having a termination. This is something that isn't easy for her to admit even now, but she's told me she'd be a liar if she said the thought hadn't crossed her mind. She was young, she still had the rest of her life ahead of her and she thought perhaps having a baby just then wasn't the right thing to do. She even went to see a pregnancy advisory counsellor. But even though she was in a very emotional state and her life was in turmoil, she just thought it wasn't right. She put the idea straight out of her head and I'll always respect her for that – and remain grateful, obviously.

Five months into the pregnancy, Mum decided to leave Keith. She packed up as much of her stuff as she could carry and moved out of the bedsit she'd shared with him. It must have been a nightmare time for her. She ended up at a mother-and-baby home in Clapton Pond, in east London, run by the Salvation Army. The place was old with grey linoleum and faded lemon-coloured walls. It reeked of pissy, shitty, pukey baby smells, but the women who ran it, always prim in their Salvation Army uniforms, were caring if a little strict. It wasn't much better than life with Keith, but at least she didn't have to put up with his violent temper.

Even so, Mum has always described sleeping there as hellish. The walls were simple partitions made of wood, or in some cases just curtains, and were so thin that you could never get any sleep. Not all the girls there had babies. Many of the residents were waifs aged thirteen or fourteen, barely more than children themselves. Throughout the night Jenny would hear screams and sobs. It was heartbreaking, although the Salvation Army did the best they could.

She remembers that one evening as she sat in her tiny cubicle, which contained only a battered bed and a chest of drawers, she didn't know where to turn. Because she'd educated herself and had a good job she knew that it wasn't the place for her, and it would certainly be no place to bring up a baby. Fortunately an old school friend, Sherrie Jeffrey, came to her rescue and let her stay at her home on the Holly Street Estate in Hackney. Sherrie was always there for Jen and they are still friends today.

Throughout her pregnancy Mum went to work, as she needed to support herself. It was Sherrie's mother who told Jenny that she should talk to Keith. 'This man has got to start taking some responsibility for you and this child.' So talk to him she did, and remembers it was an emotional meeting. Keith told Jenny that he wanted to support her and the baby. Deep down, she believed, or wanted to believe, that he really meant it – but words are easy. You can say whatever you like, but, if you don't back your words up with actions, nothing ever comes of them. Eventually, when the same old words are repeated over and over, you get sick of hearing them.

Keith told Mum he'd do this and he'd do that, but the reunion, as things turned out, was a terrible idea, backfiring on Mum almost immediately. He continued going out, often partying until five in the morning, the life of a free and single man. Yet he began to hound her and she ended up having to move from Sherrie's house, because of his late-night 'surprise' visits.

Just before I was born, though, they met up again and he promised Jenny that he would get a job and to his credit, he did. He got some temporary work at the Royal Opera House, Covent Garden, and then a little later, because his literacy skills were poor, Mum filled out an application for him to work for London Underground as a trainee electrician – a job where he could actually learn a trade. Some hope!

For a short while everything was looking rosier. Keith was working proper shifts, like a normal and responsible man. During Mum's last weeks, he popped in to see her before he went off to his job and was actually working nights when I was born. I arrived a good thirty-six hours after Mum had at last been induced at 7.40 a.m., but Dad wasn't there to meet me.

To be fair, Keith's missing my actual birth wasn't his fault.

Apparently he came straight to the hospital as soon as he could after work. Mum reckons he was expecting her to still be there groaning and pregnant to bursting but, when he came in, there she was with their tiny daughter in her arms. Mum says he just looked absolutely amazed. She just looked at him and said, 'Look what we've got.' And there was I, this olive-skinned bundle with jet-black hair, screaming my head off. Mum says the first thing I did when she looked down at me was open my eyes, and then my gob – and it's been the same ever since!

It should have been an unforgettable experience for both my parents but even the morning of my birth was marked by an unpleasant and horribly characteristic scene caused by my father – although, in some ways the incident strikes me as being quite funny. Just as I was delivered, a nurse ran up to Mum and said, 'Oh, Jenny, your husband's outside.'

Mum was surprised: 'Oh, that's funny, because he doesn't finish work yet.' Mum expected Keith to be back that morning after his night shift – but not *so* early.

The nurse was insistent. 'He's definitely outside,' she said. She showed in Jenny's 'husband' and there stood the biggest Rastafarian my mother had ever seen in her life. She was being stitched at the time and this dreadlocked Rasta took one look at her and said, 'That's not my wife,' while my Mum said, 'And that's not my boyfriend!' She says it was like something out of a Brian Rix farce, because at that time she had her legs up in stirrups!

Later that morning when Keith did come to visit, our little family was gathered in a room off the main ward. Dad was holding me when the Rastafarian walked past. As he did so, he stopped and pointed at my Mum and then gave her a thumbs-up sign. Keith went mad and started ranting like a lunatic. 'Who's that?' he demanded.

She tried to explain: 'Oh, they thought he was my husband . . .'

'What do ya mean they thought he was your husband?' he bellowed.

Mum tried to reassure him by explaining that they'd met by accident, that a nurse had introduced them by mistake. But Dad's jealousy had got the better of him once again. Possessiveness should never be mistaken for love . . .

Mum left hospital a few days after having me and we moved to a bed-and-breakfast place opposite the Rainbow, an old concert hall, in Finsbury Park, north London. She was still seeing Keith although he was far from happy with her, because she'd decided I would take her surname not his – despite his name as father being clearly entered on my birth certificate. Mum felt that, given the way he'd been behaving, Keith didn't deserve the privilege of giving me his surname. So I was called Martine Kimberley Sherrie Ponting, with Keith, or Thomas, Hemmings as the named father.

Keith, who was never married to Mum, wasn't supposed to be staying at the bed-and-breakfast, though sometimes he did. One morning he came back at five o'clock after his shift at London Underground to find Mum absolutely frantic. She'd been up all night with me. I wasn't taking any feeds. I'd been vomiting a lot and had the most terrible diarrhoea. I just wouldn't stop screaming and I'd never been like that. Usually I was very placid and slept and ate well and was pretty much contented. As I was just six weeks old, they decided to take me straight to casualty but, not having enough money for a minicab, Mum just wrapped me up the best she could in a blanket, and they made for the nearest bus station. A driver agreed to drop them off near the Whittington Hospital in

Archway. I was whisked off to the special baby unit almost as soon as they set foot in the place. Mum was worried.

When the ward sister came down a little later and said, 'Have a cup of tea and the doctor will be down to see you,' Mum became even more concerned. 'What's wrong with my baby?' she asked. She was going out of her mind. One moment she had a bouncing little baby and things were starting to go right; then, the next thing she knew, she was waiting for a doctor to tell her the worst.

The doctors did indeed prepare Mum and Keith for the worst. Quietly they explained, 'You know we're doing all we can, but we don't think your baby's going to make it – she's so frail and was completely dehydrated when she came in. She had no fluid in her body at all. We put her on a drip straight away and gave her medication. Now it's just a case of hoping that she'll be OK.' They thought I had severe gastroenteritis and told Mum she ought to stay at the hospital with me all the time – not that she had any intention of leaving me. Plainly I was seriously ill. My weight had plummeted from a healthy ten pounds to barely four.

She sat there for two agonising days just waiting to see if her baby would make it through another night. Keith was by her side most of the time and Mum says she can remember him weeping – the only time she can remember seeing such tenderness in his eyes – as they stared at the sick little girl in a cot in front of them. He was acting like a proper father – well, most of the time. He kept blaming Jenny for my illness. He accused her of not having made my feeds properly. After a few days I stabilised and the doctors seemed more positive that I would pull through – but the mystery remained as to how I could have become so ill in the first place.

*

It was three weeks later that I was eventually discharged. The council found Mum and me a room in a half-way house in London Fields, Hackney. It was very run down and far from ideal for a new mother with a tiny baby. There were three floors, each occupied by a mother and child. Mum and I were on the top floor. Bathroom facilities were minimal and the only cooker was an old thing that stood on the landing. Mum reckons our new home wasn't fit for a dog, let alone a mother and baby.

We hadn't been there long when Mum was contacted by the hospital. Some of the other babies at the hostel where we'd been staying before had also become ill. The doctors had eventually realised that there was something wrong with the water that Mum and the other women were using to make their feeds. Even though the women had boiled the kettles properly beforehand, it hadn't been enough to completely sterilise the water, and some germ had got through and caused the gastroenteritis. In a way, it was a weight off Mum's shoulders. Although she knew she'd made my feeds correctly, Keith's constant accusations that she hadn't, on top of her distress, had worn her down.

Ironically, my stay in hospital had produced an equally unexpected bonus, one that looking back I can see was the first of many steps towards my future career in show business. Even Mum wasn't the first to spot it. It was left to a photographer who happened to be lurking around the Whittington Hospital when I was six weeks old and still recovering from my gastroenteritis. He helped me to land my first job.

I was in an isolated cubicle and Mum was sitting there with me, as she did constantly, when she spied this guy wandering up and down. He came over and tapped on the window and said, 'The sister said I could come in and have a chat with you. I'm looking for a baby . . .'

Startled, Mum snapped, 'Well you can't have mine!'

'Oh no,' he replied. 'No, I don't mean it in that way. I'm a photographer and I've had a look at some of the babies here and yours is particularly photogenic, or I believe she would be. Would you mind very much if I took some photographs of her?' He explained that he was the official photographer for the local Labour Party election campaign. He said that the ward sister had given her OK, because I was on the mend and was due to be discharged soon. He told Mum that, because I was so quiet and well behaved, I could get a lot of work. So she said he could take some photos of me, and he gave her his card, saying that, if she ever wanted to get me into modelling, then she should give him a call. Afterwards, Mum spoke to Keith about it and, typically, he dismissed it completely.

Mum was really proud of what the photographer had said, but was even more chuffed when she found out that they were actually using my picture on an enormous billboard advertisement on Newington Green in north-east London. Then she discovered that the poster wasn't just on Newington Green, but on giant billboards up and down the country. At the time my Auntie Kim's husband, Graham, was a Young Socialist and was very active in the Labour Party, so one day we went down to the Michael Sobell Centre in north London to a function as his guests. Mum was walking round with me looking for Kim when Harold Wilson, who'd been Prime Minister until a few weeks before, came over, pointed at me and said, 'That's our baby.' Then he picked me up and held me. Mum, I should point out, had also been admired as a baby. But I don't know if being cuddled by Reggie Kray, who then slipped a fiver into her little hand, counts in quite the same way!

Life was only marginally easier for both Mum and me at the new place where we were living. The water may have been healthier but there was another menace to contend with: mice. They were everywhere and she'd stay awake most nights, terrified that they would get into my cot. She was virtually cracking up under the strain of caring for a baby, being convinced these mice would spread the germs they were carrying to me. The whole place was a health hazard and eventually Mum had had enough. She stormed down to the GLC – the Greater London Council – and demanded to see officials in the housing department. After she'd forcefully put her case, she was offered a two-bedroom flat on the notorious Pembury Estate in Hackney, one of the poorest places in London, but still infinitely more appealing than our current abode. We moved in just before Christmas. By then I was six months old.

The flats dated back to just before World War Two, but were still more comfortable than the place where we'd been living – and at least there were no mice and at last Mum could get a good night's sleep. She began to feel much happier and safer. The flat, which was on the second floor, was no palace: in fact, like the previous place, it was pretty dilapidated. The kitchen was an improvement on that of the last place – but not by much. There was an old butler's sink and wooden draining board. There was running water, but only cold, and there were two bedrooms, a lounge and a bathroom.

But people were really kind and helped out where they could. One of Jenny's friends gave her an old black-and-white television set, more *green* and white than black and white, because the tube was on its last legs. Uncle Laurence gave her his old settee and Auntie Kim doled out some second-hand baby clothes, an old pram and a buggy. We didn't have much furniture but it was home all the same – and it was ours. Mum could close the front door and, when she did, we felt as if we were somewhere safe at last.

Or so we thought . . .

CHAPTER 2

Everything and Nothing: My Dad

MY FIRST MEMORY of my Dad is of him dangling me over a balcony, about thirty feet above the ground. I see it in my mind's eye as though it were a photograph.

I don't feel any particular emotion or horror at the thought of being held there, and I don't remember staring down at the concrete pavement below. I don't even remember feeling terrified. I suppose I was too young, perhaps three years old. But I do remember him holding me there. To understand why a man would dangle his own daughter from a balcony so high up, threatening to drop her to the ground below, you have to understand my Dad. And that, I'm afraid, isn't easy.

Thomas Hemmings, or Keith, as his Mum and everyone else called him, was born in Ireland. He never knew his real father, a builder by the name of Frank McTay who had been the love of my Nan's life back in Ireland. But one day Frank didn't come home and Nan couldn't cope with a young son on her own, so she handed Keith into the care of her parents

17

for eight years while she moved to England to start a new life. Then, when Keith turned nine, he was brought to London to join his mother and her new husband in Hackney, east London, one of the hardest areas of the capital. At that time, the early sixties, you had to be tough to get on – and, if you weren't doing something illegal, then you didn't survive. It was often as simple as that.

He didn't do well at school, although he had a good brain. In his teenage years he fell in with the wrong crowd. There were quite a few adults in the area who'd take advantage of a poorly educated kid without much parental guidance and give them a different sort of education – such as how to make a living on the wrong side of the law. It all sounds like something from *Oliver Twist*. They took kids like him on, and then taught them how to burgle houses and sell drugs. To a kid who found school dull, it was all a bit of an adventure. Maths and English became secondary to what you could learn – and gain – on the streets.

When Mum started seeing Keith he was doing 'everything and nothing'. Among the 'everything' he was doing was drugs. There was a big West Indian community in Hackney, and Keith got involved and was out of his depth, using marijuana and hashish. Not being very well educated, living on the edge of the drugs world gave him a thrill and identity he needed.

By the time he was twenty and had first met my Mum, Keith – who they say was a dead ringer for the movie star Keanu Reeves – had settled into a profoundly irresponsible lifestyle. Yet despite that, and to this day, Mum trustingly believes that he desperately wanted to make things work between them. For a while he was very much in love with her, despite his psychotic behaviour. He'd never had anybody who loved him as much as she did, and he'd never been able to love anybody as much as he loved her. Mum says he wanted badly to cling on to their relationship, but eventually the price he had to pay was far higher than he could actually deliver. In other words, he couldn't hold down a job for longer than a couple of months. He couldn't adjust to a normal, respectable way of living. Perhaps his curse was that he didn't *want* a quiet and normal life.

By the time she had turned twenty, Mum knew things were never going to improve with Keith and that her only hope for a normal life would have to be one without him. It hadn't taken him long to find us on the Pembury Estate – even though Mum had refused to tell him our address. When he came round to see us she decided it was now or never, and plucked up the courage to tell him it was over. Keith refused to accept it. In fact he never, ever accepted it.

He'd go away for weeks on end after that. Mum would have no idea of his whereabouts until he'd turn up on our doorstep. She would fear each knock at the door in case it was him. Sometimes he'd turn up late at night – 3 a.m. was not unusual. Of course when she heard knocking at that sort of hour, she'd have a pretty good idea who it was and she'd have a pretty good idea, too, what sort of state he'd be in. Usually drunk or stoned. Or both.

Although Keith resented the fact that Jenny had me, and had to devote her time to me, Mum says that, strangely, he also loved me and was really proud of the baby they had produced. When things were better between them she would occasionally allow Keith to take me out for the day. Mum gave me, quite young, the choice of seeing my Dad or not, and in the very early days, I decided I would, because I wanted things to be normal. I wanted to have a Dad and, even if I couldn't see mine every day as most kids could theirs, I at least wanted to see him at the weekend. Everyone always said I looked like him. It was only natural for me to want stay in touch. When Mum gave me that choice, I said, 'You know, I think I will see him, but if I don't like it I don't have to keep seeing him, do I?'

'No,' she told me, 'you haven't got to do anything you don't want to do. That's why I'm asking you.'

I suppose I thought that things might be better with Dad when I was alone with him. After all, I was always really in tune with my Mum and when she wasn't at work we were bonded like superglue. We're still incredibly close today. I think that, even if Keith *had* been around like a normal father, I'd have still been a Mummy's girl. I haven't had many men in my life and have always felt very comfortable with women. Mum always treated me with respect and as a grown-up, even when I was a little girl. We grew to understand each other in the way that only two people from the same mould can. I wanted Mum and me to be entwined for the rest of my life.

One of my first trips with Keith alone was a visit to the zoo. At least that was where he told Jenny he was taking me. I must have been about three. Dad came to pick me up and off we trotted, not to the zoo but round to see one of his girlfriends. He had quite a few of those. This one was called Davine, or something like that. She was slim with red hair and lots of make-up on – about ten years older than Mum and Keith. There were quite a few cats running around her house. I don't remember the conversation, but she offered me a drink and I sat down and sipped it. Dad left me downstairs while they went upstairs. I thought they'd be down in a minute, but they weren't.

They made no pretence of keeping anything from me, because I can still remember sitting on the floor in floods, terrified because of all the noise that was coming from upstairs. I thought someone was getting hurt, because of all the screams. I didn't know what was going on, but I never forgot him coming downstairs doing up his trousers, followed by this dishevelled woman, who looked as if she'd been hurt.

Throughout my early childhood, as relations between Jenny and Keith degenerated, the flat that had been Mum's home and mine became a prison. She'd always be fearful of meeting Dad by chance in the streets, but worse, she'd be worried he might come round to the flat. Mum didn't know whether to stay in or go out.

When I was a bit older I'd often invite friends round. There was a girl called Janina, whose mother, a Turkish woman we nicknamed H, lived opposite. She was quite a regular at our place, and so was my cousin, Yasmine Hemmings, the daughter of Keith's sister, Sandra, who would often join me for a sleepover when we would drink hot chocolate in our pink pyjamas and munch bacon-flavoured snacks called Frazzles. I'd see a fair bit of another of my cousins, Carrine – Auntie Kim's daughter – who is still one of my closest friends today. She was very different from me even then, being well organised and unflappable. I love her to bits and was thrilled to go to her wedding in the summer of 2000.

At that time my Uncle Christopher, or Chrissy, was also a big part of my life. He was only about thirteen, but he was a regular at our house and he adored me. On her twenty-first birthday, he said to Mum, 'Why don't you go out with your friends, Jen? You've not been anywhere for ages. I'm nearly fourteen and I'm not a baby. Just go out, have a drink and then come home and I'll be here and look after Martine.'

Mum didn't hesitate: 'Right, you're on!'

Her friends arranged a night out and insisted it would be their treat, as it was her twenty-first. So Mum went off with her mates to the local pub, having told Chris that she'd be home by midnight. A few hours later Mum returned home to find our block of flats swarming with police. Worried silly as she walked towards the block, she soon learned she had good reason. An officer explained, to her horror, that Keith had been round, snatched me and taken me out into the freezing March night wearing just a nappy.

Chris was hysterical. 'I'm sorry, Jen,' he sobbed. 'There was a knock on the door. I opened it and Keith pushed his way in. I tried to stop him but he just punched and kicked me out of the way and then he grabbed the baby. I was so worried and I didn't know how to get in touch with you.'

It was a terrible time for Mum and my Uncle Chris, made only slightly better for her by the kindness of the policeman. He told her not to worry and to think calmly about the places that Keith could have taken me to. He then took Jenny in his panda car to find me. They drove the whole night looking in likely places. They went everywhere: to his grandmother's, to pubs, and then eventually to his sister's. She wouldn't open the door, but her husband shouted out, 'He's been here, Jenny, with the baby. We put some clothes on her and he just went off.' So by that stage they at least knew that he'd been there.

They got back into the police car and the policeman said to Jenny, 'Can you think of anywhere else?' By this time Mum was absolutely hysterical, thinking, Where is he with Martine? She's got no food, no bottles, no nothing. Finally, Mum thought it might just be worth trying my Gran and Grandad's house, although she didn't hold up much hope. But there I was – just where Keith had dumped me! Mum thinks he snatched me simply to hurt her. It then dawned on her that he would now do things to me if he couldn't do things to her directly.

I was taken to hospital for a check-up, but I was fine, other than being tired and hungry. Mum, though, was shocked and upset and from that moment on she vowed that she wouldn't let me out of her sight again. My Uncle Chris was affected by it all, too. The fact that Keith managed to get in and take me away made him feel guilty and inadequate. Mum didn't blame him but thinks he was upset for a long time. He was just a thirteen-year-old boy and Keith a grown man. Chris had done his best to thwart Dad and had taken a few knocks and bumps for his efforts.

For Mum, the time had come to move again. She'd endured endless nights when Keith would turn up drunk and hammer on the door. He'd even break in sometimes and the police became regular visitors as a result. But the crunch really came a few months later. It was a glorious summer's day. Some brightly coloured streamers which Mum had hung on the door for some reason were blowing gently in the breeze. Perhaps it was in honour of the Queen's Jubilee or something. Anyway, the perfection of it all was shattered when she heard a knock on the door. She knew who it was.

She was in the front room and I was playing happily at her feet. Keith didn't even notice me at first, because he was too busy hassling Mum for money. He said he needed cash, because he'd lost his job. To Mum it was just his usual stuff all over again. This time, though, she just wasn't prepared to listen to it. She told him to go. He then told her to put me to bed but she refused. Menacingly, he then said, 'Jenny, I've come for what's rightfully mine.' In other words he was saying that he wanted to go to bed with Mum and that, as far as he was concerned, she was his woman and didn't have a say in the matter. He shouted at her again to put me to bed, to get her clothes off and go to the bedroom. She refused. Well, that was incitement enough for Keith. His eyes switched from leering at Mum to staring at me sitting there, playing on my own. Whether he thought it was my fault 'his' Jenny was not succumbing to his demands, I don't know, but he came over to where I was sitting, picked me up and took me outside. That's when he held me over the balcony by an ankle and, screaming at Jenny, told her that if she didn't do what he asked he'd drop me. Even though he would never have done it, it was a moment of uncontrollable madness.

Mum was hysterical, screaming like a banshee and thank God she did, because somebody in the flats called the police who came quite quickly.

When he heard the sirens coming towards us, Keith knew he wasn't going to win this particular battle and brought me back inside. But in his anger and frustration, instead of placing me gently on the floor, he literally threw me across the room. Luckily I landed on the bed. Mum was sure that he'd been out the evening before and had had a hard night on drugs and drink. He was out of his tree, she tells me, and probably didn't even know what day it was.

By the time the police arrived the situation was cooling. They hadn't witnessed his threats to kill me and rape my Mum, and no charges were pressed. Instead, they escorted him away. Back then, the authorities didn't take domestic violence as seriously as they do now. It was more a case of 'Don't come back again; don't be a naughty boy'. Mum had no faith in the police: for her they were only a stopgap. They just dealt with things on the spot but then, perhaps an hour later, or a day or a week later, Keith would come back.

Even some of my few happy memories of Dad are tainted by his thoughtlessness. I'd fallen in love with this beautiful red coat – I must have been about four at the time – and had seen it in a shop in Dalston. It was a beautiful thing and one day Dad took me to the shop to buy it. Mum thought this gesture was too good to be true, and she was right, because we heard later that his redhead girlfriend had given him the money for it. Nice of her, sure, but it spoilt the illusion that Dad had saved up for something special for me.

A couple of months later, Dad took me out again. This time he promised Jenny he'd have me back home by 6 p.m. How easily he forgot such promises! By 2 a.m. I wasn't home and my frantic Mum rang the police. Officers were dispatched to try to find me. Well, Keith was a popular figure on the front line in Hackney. Strangers would stop to say hello when we went out together, and I still remember noticing sly exchanges of money and other packages. On this evening Keith's popularity must have got the better of him when we joined some of his mates in a pub. It must have been a hell of a night, because at some point Dad slipped out and went home, leaving me behind. The police eventually found me in the pub, sitting with a group of kindly Rastas at 2 a.m. and otherwise all on my own.

People have said to Mum, 'Why did you keep going back with him?' The truth is she didn't keep running back into his arms. She had no choice in the matter. One time he forced his way into our home, drunk again, and fell asleep in the spare room. Mum got up the next morning to see me crawling about on the floor. In those days Keith smoked dope, which he would hide in his sock. That morning I'd gone into the bedroom while he was sleeping it off. When Mum walked in she saw, to her horror, that I'd found the sock and was in the process of eating the bloody stuff. I had hash caked all around my face. Her shrieks of panic roused Keith from his drunken, wasted slumber.

But when he saw what had happened, we wished we hadn't woken him. He went absolutely crazy and, incredibly, accused me of stealing his stash. I was little more than a baby and had no idea what I was eating. He didn't think for one minute of the possible danger that *I* might have been in – nothing serious as it turned out.

Something like that happened pretty much every week and Mum knew we couldn't continue like this any longer. He'd frequently hit her, and yet only once did she completely lose her cool and fight back. She picked up a kitchen knife and lunged at him. He put his arms up to protect himself and the knife cut his arm. He had to go to hospital and have it stitched up. Enough was enough. If Mum hadn't decided it was time to move away, Keith would have finished up killing her, I'm sure.

So in early 1978, when I was about eighteen months old, we left the Pembury Estate and began what turned into almost four years living a nomadic life.

First we moved to Devon and stayed a while with Mum's friend Sylvia, with whom she'd shared a flat when she'd first left home. Jenny was very happy there and remembers it as more like a glorified holiday than a desperate escape. All that came to an end, though, when a friend phoned Mum to warn her that Keith had found out where we were staying and was on his way down.

Keith was devious, always managing to find out where we were. If he discovered from someone which general area we were living in, he'd be clever about finding exactly where we were. His favourite trick was to get a pass with a photograph and flash it at people saying something like, 'I've been working on the oil rigs and I've just come back and my wife and my child have moved, but I heard she's in this block of flats somewhere. Her name's Jenny and the baby's Martine. Do you know her?' And they'd go, 'Oh, yeah, she lives at number eighty-four.' Another thing he'd do was claim he was a policeman. He'd say, 'I'm from CID, I'm looking for . . .' It's amazing the methods he'd use to find us.

He always wanted the same things, of course: money, and to get back with Mum. He wanted everything a real relationship could be, but Mum knew he had nothing to offer her or me. He wanted to be able to come and go as he pleased. Hearing that Keith was on his way to the West Country it was time to up sticks and move again. For a while after that Mum worked in a pub in Chelmsford, in Essex, and we lived above it. Then the pub closed down, so the local council rehoused us in temporary accommodation in Colchester. The little Dutch cottage with a bright red door was really pretty and nice. Again, it was no palace and didn't have any mod cons. There was another old butler's sink and one cold tap, but I have fond memories of the place.

By this time Mum's friends had persuaded her to think about moving back to London. 'OK,' they'd say. 'You haven't got him on your case at the moment and he doesn't know where you are, but you've got nothing else. It's just you and the baby. Come home.' All the while Mum was working, doing whatever jobs she could get. She's a real grafter and hated being on benefit. Throughout the years we spent moving from place to place she didn't once claim the social. She worked as a barmaid, as a cleaner and then, in Colchester, in Ratner's, the jewellers.

She started off doing just Saturdays there, then, desperate for more cash, she persuaded the shop to take her on full-time.

There was another reason in addition to her work ethic that made Mum so determined not to claim benefit: every time we moved, she knew that, if she registered with the Department of Social Security, they'd ask her who my father was and Mum was worried they might contact him so he would then be able to find us again. It was all cloak-and-dagger stuff.

While we were living in Colchester, I began going to nursery school, which was great for Jenny. She managed to get me a government-funded place, so she could afford to go to work without my fees costing much. Mum would take me to school in the morning and then go to work. On Saturdays she would drop me off with an aunt, who would look after me while she was grafting. The nursery was wonderful and gave me a real chance to mix with kids my own age, although it has to be said they didn't teach me things such as reading and writing.

I had my first run-in with the opposite sex at the nursery school – at the tender age of three. There was this boy called Ryan. He had blond hair and would drive me mad when we all played hide and seek. We'd all scamper over these hollow wooden blocks and hide inside them. Ryan would always follow me and squeeze himself into the same wooden box. As if that wasn't bad enough, he would then try to kiss and cuddle me. Yuk! Needless to say, I would scream my head off every time he tried.

It was in Colchester that I broke my nose. I was out in the back room of our home one summer's evening mucking around with an old ironing board. Heaven knows why. Although we were living there, the owners were in the process of gutting the property to get it ready for whoever was going to take the place on permanently. There I was, singing and sitting on the ironing board, which I pretended was some sort of stage. Mum was talking to Uncle Laurence when I tried to attract her attention. Laurence noticed first: 'Jen, Jen – Mart's on the ironing board,' he warned. As she turned to see, Mum shrieked, 'Get her off, get her off.'

But it was too late. Suddenly the ironing board collapsed, and as it did so, it bashed against an old fire fitting which came crashing down on top of me. My uncle and Mum rushed me to hospital. I was crying and I remember touching my nose, which felt as big as my head. Blood was streaming all the way down my favourite nightie and my nose now felt as if it had spread across to my ears! A doctor examined me and said that I had broken it, but, because I was so young and my bones hadn't fused properly, he thought that it would repair itself. Mum was less sure. She was convinced that I'd end up with a huge hooked nose or something. Fortunately the doctor was right, and today you'd never know that I'd had that little adventure.

It was in Colchester also that I first got into the papers. I'd been at nursery school only a week when the mayor came to visit and a photographer from the local paper took a picture of me pretending to wash up. There was I, this tiny grinning child, in the local rag. The episode reminded Jenny of what that photographer had said when he spotted me at the Whittington Hospital. 'Miss Ponting, your daughter would make a great child model.'

So, skimming through the papers one day in Colchester, Mum saw an ad that caught her eye. Apparently, they were searching for the new Miss Pears. Younger readers might need to know that in those days a well-known soap manufacturer ran an annual beauty contest pitched at the parents of nice-looking kids. I was about three and a half at the time and Mum duly sent off a picture of me. A few weeks later we got a letter back. 'Congratulations, your daughter has progressed another stage further,' and then another one, which said I'd got into the regional finals of Miss Pears 1979. Mum couldn't believe it – but then she started to worry, because she knew that, if it went any further, I might get into the papers. She was frightened that Keith would see it and find out where we were. So Mum, thinking that I wouldn't win anyway, decided I shouldn't go through to the next round and we pulled out. But I'd definitely got the bug by then.

I began doing bits of modelling for clothes catalogues and companies such as Habitat. It wasn't regular work and it was frequently disrupted by our nomadic lifestyle. If we had to move because Keith had found us, Mum wouldn't want the agencies to know where we were going next in case he tried to track us down through them. Instead she would tell them we were going abroad so we could cover our tracks. The unwanted side effect of this strategy was that, once we moved on, the agencies couldn't track us down either.

Again in Colchester – or, more specifically, on a train from our temporary home back to London – Mum says I gave my first professional performance. I used to sing a song called 'The Elephant Goes Like This'. I can still remember it today:

> The elephant goes like this and like that;
> He's terribly big and terribly fat;
> He has no fingers or no toes
> But goodness gracious what a nose!

I sang it so often that even Mum can recite it now. Anyway, she can remember me, aged about four and a half, singing on a train as we travelled down to London one day to try to arrange somewhere to live. There were all these City gents with briefcases, bowler hats and umbrellas and I sang to them all and did the actions. As they got up to get off the train people started leaving me money. Mum was so embarrassed and said, 'Martine, sit down, darling,' and I replied, 'I'm cheering them up. Aren't they miserable, Mummy?' Then stood up and said, 'You're not miserable now, are you?' and started singing to them again. By the time we reached Liverpool Street Station these usually sober-looking City gents were just cracking up. Mum reckons it all started from then.

In the summer of 1981, when I was five, we moved back to Hackney. We got a housing trust place in Greenwood Road. We were assigned a ground-floor maisonette taking up the bottom half of a house, complete with a garden, a nice front room and a proper kitchen. Mum says the first time she went round to see it she couldn't believe it. Compared with the sort of places that we had been used to, which were really squalid, it was a palace. We'd never had anything like this before – it was all new and shiny. It felt like home straight away.

You would walk up a few steps to reach the gleaming black front door, with its elegant brass letterbox and knocker. It all looked very posh. Sadly, my bedroom let it down a bit. When the property was refurbished prior to our moving in, someone had decided to lay grey lino on the floor and stick up flock wallpaper in a tasteless shade of mouldy green. The pink candlewick bedspread and old 1950s record player we had brought with us from our travels did little to lift the décor. But little by little our own things made the place lovely to us.

There was a tree in the front garden, which sloped right down to my bedroom on the ground floor. It must have been quite a steep slope, because I remember one day waking up in the morning to find a tramp, unconscious, pressed against my bedroom window. It turned out he'd had a skinful, fallen over into our garden and then rolled all the way down until he hit the window. I remember waking up that morning and nearly having a heart attack when I saw him snoring there. I suppose I remembered too many unwelcome nocturnal visitors.

At first, every day spent living in Greenwood Road felt a little like a holiday. I remember getting my first bicycle not long after we moved in. I loved it so much I even rode it around the house, which was not the smartest thing a little girl can do. One afternoon I carried my bike, all glossy purple and yellow, upstairs. Then, while pretending I was the motorcycle stunt rider Evel Knievil – I think I even shouted out 'I am Evel Knievel' – I launched myself downstairs. Mum arrived just in time to wipe away the tears. I'd gone head first over the banisters and smashed my head open. I still have the faint scar under my left eyebrow.

Despite my attempts at demolishing the place, the maisonette was still pleasant enough to persuade Mum that our travels were over. She had family and friends nearby and she thought, Sod it – I'm not going to keep running. I'm going to kill him this time if he tries anything funny.

Of course, it wasn't long before Keith found out where we were and spoiled things. Despite his appalling behaviour, Mum had a good relationship with Dad's mum, my Nan. She was always wonderful to us. She used to say to Mum (and still does today), 'I know he's sometimes not a very nice person – but he's my son!' Anyway just before we moved in, Mum told Nan that she'd found this house in Greenwood Road, which wasn't far from her. Delighted to have us back in the bosom of her dysfunctional family, Nan replied by telling Mum, 'I'll do anything I can to help you.'

Indeed she did. As Mum needed to go to work, I used to walk round to Nan's house each day first thing and she'd take me to school. A bond grew between Nan and me that's been there ever since. She's only about five foot two or three and had black hair, fair skin and big brown eyes. She's seventy now but still has such a strong southern Irish accent that you can't always understand everything she's saying. She's a real character who loves reggae and calypso dancing. No, really – she likes her reggae so much that she only recently won a calypso dancing competition and made the front of the local paper!

After school I didn't go back to Nan's who had to take care of a lot of my cousins, and what my Mum could afford to pay her didn't stretch to dinner as well. Mum was also a little concerned about leaving me at Nan's in case Keith would pop around. Instead, I would hang around at the play centre, which was right next door to our house, and wait until Mum came home and knocked on the door to say she was back. To me the play centre was a very peculiar-looking place, I can't say why. The two women who ran it were very 'right on', yuppie types, doing their bit for the community. One was called Flo, whose short blonde hair made her look like the punk singer Billy Idol. I even told her that once, and remember that she gave me a funny look. The other woman was the complete opposite. Anyway, they ran it well.

Keith's unwanted visits continued. A typical one would

usually result in violence against my Mum, though he never hit me. There would be a knock at the door. 'Jenny, please open the door, my Mum's really seriously ill,' he would say. 'She needs to see Martine. I'm in such a state of shock.' Mum would open the door and Dad would hit her in the face without even saying hello. Mum would be on the floor, out for the count.

Apart from learning nursery rhymes like any normal kid I'd also learned from Mum how to use the phone, and she'd encouraged me to learn my name and address. In fact, I knew how to do that better than I knew most nursery rhymes. The idea was that, if Keith came round and tried to get in, I'd be able to phone the police while Mum would keep him talking at the door. I'd give them all the details, such as where we lived, and then I'd say, 'My Dad's at the door and he's not a very nice man. My Mum's trying to keep him outside. We don't want him to get in. Please hurry up and come round.'

If Keith got in he'd usually bash Mum and tell me to keep quiet and not to say anything or scream or cry. I did as he said and believe he was mystified by how the police would arrive on cue. In the end, he cottoned on that I had been phoning them, and so he accused Mum of turning me against him. He said she'd damaged my mind. Mum didn't need to do any of that, because he'd already done it himself. Mum didn't need to do or say *anything* to make me hate him. His actions and behaviour alone made that simple and natural.

On another occasion, Mum and I were just chatting in bed when we heard footsteps coming down the path. I knew even at a young age that she was trying really hard to hide the fact that she was panicking. But she was right to panic. It was Keith, of course, and as soon as he reached our doorstep he started shouting abuse and swearing, calling Mum all kinds of horrible things, including names I'd never even heard before. I just remember lying there as Mum screamed, 'Just go away, Keith. Leave us alone! I've got Martine with me. If you've got a bone to pick with me we'll do it when she's not here but please don't do this. You're not even supposed to be here.'

Mum then whispered to me, 'We'll be all right, but if Daddy tries to come in, I won't be able to keep him away so, if I say so, you've got to go and talk to the nice man at the police station on the telephone.' Then we sat there and waited. It was quiet for a bit, but then Keith's shouting started up again, getting worse as each second passed. I'll never forget getting out of bed and going to the front door. I flicked open the letterbox and peered outside. I still remember seeing these two eyes looking back at me – it frightened the life out of me. I just thought Dad was evil. I really believed he was evil.

My Mum was crying and beginning to get into a bit of a state when he started kicking the door in, literally smashing his way through it. I was trembling as the wood splintered under his blows. I ran upstairs and dialled the number. A policeman answered and I told him, 'My Dad's smashed his way into our house and I can hear Mum being hurt downstairs.'

By now my Dad had demolished the door and was inside. 'Try to calm down,' the policeman said, 'because Mummy is a grown-up and everything will be fine, but it's important that you stay upstairs.' Then he tried to distract me from what was happening downstairs. 'Have you got a piece of paper?' he asked. 'Can you draw me a house? What's in the house?'

I was shaking uncontrollably and sobbing. 'I've got to go,' I stammered. 'I can't draw this house any more, because Mummy's screaming and Mummy sounds like she's being hurt.' The policeman did his best reassure me: 'People will be there in a minute. Please don't go down,' he pleaded. I just hung up the phone.

I was only five years old at the time, yet I can honestly say I truly wanted to kill my father. I wanted to kill him, and can quite see how other kids have hurt people because of their parents. I even thought about getting a kitchen knife to protect myself in case he came and tried to hurt me. I sat on the stairs shaking, and then it all went quiet, deathly quiet. I was trembling and thinking, What's happened?

The next thing I heard was this dull thudding. I didn't know what it was. I hadn't heard it before. So I went downstairs and saw him hitting my Mum's head on the bathroom sink, over and over again. He looked at me and said coldly, 'This is what happens when you're bad.' And he just kept doing it. I was screaming. Then he got up and left and I went to look after Mum, who was lying unconscious on the bathroom floor. The police arrived shortly afterwards but Keith was gone. Mum was rushed to hospital.

There were a couple of other dreadful beatings like that, but none in which I'd ever seen that sort of damage inflicted. Mum would still go to work on a Monday morning whether it was with a terrible black eye, split lip, or whatever. It was around the time when the Human League were in the charts with 'Don't You Want Me, Baby?' and Mum had a blonde flick, fashionable then, along with the make-up and the glossy lips that went with it. She used to wear blue eye shadow and I remember one day thinking that you couldn't see where the blue eye shadow ended, because she had this big blue bruise on her face.

I didn't realise it was a bruise at first and I said, 'I think you've put too much blue eye shadow on.'

She said, 'No, don't touch it, it's Mummy's bruise,' and I just said, 'Oh.'

She tried so hard to protect and shield me from my father's rages – and she did a good job, too, because I was much older by the time I heard about the worst night Jenny had to endure – but it was also probably the last attack of such violence.

She was in bed one night and thought she heard something outside. She ignored it, though. After all, it was an old house and with any old house, you often hear lots of creaks and strange noises. But this was no ordinary creak for on this night Keith had broken in through a window downstairs. He was more out of his mind than Mum had ever seen him before. She was very frightened – terrified – because, although he was incoherent, Dad was also making threats that were all too easily understood.

He pinned Mum to the bed and told her to keep very quiet. He said if she didn't then he would wake me up and make me come and watch what he had in mind. It was blackmail – but that was only the beginning of the nightmare. To put it bluntly, he forced Mum to give in to his depraved sexual desire. I have a good idea about what happened that night, though it's understandably something my mother finds very difficult to talk about. I know he burned her body in various places with a cigarette. It was truly horrible, disgusting, degrading. And yet, throughout everything he did to her that long, agonising night, she kept quiet. She never uttered a sound, not one murmur, because she didn't want to betray or alarm me.

In fact Mum remembers that the next morning, when it was all over and he was asleep, the inside of her mouth was still bleeding from where she'd literally gritted her teeth all night to stop herself from screaming. It was at that point that she thought, This can't go on. This is really ridiculous now.

Keith had said to Mum during the night, 'Why don't you

37

just accept things the way they are? You're never going to get away from me. You're always going to belong to me. I'm always going to be able to do what I like, when I like, and you should just accept it.'

At the time, in the middle of her ordeal, Mum just agreed with him, but deep in her mind she was thinking: This is the last time you're ever going to do this to me, you'll see.

CHAPTER 3

Mum

SOMEHOW, IN BETWEEN Dad's acts of domestic terrorism, I managed to do nearly all the things a little girl should do. I suppose my Mum's incredible strength and devotion enabled me to learn and grow pretty normally under the circumstances. I was a proper Mummy's girl. She encouraged me to sing along to records on our old gramophone and we would watch all the old black-and-white musical films together. I picked up the lyrics easily, but singing and acting wasn't my first career choice at that age.

'What do you want to be when you grow up?' is a fairly normal question to pose to a young child. Boys often come back with answers like 'a fireman' or 'an astronaut'. Young girls, on the other hand, might say 'a nurse' or 'a vet'. Me? Well, I wanted to be a stripper! Honest to God, I did.

I can still remember walking around the East End as a child, when I was maybe five or six years old, and passing a pub not far from Bethnal Green. I think it was called the Green Man. On this particular day I noticed a woman in front of me dolled up to the nines. Now I'd be lying if I said I didn't always love make-up, and liked the smell of it as much as the smell of perfume. I loved heels that went clippity-clop. I loved it even more when the heels used to scuff on the floor in rhythm. I loved anything feminine, then, and still do.

Anyway, this woman looked incredibly glamorous to me. She was wrapped up in a fur coat and looked impossibly rich and classy to my young eyes.

'Oh, Mum,' I said, 'doesn't she look lovely?'

Mum looked bemused. 'No, Martine, she doesn't.'

'Yes, she does,' I insisted. 'I think she looks lovely.'

Again Mum contradicted me. 'I don't think she does, Martine. Now come on – let's get a move on.'

'Why are you being so horrible about her, Mum?' I asked.

She stopped, turned and looked me straight in the eye. 'Martine, do you know what she does for a living?' I shook my head, already starting to feel a little stupid. 'That lady is an exotic dancer. An exotic dancer.' Mum turned on her heels and began walking on again. It took me a while to catch her up.

'But what's an exotic dancer do, Mum?' I asked, again in that way only a young girl can.

'Well,' she said, 'she's a lady who takes all her clothes off and then dances naked in front of men for money.'

I kid you not when I say that I grabbed Mum's hand and looked up to her slightly embarrassed face and declared quite passionately, 'I want to be an exotic dancer, too!'

Mum was dumbfounded. 'They're called strippers, too, Martine.'

'Why's that?' I asked.

'Because sometimes they take their clothes off very quickly,' she explained, by now almost dragging me away down the street.

'Oh,' I said. 'I'd love to be a stripper if I looked like her. I'd love it. They do get to dance?'

I can still remember Mum saying, 'Yes they do, Martine, but I can't believe you're coming out with this. There's no way you're going to be a stripper!'

Despite all her best efforts to dissuade me, I was completely hooked on the idea of clambering up on stage in a fancy costume and then ripping it off for an appreciative audience. For quite a while after that unexpected bit of careers guidance, when people asked me, 'What do you want to be when you grow up?' I'd reply, dead straight, 'A stripper, thank you very much.'

Not long after that I first learned about Gypsy Rose Lee, from watching the musical *Gypsy*, and I was off again in my fantasy. This time I thought about copying Gypsy Rose, who I'd heard did exotic dancing with the most beautiful feathers. She held the feathers carefully so she never had to reveal too much. In the show – the first I was to see of Gypsy Rose was in the film, with Natalie Wood in the part – everyone thought that Rose's sister Baby Jane was going to be the star. But it was Gypsy Rose who ended up making it big. I can remember saying to Mum when I first laid eyes on Natalie Wood that she was the most beautiful woman I'd ever seen. And as Gypsy Rose she showed her Mum, she showed *everybody*, that she could make it and be a star, even if it meant stripping in a burlesque house.

My Mum doesn't often mention that little episode in my life – I suppose she's embarrassed by it. However, when I began this autobiography, I wanted to show how inspirational certain things can be in a person's life. Sometimes something quite surprising or insignificant to others can prove to be a major turning point. Now I'm not saying every little girl out there who reads this book should aim to be a stripper, but there's nothing wrong in having dreams – dreams of proving that you *can* make it in this world.

I was very fortunate, too, to have received encouragement for my showbiz fantasies at school. I loved school – Shacklewell Infants' School in particular – then back at home I would hide from the horrors around me by watching that old black-and-white telly, slipping off into my own little world, where the women wore glamorous frocks and everybody danced gracefully. Even as a tot I knew loads of Broadway standards off by heart, thanks to singsongs with Mum. But it was thanks to school and mixing with kids from all sorts of different cultures that I learned more contemporary numbers.

I should also say a word about my first teacher, Miss Wright, whom I still remember fondly for her affection as much as for anything else. I used to love writing stories in infants' school and would let my imagination run riot, but one particular essay prompted Miss Wright to ask my Mum to come and see her at school. My teacher was concerned, it transpired, because of something I'd written in class, a little horror story. She said she was worried about what was going on in my head. She wondered how a five-year-old girl could be writing such a thing.

'I don't think Martine should be writing stuff like this,' she explained.

I can't remember now what it was I wrote and I've since lost my early exercise books, but it had obviously been inspired by something that had happened with my Dad. I suppose my imagination had gone into overdrive and I'd poured all my confusion into this rather disturbing story.

Mum was shocked. 'I'm dreadfully sorry,' she told Miss Wright. 'We've had a bit of trouble at home and it's probably been playing on Martine's mind. I'm trying to do my best to keep her away from all of that but it's obviously affecting her.'

I had been at infants' school for about six months when I got to perform in my first play, *Away in a Manger*. OK, so it wasn't a proper play – not like the stuff I would do later at junior school – but it was staged in front of an audience of proud mums and dads and I absolutely loved it. We didn't have a proper stage. Instead, each of the children would play their part standing on these rickety old wooden blocks. There was no time for nerves, since you were more worried about falling off the blocks than getting your lines right. I was cast as an angel and Mum often embarrasses me by reminding our friends of my less-than-celestial behaviour. Apparently, my tinsel halo wasn't as big as that of one of the other girls so I nicked hers just before the show started!

I do remember feeling very excited, very comfortable and quite relaxed during the performance – I get more nervous now than I did then – although seeing my Mum weeping as Miss Lock, the pianist, pounded out the carols gave me a bit of a shock. Miss Lock was very funky, all blonde hair, silver chunky jewellery and a permanent suntan. She noticed me looking confused as my Mum broke down in floods as if to say, 'Don't worry, Martine, your mother's fine.'

Every year I dreamed of playing Mary in the infants' nativity play, but I never got the part. That's showbiz for you. Anyway, my performance as the angel all those years ago has left me with a lasting nickname. Mum had other nicknames for me that were twice as embarrassing. Doughnut, for example, which started when I was four, because I was so soft and sweet – ah! – and she still calls me that today. But Angel really stuck. We later named one of our companies Angel and I also have it tattooed on my right ankle.

When I moved up to Shacklewell Juniors, aged six and a bit, I got my first taste of performing in a proper play – and my first experience of envy from all the other kids, who got the hump because I soon landed all the lead parts. The teacher who inspired me then was called Miss Smith and our first project was a production of *Noah's Ark*. We had this big boat, which everyone had painted, and we were getting stuck into rehearsals. There was a girl there called Leigh and she was supposed to sing, 'So you boys can see my bloomers, thank you. No, I'd rather not . . .' And then she would flash a little bit of her knickers.

Well, Leigh wouldn't do it. She was shy, I suppose. Instead of giving a quick flash all she managed was to lift her skirt a little bit to the knee – as you would at that age. Miss Smith was sensitive to Leigh's unease and told her, 'You're not really comfortable with this, are you, Leigh? Would you rather someone else do it?' Leigh, who looked as if she was going to cry every time she opened her mouth, nodded at Miss Smith. The teacher then asked if there was anybody else who would like to do it. Because I was a bit of a show-off, my hand shot up. I was waving and jumping up and down with unbridled enthusiasm.

'OK, would *you* like to have a go?' she asked. 'What's your name?' I said, 'It's Martine, miss, and I'd like a go.' Miss Smith began playing the piano. All I could see was her head above the piano and her arms going up and down as she bashed the keys. At that time my Mum always bought me socks and knickers with cartoons and slogans on them. So I got up on the chair, stood up so everyone could see me and sang my line: 'So you boys can see my bloomers, thank you. No, I'd rather not . . .'

I wasn't quite expecting the reaction of the class when I turned round and pulled my skirt up. I bent over and gave everyone a flash of my knickers. That instant the whole class went into uproar because my knickers had 'Sunday' written on them – and it was Wednesday. Everyone was laughing their head off. Miss Smith didn't know what to do. She stopped playing the piano as if she was in shock and said quietly, 'I think that's great, Martine, but I feel you should change your knickers for the performance, because it definitely won't be on a Sunday.'

As I got more and more lead roles in school plays I made a few enemies. I remember that a girl in my class called Pippa took a big dislike to me for a while and gave me my first taste of bullying. I was only four foot seven for years and everyone used to say I was a real titch, until I suddenly shot up by about five inches in my teens, not that this made me exactly lofty. My Mum is tall and so is my Dad. I reckon I must have taken after my Nan, Keith's mum, who is really small.

Anyway, Pippa was much taller than I was. But for some reason she started to tell people that I was bullying her. If you'd seen the size of her and the size of me you'd realise how ridiculous that very notion was. I'd have had to be the thickest, stupidest girl in the East End to want to pick on big Pippa, because I'd have been squashed in one go if I'd tried. The strange thing was that people *did* believe her and I kept getting called to see the head teacher, who'd say sternly, 'Martine, you're making people upset.' And I would say, 'No, no I'm not' – and I wasn't.

Things came to head one day as we were standing by the

sunflowers we were growing for a project. We had to measure them with a tape rule. Pippa was hiding behind one of them and looking at me, her eyes filled with hatred. All of a sudden she put her arm in her mouth and bit herself, leaving deep teeth marks and I instantly worked out what she was up to.

'Don't you dare go and tell Mr Ward that I did that,' I screamed. But, of course, that was exactly what she did. She was the most amazing actress you've ever seen in your life – and I've seen some. She even made herself cry. I was called over and asked if I'd done it.

'I promise I didn't bite her,' I pleaded. 'She's just bitten herself over by those sunflowers. Check the teeth marks – they won't match mine. I have not bullied her. I have not bullied her,' I repeated.

The matter went away, but for only a while. After that episode she used to smirk at me every time she saw me, and when she said things about my size, I'd hit back with, 'At least I'm not a giant. I'm glad I'm just a shrimp when I see you!' Yes, it was childish stuff – we were children. But that wasn't the end of it.

One day I was playing with my friend Angelique at her house. There was a knock at the door and we went to see who it was. There outside were Pippa and her mum, of all people. I could sense there was going to be a confrontation, but had no idea what had prompted it. Pippa's mum said to me, 'If you ever, ever lay a finger on my daughter again I will go mad' – which she promptly did, right there on the doorstep.

I burst out crying as Angelique's mum raced to the rescue to try to placate her. 'Listen, Martine's just a little girl,' she explained. 'Why are you getting involved?'

But Pippa's mum was having none of it. 'She's making my daughter's life a misery,' she ranted.

For my part I honestly didn't know what was going on –

I really didn't understand it. I knew I'd said horrible things to Pippa but only after she'd pushed me to the edge. I was being sent to see the headmistress for all sorts of things Pippa had accused me of, none of which I'd done, and all because this Loony Toon had bitten and kicked herself and done these nutty things to get attention.

Maybe it was because I was doing OK at school. I simply didn't know, but I was deeply upset by the whole situation. It seemed to be getting out of control. Anyway, after mother and daughter had had their say, Pippa's mum nudged me quite hard and let off a final volley of abuse right in my tear-stained face.

Later that evening I told my Mum what had happened. 'I am not having it,' Mum raged. 'I'll take care of this.'

She went round to Pippa's house so fast you'd never have seen anything like it in your life. Mum knew where they lived, because she'd been out with Pippa's mum on girlie nights. She knocked loudly on the door, and when a little kid answered she said, 'Get your mum and get her out here now.'

Pippa's mum appeared a few moments later. 'How would you like it if I treated you like you treated my daughter?' Mum asked her. 'You might be bigger than my daughter but I'm bigger than you. Who do you think you are, picking on my daughter? You're an adult, for goodness sake – you should know better. If you lay one finger on my daughter again, I swear to God you will regret it for the rest of your life.' Mum raged on: 'You're sick. Why are you bullying a little girl over problems between kids? You're just a big bully yourself. Martine has never done anything to Pippa, so I don't know what Pippa's problem is. I've asked the teachers and nobody's ever seen Martine do anything to your daughter. She's making the whole thing up.' Mum just flipped the minute she'd thought someone had hurt me.

Sadly, my experience with Pippa wasn't the only time I got bullied. There were a couple of girls I always used to hang around with at school. We were quite good friends until I started getting the bigger parts in school plays and singing more solos. Then they started turning nasty. Usually they'd get me in the toilets and take their frustrations out on me. They'd push me around a bit and give me a sharp whack. It was horrible. They didn't punch me but there would be plenty of slapping and hair-pulling. Afterwards I'd have to go back to my class as if nothing had happened, because they'd said that if I dared mention it to anyone then they'd just do it again. A lot of kids have the same experiences at school. To grown-ups, bullying can sound quite trivial but they should never forget the harm that fear and unwarranted beatings can do to a young mind.

I had some *good* friends at junior school, too, and grew particularly close to three Afro-Caribbean mates, Ayo – a big girl who had boobs even in junior school, I swear – Ada and Charmaine. We used to bring tapes into school, stick them in an old Fisher Price cassette player and dance to Bob Marley in the playground

Another really happy memory for me at around this time, when I was six or seven, was the arrival of Pouchie, a little puppy Mum bought for me. Pouchie looked just like Gizmo from the *Gremlins* movie. A lot of people say their dogs look like that but my dog really did. I called her Pouchie, because originally I wanted this cuddly *toy* dog with pink ears and paws: 'Little Pouchie, lovely little Pouchie' – I think that's how they described her in the Argos catalogue. I used to look through that catalogue every year in the run-up to Christmas. And, like any little girl, I'd go, 'I want that, I want that, I want that and that and that,' with my fingers rushing from one shiny new toy to the next one. Ah, Argos – a kid who had everything in that catalogue really could have a perfect Christmas. They'd be totally spoiled, too, but isn't that what Christmas is all about? Anyway, Pouchie was in there and I remember Mum coming back from work one day – I had short spiky hair at the time – and in her arms she was cradling this beautiful little dog.

She told me straight away that the little puppy was not the pink Pouchie in the catalogue in case I got disappointed, but she then said I could call her Pouchie if I wanted.

I looked up at Mum and went, 'But Mum, isn't it Gizmo?' Its little rubbery face really was a dead ringer for Gizmo's.

'No,' she said. 'It's not Gizmo but she does look like it, doesn't she? It's a little girl puppy!'

I was absolutely ecstatic. She was beautiful, little Pouchie. I had her until I was about eighteen. Oh, and when I think of the things I used to do with her, well, it's so embarrassing. I used to put her in my doll's pram and take her for a walk. Then, when I was a little older, she was put on the back of my bike while I pedalled around. The poor dog used to be hanging on to the back for dear life, her little paws desperately trying to grab hold of something to stop her hitting the deck. It must have nearly killed her! Honestly, I laugh about it now but Mum used to say, 'Martine [or Doughnut], that dog's walking funny. Have you put her on the back of that bike again?'

'Of course not, Mum,' I'd reply lying through my little back teeth.

I say lying through my back teeth, because I didn't really have many other teeth to speak of at that time, owing to a little accident that had happened a couple of years earlier when we first moved back to London. We used to travel everywhere by bus when I was really young, not the flash modern buses but the old-fashioned ones with no doors, just a platform you hopped on to at the back and a staircase to the top deck. Like most kids I loved travelling upstairs, right at the front where there was this big metal bar running from one side to the other, covered in white tape for people to grab hold of when the bus got going.

I used to like playing with that bar and would spend entire journeys lost in my own little world, gnawing on it as if it were a giant Milky Bar chocolate. It drove Mum nuts! Well, on one trip, I was in my accustomed place at the front, chewing away at the white tape, when Mum started having a go at me.

'Don't bite that,' she said. 'It's disgusting. It's dirty! People's dirty hands have been on that. Martine, take your mouth off!'

Of course I just ignored her and carried on until, at the very moment when Mum stopped shouting, the bus came to a sudden stop. The ferocity of the brakes sent a judder all the way down its chassis, a jolt that was so strong it literally smashed all my front teeth out on the grab-rail! What a 'nana I felt! I can see the funny side now but, if you were to flick through all my infants' school pictures, you would see that I've got no teeth. My baby teeth were completely knocked out and, instead of looking like a cute kid with long hair and a sweet little smile, I looked like a gummy old granny.

I think all little girls are interested in their appearance long before they become teenagers, and I was no different. There was a woman across the road who had the same size feet as mine. I can't remember now whether that was because she was especially small or whether I had giant plates of meat for a kid. One day, when I was about six, she came over and handed me a pair of her old high heels, as there was a hole in the sole of one of them. Holes in the sole? Not a rarity round our way. So I grabbed the shoes and did what Mum used to do when she had a hole and couldn't afford to go to the cobbler's. I got an empty corn flakes box and cut out an insole to fill the gap and off I went – or rather didn't. It must have taken me about forty-five minutes to totter to school that morning, not the usual fifteen – and my Nan was going spare: 'Jesus, oh, Jesus, oh fucking Jesus!' she'd moan in her pronounced Irish accent. 'Martine, if you'll be taking forty-five minutes to walk to school I'm going to tell your mother of you when she gets home.'

'Tell her what you like,' I cried back, because I was loving every painful, wobbly minute of it.

After that I was hooked and started nicking my Mum's high heels to walk to school, padding them out with paper to make them fit. I don't think Nan knew what to make of it, me being such a little lady. When it was autumn she'd point out the horse chestnut trees in the park on the way to school. Now you'd expect most kids to start scrabbling around picking up the conkers. Not me. I'd stand there all proper and grown up in my high heels, aged six, while Nan would be on her hands and knees picking them up like an enthusiastic child.

I suppose when I look back that there were times when I could be a proper little madam. One Christmas, the one before my seventh birthday, I wanted a pair of disco roller skates more than anything. Just before the big day I was in Mum's bedroom, looking through all her clothes and high heels, when I noticed a white cupboard behind her wardrobe. 'An adventure!' I thought and squeezed myself behind the wardrobe to get to the cupboard. There I found carrier bags full of presents for me. I was in seventh heaven but also terrified by the spiders and cobwebs and other creepies. I rummaged through all the bags until I found what I was hoping for – my roller skates. I put them on, laced them up and was skating around the room when I suddenly heard

Mum coming up the stairs. I stopped and began to tug at the boots but couldn't get them off. I was getting into a real panic as I struggled to undo the laces. With Mum almost at the top of the stairs, I decided to try to conceal my behaviour by tucking my feet under the mattress on the opposite side to the door into the room. Mum must have sussed that I'd been up to something from the strange way I was sitting, with only my head and upper body showing above her bed.

'Martine,' she said, 'have you been having a rummage?' I denied it all, of course, but then she noticed some tissue paper and the corner of the skates' box poking out from under the bed. 'Is that the box to what I think it is?' she asked. I couldn't think of anything to say. Mum told me to stand up but I couldn't, because my wheels and the stoppers had got caught under the mattress.

'I can't, Mum, I'm stuck.'

'Don't start, Martine. Stop mucking me around. Stand up now,' she said, her voice barely concealing her anger.

'I can't,' I protested again. 'The wheels have got stuck . . .' Oops!

'So you *have* got 'em on, then,' Mum barked. 'Get them off now and put them back in the box. I'm taking them back to the shop. If you can't be a good girl and not rummage through things that are supposed to be a surprise, then you're not *getting* any surprises.'

I pleaded with her but in vain. She put them in the box with a smug look on her face and took them downstairs. She relented, of course, and I did get my roller skates that Christmas – until then I really wasn't sure whether or not Mum would let me have them – and I remember posing in them for a picture, trying to give the same smug look that Mum gave me when she took them away.

*

My mother had her own life away from Keith, too, but his surprise appearances hung over us both constantly like a horrible black cloud. That said, she still managed to have some fun. She was a very attractive young woman and a lot of men were interested in her. She was also very aware of the damage, the mental harm, that Dad had inflicted on me over the years.

She was so protective towards me that when she went out on a date she did her best to keep it from me. There were times when I was left with a babysitter and, as the evening wore on, I'd peek out of the window to see if she was coming home. Sometimes I'd see her outside and catch her giving some man a goodbye kiss on the cheek, the kind that says 'Thank you very much for taking me home' or whatever. But she wouldn't let them in the house. That didn't make much difference to my attitude towards them, because I used to hate them all – any man who paid Mum attention. I used to give her such a hard time when she came in. It's all quite understandable now that I look back, but at the time it must have hurt her. Who wants to come back from a date to have their little girl shouting things like, 'What's he want from you, Mum? Why is he bringing you home? I don't like him! I hate him!'

There weren't that many men, but one in particular sticks in my mind. His name was David and my Mum was very keen on him for a short while. He looked just like the mustachioed actor Tom Selleck. I'd say she was more in lust than in love with David, but I absolutely hated him nonetheless, for when he did come into our home, he would try to hug Mum in front of me.

That would set me off straightaway, not just mentally but also physically. It would upset my whole system and I'd get in a right state about it. I hated seeing it. It had been years since she'd had a proper romance and David would sometimes stay the night. I think when my Mum realised just how much it was affecting me she pretty much knocked her relationship with David on the head. Young as I was I knew somewhere in my heart that Mum was perfectly entitled to have a loving relationship, but to me, at that time, well, I thought they were disgusting. Not just disgusting but dirty. I couldn't sleep at night for thinking about it. I'd be lying there with my headphones on, saying to myself, 'I hope I don't hear him hurting her again,' because to me the sound of two adults making love had been twisted into something else, because of Keith and his violent assaults on my Mum.

Sex and violence had become quite confused in my little head. All I knew at the time was that I loathed David. Whereas I was used to being in bed with Mum, it was David who was now sharing her bed. Jenny really couldn't have done more to reassure me. She explained quite patiently how no one was replacing me in her affections, but at the same time she also pointed out that, as I was growing up, it was time I slept on my own. She was trying her best to raise me as normally as possible under the most abnormal conditions.

It's funny now I think about it but at the time those conditions felt quite normal to me. I can remember almost bouncing to Shacklewell Junior School during the summer, happy as could be. I can also remember the terror of Dad's visits. Yet, even allowing for the vicious ordeal he had recently inflicted upon my Mum, there was even worse unpleasantness waiting to strike us.

Shortly after the night Dad tortured my Mum, my aunt – Keith's sister – told Jenny about a solicitor who would listen to her and may be able to help sort things out with Dad.

Mum went to see him and told him the full story. The solicitor immediately got an injunction that prevented Keith from coming near our home. Mum was worried that it was just a piece of paper that didn't mean anything, but he assured her that it did. And indeed Keith did violate the injunction on several occasions, but he knew that when he did so the police were always only one step behind him. Whenever he'd turn up, Mum would phone them and tell them he was outside ringing the doorbell, and they'd arrive straight away. He knew that making a call to the police would be the first thing Mum would do when he turned up, so he didn't stick around long. He was usually gone by the time the squad car arrived.

Now that he was unable to terrorise us in the old ways, it wasn't long before Keith decided to exact his revenge. A few weeks after the attack on Mum, he broke into a house in the district and abducted a friend of Mum's. She was sixteen at the time and a beautiful young woman. What happened during that abduction wasn't very pleasant, but even weirder was that, throughout the entire ordeal she underwent at his hands, Keith kept calling her Jenny. He released her the following day and took her home. Once free of his clutches, she told Jenny what had happened and my Mum took her straight down to the police station.

She has never gone into the full details of what happened that night, but she told Mum, 'He kept thinking I was you, Jen, he kept saying your name.' I don't know what drugs he'd taken, but obviously something had flipped inside his brain. Knowing some of what had happened to Mum the last time Dad broke in – the torture, the cigarette burns – I dreaded to think what he had done to her.

Mum has told me that the police were brilliant, particularly a detective sergeant called Chris Coomber.

Mum's friend made a statement, during which she revealed that on the morning that he released her, after the drink and drugs had worn off, he told her that he was going to kill Jenny and me. '"Nobody's going to stand in my way," is what he told me,' she explained.

This time the police didn't hold back. They installed a panic button where we lived and told Mum that, if Keith did ever come back, then she need only press that button and they would be there within seconds. They also put a warrant out for his arrest but, since Keith was still on the loose that night, Mum, the friend and I went to stay with another of Mum's friends, Pamela Paris, who had been a good mate of ours for years and lived at the end of our road. Somehow, Keith found out where we were.

At three o'clock in the morning, with me sound asleep, Mum and Pam heard noises outside. Pam looked out of the door, saw it was Keith and phoned the police. They arrived in minutes, but by then he'd moved round to the back of the house. Pam opened the door to the officers and told them he was at the back, so they rushed straight through the house into the garden. But Keith was gone. He had managed to jump over the garden fence and escape.

It seems, though, that he had meant what he'd said about his intention to harm me and Mum, because he left an array of weapons he'd planned to use on us behind him, including battery acid, a knife and some lead piping. It's frightening to think what would have happened if Mum had opened the door to him. Afterwards, Mum and Pam didn't get a wink of sleep, while the poor friend, who had fled upstairs as soon as she heard the commotion, remained in hiding, terrified that he was going to get her again.

The following day, Keith turned up at my Gran's house as if nothing had happened during the previous forty-eight hours. The friend phoned us later and told Jenny that he'd said he was going to wait in the pub for her. Mum knew what he'd say. He'd conceitedly think that, despite what he'd done, she'd go down there and everything would be fine and happy ever after – but Mum had wised up by now. Instead of going to see him in person, she called the police, who turned up at the pub instead and arrested him. Dad was charged with threatening behaviour and was remanded in custody. It was a good example of his Jekyll-and-Hyde character. When he wanted to seem a charming man who loved his family, he could, and no one would have thought he was ever any different. Everybody who met him said what a wonderful bloke he was, until he went on the turn and things didn't go his way.

Keith was in custody on remand for six months and Mum says that those were the best six months of her life up to that time. The case first went to a committal hearing at the magistrates' court, where the bench decided that there was indeed a case against him and a date was set for the trial at the Old Bailey.

That committal hearing was painfully significant for something unconnected with Keith. Mum's brother, my Uncle Chris, seemed particularly depressed during the proceedings. Softly he told Mum, 'I don't think I'm much longer for this world.' Thinking he was just very nervous about the prospect of having to give evidence in court, Mum assumed he was just fed up with it all, which was totally understandable. The whole family had been through a horrible time. 'Oh, stop being silly,' Mum told him. 'You're only seventeen. You'll be fine.'

Tragically, it proved to be the last conversation they ever

had. Two days later Mum got a phone call from my Gran saying that Chrissy hadn't been to work that day. Mum rang my Uncle Laurence: 'Nobody can find Chrissy,' she said anxiously. He was staying at a friend's flat not far from us. Laurence told Mum he'd go round there and check he was OK. Laurence looked through the letterbox and saw someone lying on the settee. He couldn't see a face, but saw there was no movement. Worried, he called the police, who arrived not long afterwards and promptly kicked down the door. Laurence brushed past the officers and found Chrissy lying there, dead. He was the first to see the body of his brother. Mum thinks seeing his little brother like that has stuck with Laurence ever since. He's never really got over it.

Chris had died just a month before his eighteenth birthday and it was an immense tragedy for our family. Mum remembers Chrissy as a sensitive, handsome boy, who had done quite well at school and afterwards had landed a job as an apprentice. But he'd found it hard living at home with his Mum and Dad and had fallen in with the wrong sort of gang. He began glue sniffing and smoking the odd bit of dope. He was a bit of a mod, who loved listening to music from the likes of the Jam, even if he looked more like Suggs from Madness.

From dope, his drug intake escalated to barbiturates, uppers, downers – whatever, really – and we later found out that this was what had killed him. He overdosed on barbiturates, but, apparently, when the post-mortem took place, the doctors discovered that his lungs had been virtually destroyed by glue sniffing and the heavy smoking.

He was seven years younger than Mum and I adored him. Chris had been around from when I was born. He loved all the kids in the family, but especially me, I think, his little niece. He'd babysit me sometimes and was kind to Mum. He was a big part of my life and used to show me nothing but love. He was the type that loved to laugh, but didn't laugh that often.

We can only guess what was going on in his mind when he did what he did. The pressure of the court case was probably the final thing that got to him. The great irony was that Chris had been a huge support for Mum, and had been a key to her instigating legal action against Keith.

His funeral, like all funerals – but particularly when it's a young person's – was solemn. His sister, Carol, was utterly distraught and screamed and wept through the service. Like Mum and Laurence, she and Chrissy had been very close. She and Chrissy were the ones who had lived at home with their parents when Mum and Laurence had stayed with their aunt as children.

I didn't go to the funeral. When Mum told me Chrissy had died I shut myself in our loo at Greenwood Road, sat down on the toilet seat and wept my heart out. Mum was distraught too, and began a one-woman campaign to highlight the dangers of drug abuse – which was not as common back then before the rave scene came along and threw up tragedies like that of Leah Betts. She even got on London's Capital Radio to speak about the tragedy of Chrissy and the dangers of drugs.

The case against Keith was still set to go ahead. But then the friend vanished. Mum got a call from Detective Sergeant Coomber saying that they couldn't find her. Mum said she was sure she was around. It transpired that she was so terrified of giving evidence against Keith that she'd upped and left – and Mum hasn't set eyes on her since. She phoned Mum once, a few years later, after she'd married John

McCutcheon, to tell her that she'd had her fourth child. There's no rift as such, although her friend's disappearance loused things up for Mum at the time. After that the two of them simply led separate lives and presumably always will.

This friend's evidence was key to the case against Dad, and the police were beside themselves when she vanished. The jury had already been sworn in, everything was up and running and all the written statements had been put forward by the prosecution. There was the battery acid, the knife and the lead pipe as evidence as well as answerphone tapes containing various messages in which Keith had threatened to kill Mum. They had everything they needed to send him away but this friend's evidence was, as I say, crucial. Without her the prosecution felt they could not go ahead.

The police were devastated at not being able to find her, but they couldn't, so the case had to be dropped and Keith was a free man again and back on the prowl. Mum, understandably, was distraught. As far as she was concerned, this had been her one chance to get rid of Keith for good, to remove him from both our lives and to pay him back for all the things he'd done to us.

CHAPTER 4

Dad Again

WITH THEIR CASE against him in tatters, the police had had no alternative but to release Keith Hemmings from remand – bad news, but there was also something good in the air. During all the misery and distress that had led up to Keith's release, Mum had met a new man. His name was John McCutcheon. Mum had first met John at a dinner dance at the King's Head pub in Hackney. John was stocky, averagely tall and came from Glasgow. He had a wonderfully rich accent, but his hair was dreadful in those days, a bad perm with blond streaks!

They'd been out only a few times but she must have felt that there was something special between them. After a few weeks Mum decided she needed to tell John about everything that had been happening in our lives. It was quite a brave move on her part, considering how her past more often than not had put prospective men friends right off. But John, who at that time was working in antique-furniture reproduction, took it all in his stride.

'Right,' he said. 'We'll face this together.' He knew the full story and reassured Jenny that he'd stay by her side through it all. Their relationship was perfect for Mum, who soon invited John to move into our home in Greenwood Road.

John was very good for Jenny, and in time I became pleased for her, though it took a while before I warmed to him or came to terms with our having a man about the place. I began to realise that it was about time she found someone nice after all the horror she'd had to endure. For years we'd been moving round, living here and there, never stopping at one place long enough for Mum to form a proper relationship before we'd have to pack up and move on somewhere else. Either that or she would meet someone and try to start a relationship with them, only for Keith to turn up suddenly and ruin it. Nobody, until John, wanted to take on the baggage that came with the pair of us. Mum never blamed anyone for that. She understood. After all, who would want to take on a woman like Jenny with a crazy psychopathic ex-boyfriend on the loose?

As I said, I didn't like John much at first. In fact I absolutely hated him. That feeling slowly subsided as time passed and I became quite nonchalant about it all. Then, in the midst of all the trouble with Keith and the courts, my Mum said to me one day, 'Martine, I want to ask you something. What would you think if me and John got married?'

I answered quite truthfully at the time by saying, 'I don't care, so long as I'm a flower girl and get a nice dress,' because that's the way you tend to do things when you're that age. I think my offhand response quite upset Jenny.

'Oh, please don't be like that, Martine. If you're not happy, just say so.'

But I said, 'No, I don't care, I don't care what you do. Do what you want.'

If I sounded a little beastly I soon learned better. After a while, you see, I started to realise that, with John around the house, Keith didn't come and visit us any more.

John was a very old-fashioned guy, not especially emotional – at least not on the surface – but he was somebody who seemed very strong, very steady. In short, he was somebody with whom Mum felt safe. I think she was in love with the idea of our being safe – of no longer having to pack up and move – and with the sense of security that came with having a man about. She was also in love with the notion of having a house and a nice car. Yes, she was in love with all that, but I don't think she was ever truly in love with John, whereas the minute John met Jenny he was smitten by her, and you knew she was just what he wanted.

John had been married before and had a daughter, Isla, but his marriage had collapsed. When he had met Mum, they struck an immediate bond. They both needed each other at the time. I soon grew to love having a man around I could call Dad and I knew he loved Mum so much. He treated her properly. John helped us both in so many ways. His wages at that time weren't half bad and I got the best Christmases I'd ever had. It was great just being able to send Christmas cards addressed to 'Mum & Dad'. But things changed in another way, too, because for years I had been able to step out of the bath, say, and run around the house naked. Now I knew I had to be careful and wrap up in a towel before dashing to my room, because there was a man about the place.

For me, though, by far the most important feeling I got from having John around was that I started feeling safe for the first time in my life. Selfish, I know, but there was something for me in all of this as well as something for my Mum. John, it soon became clear, was nothing like my Dad. Here was a man who wasn't going to take what he wanted, then turn nasty and go away.

So marry they did, and in the best tradition there promptly followed a honeymoon, a two-week break – originally intended as a two-week break from me as well. Yours Truly was dropped off at Uncle Laurence's and off Mum and John went – first for a week in Devon, then for a week staying with one of my aunts, Kim, in Wales. They had planned a more expensive honeymoon, but this would have to do for now.

Well, at the end of the first week Mum missed having her little Angel around so much that I ended up joining them for the second week. They came back and picked me up from my uncle's house in Essex and took me to Wales with them. What a week! We were staying near a golf course and I went off to follow my Auntie Kim as she hacked her way around the greens and fairways. 'Stand back, Martine, stand back,' Auntie Kim shouted as she sized up her shot.

But I must have been in a world of my own, because I don't remember her shouting at me at all. Instead I just wandered closer and closer to her until – *whack!* Auntie Kim's golf club hit me straight in the eye. So my main recollection of my Mum's honeymoon was getting smacked in the face with a golf club and receiving a souvenir shell lamp from their week in Torquay. The marriage had begun with a bang all right.

Things were ticking over remarkably well compared with the horrors of before. I should have known it was too good to last. We all should have known, because, just as we were getting used to leading a normal life, we got hit with the proverbial bolt from the blue. It still sounds almost unbelievable, considering what he'd done, but Keith served Mum with a summons for access to me!

She went straight down to the solicitors who had issued

the court injunction against Keith to seek their advice. Then, a few days later, Keith had the audacity to phone us at home. He spoke to John first and said menacingly, 'I think we need a little meet, mate, don't you?'

John thought it better to confront the beast, and so arranged to meet Keith in a pub on a corner near to wherever he was living at the time. Mum bravely decided to go with him, while I was left with a babysitter.

Keith had plenty of surprises in store. After spending thirty-odd years living as Keith, my Dad had suddenly decided to revert to his proper first name, Thomas. Mum thinks it was as if my father was trying to make a statement along the lines of, 'I've grown up now – I'm no longer Keith the dodgy, druggy woman beater. I'm now honest Tom.'

Down at the pub he began by telling John that, while he was Jenny's husband, he would never be my Dad, and that as my natural father he had every intention of seeing me. Mum told Keith flatly that I didn't want to see him. Instead of slugging it out in the pub at the end of the night, as was his habit, Keith, Tom, Dad, whatever he called himself, slipped quietly into the night to consider his next move.

And that next move was his decision to go ahead with his threat to fight for access to me. Not just access but, unbelievably, Dad and his lawyers were preparing to fight for sole custody, effectively removing me from the care of Mum and John and placing me almost entirely in his hands. The shock was so overwhelming it floored me. I was baffled, unable to conceive of what life might be like if he won. The court papers were issued via Mum's solicitors. The case was to be heard at the Old Bailey, of all places.

I was just nine years old at the time and blessed with a very vivid imagination. To say it was weird being at the Old Bailey would be a huge understatement. People had been telling me that some of the biggest villains and murderers of all time had been tried at this court, the most famous in the land, so there I sat with my imagination running wild as we waited for our case to begin.

I was nervous about meeting the judge, really quite scared. I remember thinking that he must have laid eyes on all these evil people and hoped he didn't think I was an evil person, too. The case was quite hard for a nine-year-old to follow, but I remember Mum's barrister saying all these things about our past to the judge. At the end of that the judge said that he wanted to talk to me privately in his chambers. Mum explained quietly, 'Martine, the judge wants to talk to you. He wants to know why you've made the decisions you've made about who you want to stay with. Do you want to do that?'

So I said, 'Yeah, OK, I'm a bit scared, Mummy, but all right, I'll see the man.'

Mum was brilliant. 'Oh, you've got no reason to be scared of him, Angel,' she whispered gently. 'He's a good guy.'

So there was I, this little girl, tottering off into the judge's chambers. I walked through the court, passing Mum on one side and my father on the other. He actually looked very smart, but that was not surprising: I always remembered him as being very smart when I was younger – smart and handsome, too, always popular with the ladies. That day he stood there in a suit – quite a dark, formal suit. I was in a little cream dress which Mum had bought me from somewhere near the Alfred Marks employment bureau in Victoria where she worked. It was a chiffon number that was completely out of fashion by the eighties. It was horrible. It had an elasticated waist built in and a little belt that you put in through the hoops. That was topped off with little white lacy ankle socks and black patent-leather shoes. If the judge was presiding over a fashion contest, I would have been on a complete loser.

The judge, I have to say, was particularly nice. I thought he looked a bit like Father Christmas. He was old and grey under his wig and had big cheeks and twinkly eyes. I stood in front of him in this horrible chiffon thing and listened attentively as he said, 'Please, young lady, would you sit in this chair.' He pointed to a big chair next to his, which I thought was absolutely massive. The next thing the judge said left me gobsmacked. 'That's a nice dress. Where did you get it from?' I suppose he was just being nice so that I wouldn't be too overwhelmed by it all. Either that or he needed glasses.

'Do you understand what you're here for today, Martine?' he asked. I said I did. 'We just need to decide whether you want to spend time with your Daddy or not,' he went on in his deep judge-like voice.

I said that I didn't want to spend any more time with my Dad ever. Without batting an eyelid he replied, 'Why is that?'

And I explained that it was because he kept doing horrible things to my Mum. 'Sometimes he comes in and says nasty things to me, too, when he thinks that I'm asleep. He'll come in and say something that he's done and I'll be upset and run into my Mum's room.

'He'd say weird things like; "I suggest you go in and see Mummy now, because she's been bad again," and then I'd run into Mum and see that she was crying. And I've seen him hit her, too: I saw him smash her head on the sink.'

I told the judge that we had panic buttons installed in the house by the police and that I'd hear Mummy screaming when Dad came round to hurt her. I described how she'd sometimes even have to go to hospital after the beatings. 'I just don't think Dad's a nice man,' I said. 'I don't want to be with him any more, please.'

The judge sat and listened to it all and then looked at me in a kindly sort of way: 'Do you know what, Martine? I'm going to tell you something and I hope it makes you very happy,' he said.

'What's that?'

And then he told me: 'You will never, ever have to see your Dad again.' I responded by bursting out laughing because I was so happy. I giggled with delight, and then asked, 'Really? Really? Are you telling me the truth? Can you really do that?'

And he replied, 'Yes, I can do that. Then when you're eighteen —'

But I interrupted him again and said precociously, 'That's ages away.'

'I know,' the judge said coolly. 'But when you are eighteen, you'll be a grown-up and can make up your own mind about whether you see him or not. But until then he's not allowed within a certain distance of you.' He proceeded to ask me if that made me happy, and I said that it made me feel *much* happier.

Unbelievably, I then told him there was something else I didn't want to put up with any more. The judge fixed me with a hard but reassuring stare: 'And what's that, young lady?'

Quick as a flash I said, 'I don't want to ever have to eat Brussels sprouts again, either!'

Now it was the judge's turn to burst out laughing. With a huge smile he told me, 'Well, Martine, that's something you'll have to talk to your Mum about, I'm afraid. There's nothing I can do about that.'

He gave me a little pat on the knee. 'Well now, young lady, I suggest you go outside and wait for your mum and give her a big cuddle.'

I did just that. I got down from the big chair and a nice

lady, who was probably an usher, walked me out and waited with me until Mum and John came over. I looked at my Mum and my Mum looked at me. I didn't say a word, but gave her a little wink instead and she started laughing. I walked out hand in hand down the court steps with John and Mum, and that was that.

As we made our way I had to walk past Dad, but I couldn't look at him. I could feel him looking at me but I averted my eyes. I haven't seen my father since and I have no wish to – and he's seen me only on telly. I'd like to say I've never heard from him again but that wouldn't be quite true.

Keith was denied any access to me. He was also told he could never apply for it again. With business done we went off to celebrate. We went to Ridley Road market, in Dalston, where I was treated to a little hamster, which I named Harry. Sadly, he didn't last long, because he kept biting me every time I tried to feed him. He ended up starving to death. I cried and cried for weeks afterwards, thinking that I'd killed him. Mum said, 'You're supposed to feed and water him – what were you thinking of? Whenever I checked that you'd put food in there —'

'Yeah,' I said, 'but he used to knock it over when he used to run in his wheel and then he couldn't find what I'd given him. Whenever I used to go and put more in he used to bite my hand.' He was a vicious hamster for sure and I said to Mum, 'I wish we'd never bought him!'

Not long after the court case, Mum, John and I changed my surname to take on John's, McCutcheon, so that for the first time in my nine years on this earth we could all be a proper family. It felt great. Mum has since said that I gave a self-assured performance that day in court and, apparently, I'd also told the judge about wanting to be an actress and a singer. He told Mum after the case that I was the most level-headed nine-year-old he'd ever spoken to in his life. My confidence comes from my Mum. She's a strong, determined woman.

Funnily enough I don't remember telling any strangers about my dream of becoming a singer and a dancer in such a serious way before meeting the judge. Lots of young people have such dreams when they're little, but there was no doubt that I was getting increasingly serious about going for mine – despite my tender years. Mum knew that it wasn't idle talk. She had recognised the fact that I was something of a natural when I was only a few months old, and had had my picture taken for the Labour Party poster.

Obviously, money was tight when I was a kid, but one of the things I *could* do was watch films on television and later, when I was a bit older, on videos – when we could afford to rent them. I think it was these that pretty much made me decide that I wanted to become an actress. I adored watching films like *Hello Dolly, Funny Girl* and *The Way They Were*. I was hooked on anything to do with Barbra Streisand. Mum had lots of her records and we had this big old record player. It was like an old sideboard from the fifties on which I'd forever be playing her records and singing along.

Mum was a big Streisand fan too. She was also a fan of many other singers such as Crystal Gayle, Dolly Parton and Meat Loaf, and I used to sing along to them, too. I've always had a real knack for picking up the words from songs, but back then I used to sing them in my own way. Mum says I was a bit of a daydreamer, an understandable reaction to living in fear of my father for so long: music and movies continued to be my fantasy world, my escape route.

CHAPTER 5

Charity

SCHOOL PLAYS, MODELLING jobs and those fabulous movies from the forties and fifties had given me more than just a taste for show business. I was fascinated and intrigued by it, and was beginning to do more than just dream about following my heroines – such as Streisand and Marilyn Monroe – on to the big screen. Where I think I was luckier than most kids from my kind of working-class background was that I received so much encouragement. Not in terms of being pushed into making a career choice at nine – that would have been ridiculous. It was more in terms of doing extra classes in dance outside of school. Indeed, if I ever said, 'Listen everyone – I want to be a star!' the grown-ups would simply nod and say, 'Of course you do, Martine.' No one, not even Mum, ever believed I could make a living out of it.

I was incredibly lucky to have had their tacit support, though, and, as I mentioned earlier, to have had plenty of encouragement from the age of five or so from the teachers at Shacklewell Infants' and then Junior School. Some kids hate school, but I was never one of them. I absolutely loved it, from games in the playground to the crisp smell of new exercise books, which I can remember even now. My teacher, Ann Smith, had played a big part in boosting my confidence, which, considering the sort of childhood I'd had until then, was a huge help to me as a youngster. And, of course, my Mum did more than most parents in terms of helping me realise my dreams. Once she accepted that I was serious about being a singer and dancer – that it wasn't just fun, fun, fun any more – she really got behind me and gave up much of her time to help and encourage me. Lots of little girls want to be stars, I know; lots of little girls want to be dancers or ballerinas or actresses, but only very few avoid being side-tracked from that dream as they get older.

And let's face it: there are plenty of interesting sidetracks out there. There are boys, for instance, and having a family – which I would love to do one day – but for me the only true fulfilment and enjoyment I'd experienced was from my work. I do believe that, nine times out of ten, if you work as you've never worked before at something and you truly, truly put in everything you can to make yourself succeed, then you will. I'm not saying you'll be a star or a celebrity but you will achieve some of your dreams. I was very lucky in having those two people, Mum and Ann Smith, to give me the confidence to fulfil mine.

My school plays and performances were among the most enjoyable experiences I'd had at Shacklewell. My love affair with singing and acting had become so strong, I was yearning to take it further, and a couple of teachers I had been seeing privately provided the key. I had started these extra dance classes three years before, just before my sixth birthday, and had had some success in such things as local disco-dancing competitions. One class was held in Mare Street, Hackney, run by a remarkable woman called Wendy Foley, a thin older lady who smoked like a chimney and was always tanned, even in the depths of winter. She was great character. 'Come on, girls,' she'd holler. 'Get your Latin American shoes on – we're going to do a class today. Come on, we ain't got all day.' And as she spoke her cigarette ash would be falling all over the place.

There was also a guy called Mark who used to teach me. I was always a bit wary of him, because I didn't like having a male teacher. Again, this was probably because of my Dad. But Mark was a lovely guy. We used to do all sorts of dancing, from disco and ballroom to jazz and Latin American. I absolutely loved it. The classes at Wendy Foley's coincided with various people encouraging me to go even further. They would say to Mum, 'If Martine wants to do jazz or tap or whatever, she'd be really good.' Everyone used to say that to Mum, along with the magic words, 'She should go to stage school, you know.'

But not many kids from our sort of background went to stage school and Mum didn't really know anything about such places. Of course, there are actually a handful of schools in London where kids can go and do normal lessons half the time and then learn singing, dancing and acting the rest of the time, but back then neither Mum nor I had heard of any of them. I thought becoming an actress or a dancer was really something that happened only in America. In fact I used to think that *everything* happened in America and that nothing ever happened in England. The television programme *Fame* – set in a New York performing-arts school – had come and gone, while the movie *Flashdance* held me spellbound. I loved it.

I've really got to thank Wendy Foley for what happened next, something that set me up for where I am today. She told

Mum, not long after the court case concerning Keith and my custody, that if I wanted to do ballet, tap or jazz I ought to go to a young woman called Zayni Halil, who ran a dance school in Stoke Newington a few miles away. Zayni was a Turkish girl who had enjoyed a brief professional career as a dancer but was unable to remain in the business because of family and religious pressures, although her parents allowed her to run a school.

When I first met Zayni she had a little dance school. She was a petite, very beautiful girl. I thought, I hope I'm like you when I'm older. She was very slim and gorgeous-looking, and was an amazing dancer. She had once got on to the *Morecambe and Wise* TV show to tap dance. And that was quite a claim to fame then, because they were regarded as one of the greatest entertainment double acts of all time.

She'd also been to a London stage school that at the time I'd never heard of, called Italia Conti. She'd done loads of jobs dancing, but the *Morecambe and Wise* show was the one that I remember most, because she gave me the outfit that she'd worn for it. It was a top hat and tails with a difference – the outfit had a sequinned waistcoat and a white bow tie with a little leotard and fishnets. It was a great outfit and you can imagine how tiny she was if it fitted me. I was only nine at this time and she was about eighteen or nineteen – but it fitted both of us.

As the weeks went by Zayni would regale me with tales of her life at the Italia Conti school, where you did normal academic lessons while training in dance, drama and singing. 'You would love it,' she said to awe-struck students. 'It's full time, which means you get to dance and sing and act and train every day as well as doing your normal lessons, in the morning or in the afternoon, depending on what day it is.'

Zayni knew all about it, and even had their prospectus and

a video of some of the students who were already there. She gave me the rundown on the place: how it was near the Barbican in the City of London, how strict it was and so forth. She even phoned them for Mum and me, and asked them when their next audition dates were for the following year's intake of new children.

After I had spent a few months with Zayni, she had to close her little dance school, but she offered to tutor me at her home to help me. Armed with the information about Italia Conti's auditions, we had a target to work towards – and it was only eight months away. Because of the limited time, Zayni said she wanted me to come to her home every Saturday to help prepare me for the auditions.

So from then on, every Saturday, Mum would drive me over to Zayni's house in Southgate, which took about an hour, and when I got there Zayni would put down wooden boards for me to dance on. We used to drive there in this horrible old bogey-green Granada. The door used to nearly fall off its hinges. In fact it was such a dodgy door that Mum had to tell everyone, 'Sorry, you should pull the clasp, lift the door and then open it out,' because if they had just opened it in the conventional way the door would have snapped off!

We used to have a good old singalong on the way to Zayni's. Mum would sing to 'Rock With Me Tonight' by Freddie Jackson and 'Always' by Atlantic Starr. She wasn't half bad, either.

Once I was there, Zayni would spend all day coaching me in tap, ballet, improvisation, singing. Everything she taught me was geared towards my getting to a standard acceptable to Italia Conti. She was an excellent teacher, pushing me quite hard and always throwing new things at me to learn. For tap, she taught me a routine to 'It Don't Mean a Thing If It Ain't Got That Swing', including incredibly complicated time steps. Somehow, I managed to take everything on board, and it all did wonders for my confidence.

Eight months later Mum filled out the forms for two different stage schools, Italia Conti and Arts Educational, and a few weeks after that I got the dates for the auditions through the post. They were to take place on two separate Saturdays. Italia Conti was my first choice, because I'd heard such good things about it, and I was less keen on Arts Educational, because it was so ballet-orientated. While I'd loved ballet ever since I first saw *Flashdance* on the telly while aged nine, I really wanted to be an all-round performer and not a disciplined classical ballet dancer. Not only that, but I was also growing a bit more by then, so it was already looking as if I might be too tall to be a ballet dancer anyway.

My teachers at school followed my progress and were always very encouraging. Yet, when some of the other girls found out I was about to audition for stage schools, the bullying began again with renewed vigour. They set about making my life a misery for the next few weeks. Some of them ganged up on me and gave me a real hard time. I couldn't understand why, because I hadn't done anything to them. I was just trying to do something I loved doing and it wasn't hurting them in any way. Looking back now, more than fifteen years on, I guess it was just jealousy, but why I don't know. After all, I'd had no better start in life than the girls who were being cruel to me – in most cases I'd probably had it much worse.

Bullying is something you have to nip in the bud if you can. You have to make sure the bully knows that you're not going to stand for it. There's nothing like developing your own independence and your own strength when it comes to standing up to bullies. I learned to deal with it by laughing in their faces. Once I laughed at them, it made them feel stupid.

*

The day of the audition for Italia Conti was upon me. I was nearly ten. Mum took me along, into a room that seemed absolutely huge, with a group of nine other youngsters. There was a panel of grown-ups there, too, all from Italia Conti except for a representative of the Inner London Education Authority (ILEA), which in those days was able to award discretionary grants to a very limited number of students every year to help them go to a special school like this.

If the stage school put you within their top three or four places, and if you lived in the right borough, then you automatically got a grant from the ILEA. Fortunately, we did live in the right borough, which was just as well, because without the grant there was simply no way my Mum could have afforded to send me to either school, since the fees ran into thousands of pounds a year. In fact the fees were more than she'd earned in God knew how long.

We were there for the whole day and I had to do a bit of everything. A bit of drama – I did a speech from the film *Hello Dolly* – and a piece of ballet, which I did to the Phil Collins hit 'Against All Odds'. That had the examiners in fits, because every other hopeful candidate danced to really conventional classical pieces such as *The Nutcracker* or *Swan Lake*. My modern-dance routine was an interpretation of Donna Summer's 'Hot Stuff'. There was some tap and a song. I chose 'The Lady Is a Tramp'.

You were supposed to wear what they described as a neutral outfit to the auditions – but not little Martine. Oh, no. Even my Mum didn't know that I'd slipped my favourite gold catsuit – covered in gold sequins – and some gold shoes into my kitbag. For some reason I also hid a tube of that gold face glitter inside, but never said a word.

There was a break before I had to sing my piece and I took full advantage of it. I went off to the toilets to make my transformation. The loos and changing rooms ponged of stale sweat and struck me as very dark and dreary. Nevertheless, I must have been gone quite a while, because Mum was waiting there, too, when I emerged. She took one look at me, dressed top-to-tail in gold, with glitter all over my face, and was horrified.

'*Martine!*' Her voice was half-way between a scream and a sob. 'What are you doing? That's not your uniform. You've got to take it off now. Take it off now!'

I stood my ground. 'No, Mum,' I said firmly before adding preciously, 'At least this way they'll remember me, good or bad. There's too many other talented kids here and if I don't do something to make them take notice then we might as well go home.'

By now someone from the school, one of the teachers, had joined us in the loos. She must have picked up on what we were arguing about, because she told Mum, 'It's all right. Let her wear it if she wants to.' As I remember, this teacher was almost in hysterics – I must have looked quite a sight in my sparkly gold outfit.

Back upstairs for the audition, I was given the number one. Oh, no, I thought. I'm going to have to go first. Another wave of panic swept over me. But I need not have worried. The number didn't relate to anything except identification. I sat back down as the other mums exchanged glances and no doubt passed a few catty comments about my costume.

As I left Conti at the end of that day, I was thinking that the audition had gone quite well. I did screw up a poem they wanted me to read, 'My Mother Said', saying 'Thrance' instead of 'France'. I also recognised how good a lot of the other kids were, so it was hard to judge whether I'd get in or not – and even if I did get a place it was vital that it should be a high-ranking one in order for me to qualify for the grant.

A letter came through from Italia Conti a few days later – I knew instantly it was from them as I picked up the post from the doormat, because they had their own envelopes with the school's name and address printed on them. I gave it to Mum.

'You open it,' I said.

'No, you open it,' she said.

'No, you do it, Mum.'

And so it went on.

Finally she told me, 'Go on, Martine, it's your thing . . .'

I was too nervous and excited to do anything, so finally Mum just tore open the envelope and screamed with excitement. 'You've done it!' she said. 'You're in!' I couldn't believe it.

Italia Conti, one of London's top stage schools, had given me second place so, I was in, *and* I would get a grant. I had it! I was so excited. That night we celebrated in style. We spent a fiver on a Chinese takeaway and to this day I can still remember what we ate: sweet-and-sour prawns and special fried rice. Things seemed to be finally coming right. But our joy was to be short-lived.

When Mum contacted the ILEA to confirm the details of the grant she was told that I wasn't going to get their financial assistance after all, because of a new initiative to encourage ethnic minorities. They said they couldn't give the grant to anyone other than those from minorities, because that was their new policy. I was heartbroken, utterly heartbroken.

I'd got a place at Italia Conti only for the council to change their rules, something we were not informed of at the beginning. We should have been told. Mum was devastated, too, and she had the tough job of breaking the news to me. 'I don't know how to tell you this,' she said, her voice cracking slightly. 'You've got in the school but I'm afraid you haven't got a grant.'

I simply couldn't understand what the problem was. After all, I'd done everything I was supposed to do.

'What do you mean?' I said. 'I've got into the school and they said if I got into the school and came in the top three or four then I'd get the grant. Where did I come?'

'You came second,' Mum replied despondently.

'Well if I came second,' I continued, 'then I should have easily got the grant. I don't understand.'

Mum tried to explain it to me, but I couldn't comprehend. It seemed so unfair. I was in tears for days, because I'd worked so hard. Zayni didn't know what to say either. 'It's just politics, Martine, it's just politics,' she explained as she tried to comfort me.

I had to get my head round the fact that I wasn't going to be able to go. Even worse, I started contemplating the alternatives: that I was going to end up at Kingsland, the local comprehensive, for instance, and a tough old place at that. Mum, though, refused to give up and told me firmly that it wasn't over yet. She was determined to do everything in her power to help me. First she arranged for me to begin attending Italia Conti's Saturday classes, for which she could just about scrape the money together.

'We won't tell them you haven't got the money for the rest and by hook or by crook we'll find you this money,' she vowed. Mum was more confident than I was because, while she was saying this, I just kept thinking, It ain't going to happen. There were no scholarships available, either. Everywhere we looked, we hit brick walls.

I really didn't want to have to go to Kingsland Comprehensive School. It was scary if only because the kids there were so big. You used to see people mucking about and having fights outside the gates. As a kid, you think, That's *big* school, and I admit I was terrified of the whole idea of it. The areas from which the school drew its pupils were slowly but surely going downhill and getting worse year by year. Holly Street Estate, which was near us, was typical: it had the most terrible reputation for drugs and violence. It's since been bulldozed – need I say more?

That said, there was still a small part of me that quite fancied the idea of going to Kingsland, as it was a place that all the girls over the road went to and a lot of my friends were destined to go there. But we were getting deep into Thatcherism at this time, and the emphasis was on choice, so many people who wouldn't normally have had the opportunity to send their kids to a private school were now beginning to do just that – so long as they could afford to, of course. For example Angelique's parents didn't want to send her to Kingsland School, so she went elsewhere. These were just normal people who wanted the best for their kids, and, because the local schools were so bad, they were forced to try to find somewhere else for them, to give them a decent start in life.

Mum remained determined to do everything in her power to help me fulfil my dreams. Someone had told her about a book of grant-making trusts that was kept at the public library. This tome, she was told, listed hundreds of trusts, scattered throughout the country, that helped people improve themselves – churches, businesses, even Laura Ashley – all of them prepared to invest in somebody because they believed in them.

So, every Saturday after I'd finished my class at the Conti at 3 p.m., Mum would take me down to the library for the rest of the day and we'd sit in the reference section and wade through this massive book, looking for trusts that might be willing to help me. We looked at every single one, and there were literally hundreds to write to. I'd write out the trust's address and then stick stamps on the envelopes. Mum had written a standard letter which she'd photocopied at work. At the library she would address it and add the date. I'd slip it in the envelope and on the way home we'd stop off at a post box and send them off, always enclosing a stamped, addressed envelope with each application.

Mum's letter simply explained why she hoped they would consider helping us. She told them about her little girl, whose life revolved around singing and dancing and acting and who'd been offered a place at a stage school but wasn't going to be able to go, because her Mum couldn't afford to pay the fees. Despite her efforts and outward optimism, Mum was actually far from confident that we'd be successful and find anyone to assist us. After all, I was now ten years old and I probably was, as far as they were concerned, just a precocious child who had this idea in her head that she wanted to be a star. Mum must have copied and prepared well over a thousand letters. That's no exaggeration.

It wasn't long before we started getting replies. In fact the postman must have thought the Christmas rush had started early at our house, because we got sackloads of mail. Every day, with every post, more and more letters would arrive, invariably bringing more and more rejections and usually starting, 'Thank you for your letter but regrettably . . .' They were all very polite and apologetic but the result was always the same: they couldn't help.

Mum never actually got to speak to anyone at any of these organisations. Perhaps it would have been easier if she had: at least then she would have been able to get my case across more clearly. But they all insisted on contact by letter, as the correspondence could then be presented to a board of trustees who would meet to see if you fitted their criteria. They all had very tight rules on whom they'd give money to. Some, for example, would help only boys, some only girls from a certain area, while some helped only people trying to study for a particular career in a subject such as engineering or medicine. The arts, sadly but predictably, didn't seem to figure very highly on anyone's list of deserving causes.

It was extremely demoralising, to put it mildly, but Mum did her best to remain cheerful about it (though I knew she felt the same way as I did). I'd come a long way to get offered a place at Italia Conti and now it was looking very much as if that would all have to be forgotten, because we were flat broke. Talk about unfair!

But Mum refused to be beaten and kept writing those letters. One of the very last ones we posted was to a Church of England charity based in Moorgate, called the Reeves Foundation. This was a small organisation which usually gave grants to young lawyers doing their Bar exams, medical students needing extra help to pay their way through medical school, or people training to become professional classical musicians such as flautists or cellists. To even be *considered* for a grant from them you had to live in the Smithfield area of London or have worked in the Smithfield or City area. Mum, thank heavens, had worked in the City most of her life with the Alfred Marks employment bureau, and at various other places doing cleaning jobs, so off went one of our standard letters. I'd almost given up hope by now and could think of nothing more than starting at Kingsland in September.

Within a week we had a reply – our first breakthrough. The Reeves Foundation was arranging a board meeting and intended to discuss my case and consider me for a grant.

They planned to take into account my history and background, what Italia Conti had made of me and why I'd got into the school in the first place. We were ecstatic, even though we were not out of the woods yet. They hadn't said they *would* give me a grant, but at least they were considering me. Progress at last!

The days leading up to the Reeves Foundation board meeting were exciting but also nerve-wracking. I knew this was my very last chance. I'd been going to Italia Conti's Saturday classes by then for about three months and Mum was already finding it tough having to scrimp the cash together even for that. She was in arrears with my fees by a couple of weeks. John was earning but, with businesses struggling against the recession, doubted he could have funded me through somewhere as expensive as Italia Conti.

It felt like an eternity before the letter from the Reeves Foundation we were praying for dropped on the doormat. Mum could barely pluck up the courage to open it. We were standing there in our living room at Greenwood Road, next to a very dodgy-looking bar we had been given by friends. It was in the shape of a ship and wouldn't have looked out of place in Del Boy's flat in *Only Fools and Horses*. I remember her reaction as she ripped open the envelope and pulled out the letter it contained. This was my moment of truth.

The letter was signed by one Carol Goddard, the administrator of the charity, and it was just the news we wanted, not to mention *needed*, so desperately. She said they had considered my case and they were delighted to confirm that they would be able to help. They would pay my school fees, which at that time were £1,260 a term, and they would do so until I was sixteen.

We couldn't believe it. After all we'd been through, at last someone was willing to help.

CHAPTER 6

Stage School

AFTER MONTHS OF sweating it out and wondering if I would ever get to go to Italia Conti, the last few weeks leading up to my first term there were unbelievably exciting, like living in a fairy tale. Every minute of every day, my mind would be racing, counting down to the big day. There was much to do to get ready for school and plenty of rules and requirements to keep me and Mum occupied.

Everyone had to wear a uniform – not just any uniform from any old store but a really smart outfit from a little shop in Stepney run by a Jewish couple. The guy was quite eccentric and made Mum wait for ages before he served her. Everything he brought out was too big for me – and he said to Mum, 'Your daughter is too thin – we've got nothing to fit her!'

Mum told him, 'Well *make* something to fit her – she can't wear that kilt, because it's round her ankles.'

The uniform was beautiful. It consisted of a kilt of light-blue tartan with a dark-blue check running through it. You had to wear it with white socks and black shoes. Then there was a blue shirt and a dark navy tie bearing the school's logo: a tiny 'I' set inside a bigger 'C' for 'Italia Conti'. Pupils also had to have a royal-blue jumper, a V-neck with a light-blue stripe in the V, and, best of all, a navy-blue blazer with the IC logo on the left breast pocket. But this time the logo was different. Squeezed between the gaps of the I and the C on one side would be the figure of a ballerina and on the other side the image of an actor. The last must-have item was the school raincoat, if you can believe that.

All in all, it made for quite a strict but incredibly smart uniform. There was more to buy, though, such as performance clothes. These consisted of a black leotard with a certain neck style, and a straight, horrible tank-top-shaped thing, very unflattering, worn with equally horrible thick pink tights. You always had to have your hair in a bun for ballet and wear pink leather or satin shoes with ribbons on your feet. For certain classes you could have elastic-sided shoes, because it was easier to put them on, but really you were expected to wear the shoes that had ribbons.

For tap you had to wear black tights, black leotard, black socks and black tap shoes. For acting it was a little more relaxed. You wore the Italia Conti black T-shirt and a long black acting skirt worn over black leggings or tights, the idea being that, if you were playing a guy, you could take the skirt off and walk around in your leggings; if you were playing a woman you kept the skirt on.

The shopping was done. It must have strained Mum's finances dreadfully but now it was time to start.

We had just moved to a lovely three-bedroom ex-council house in Forest Gate, east London, under Margaret

Thatcher's right-to-buy scheme. Italia Conti was at the Barbican in the City. On the first day Mum took me but after that I'd get a mainline train to Liverpool Street and then a tube train to the Barbican, which meant getting up every morning at 6.30 to get dressed and washed and ready to go. After I had been going there a while, I was able to link up with other kids, and the journey became a bit more fun.

On that first day, I was done up to the nines in my brand-new uniform. Mum reckoned I looked a picture, but I'm not so sure: I had a little grey carpet bag that weighed a ton, my feet were a bit big at the time, I had skinny legs and my uniform was too big for me. I'd also curled my hair for school the night before and put a little bobble in it. I was very excited – and more than a little nervous.

The school itself was spread over eight floors, like a low tower block. The academic classes were on the second floor and that was also where you'd find the headmaster's office. Up another flight there were more classes. The third floor also contained the staff room, the canteen, the public telephone box and the first performance studio, though that studio was used mainly by older students. There were more studios on the fourth floor. The fifth and sixth storeys were where you'd find several activities taking place, be they script-reading, Shakespeare study, ballet, tap or jazz. There were a lot of studios to use, so that many different classes could go on at the same time.

The school also had a unique smell, which I can still feel tingling in my nostrils whenever I cast my mind back to those exciting first days. It was the scent of stale sweat combined with resin. Resin is used in dance classes to give ballet shoes more grip, but its odour, once mixed with the niff of smelly feet and sweaty bodies, is quite unforgettable and spread through all eight floors of the school.

To cater for the wide variety of abilities – a second-former might be strong in dance but weak in acting, for instance – different year groups would be mixed in the various performance classes. The first, second and third years would generally be grouped together, as would the fourth and fifth years. The youngsters would do their performance classes in the morning and study in the afternoons, while the older ones did things the other way round, but the head would frequently mix things up, at least two or three times a year, to keep the timetables varied.

I can remember as clear as day sitting downstairs doing maths and having the teacher banging on about Pythagoras's theorem while all I could hear above me was tappity-tap, tappity-tap as the older kids went through a routine. I'd be sitting there daydreaming, thinking, Oh, I wish I was up there.

There were about twenty-five of us in my year, mainly girls along with four or five boys, but I reckon I was the cheekiest, especially if my first day was anything to go by. The school had its own agency, which put pupils up for jobs in television productions, theatre and adverts, and in a break on my very first day I marched straight into the agency on the first floor, strolled up to the woman in charge and said, 'Hello, have you got any work for me?'

The woman was gobsmacked. 'Who are you?' she demanded.

'I'm Martine, Martine McCutcheon, miss. Have you got any auditions or anything I can go on? Because I don't want to go to normal school. If you can get me out of schoolwork that would be brilliant,' I said. 'I don't want to do any of that.'

I was just so excited to be there that I wanted to meet everyone. I gave the woman, who sat there speechless, a big smile and said, 'Well, if you get anything for me then please let me know.' And then I turned on my heels and walked out.

It wasn't long after that little display that I discovered that the woman I'd seen was Gaynor Seward, who ran the agency, and most of the other kids were terrified of her. And there I'd been, on my first day, asking her if there was any work going! Years later she told Mum she remembered me doing it. And in a way it worked, because the day after that I was sent out for my first audition.

Whenever I'd see her, Gaynor would encourage me to speak more correctly. 'We'll get you talking standard English if it's the last thing we do,' she'd say – and they did. I spoke beautifully when I left the school. It was only when I got into *EastEnders* that I went back to my old habits. Oh, well. At least I know I *can* sound posh if I have to.

One of my first auditions was for American Kool Aid. I got it and ended up doing six adverts for the drink, a synthetic-tasting product that was immortalised in the sixties when it was laced with the mind-bending drug LSD by the first hippies. Gulp! At least none of the samples I tried sent me funny. Mind you, it was hard to tell by the time they had made me up for filming. I had to wear a blue catsuit while almost every bit of exposed skin was painted blue to match. Even my eyelids got the same treatment. We filmed it against a blue background, the idea being that only our hands, feet and head would show up.

The storyline, if you can call it that, was that I had to catch the Kool Aid in my magical blue hands. The drink can was tied on to an invisible string. The guy who was in the ad with me, who was also painted blue, would have put the English cricket team to shame as he caught his drink every time. I, on the other hand, found myself suffering from technical problems. Technical problems? Well, the bloke off camera who was throwing my drink cans to me had the worst aim in the world. Kool Aid was flying literally everywhere except into my mitts as it bounced around on the end of this piece of string connected to what looked like a giant fishing rod. The guy who kept throwing it at me was missing me by a mile and just muttered 'Sorry' each time it passed me by.

It wasn't the best first advert to do and afterwards I thought, I don't know about doing any more! I mean, I looked like a right idiot, even if I *did* get paid £350.

My first school friend, Claudia Hill, didn't fare much better with her first ad. Her family were really glamorous. Her Mum and Dad drove beautiful cars such as Shogun Jeeps, or something similar. I can't remember now what her ad was for, but Claudia ended up hanging around all day waiting to do her bit. She had this gorgeous head of hair, and Jackie, her Mum, made sure that it was all washed and perfectly styled the night before.

When the time came to step in front of the cameras an assistant passed Claudia a cardboard box. 'What's this for?' Claudia asked in all innocence. 'It's to stick over your head,' the assistant replied. So Claudia's first TV ad saw her wear a box on her head! Her Mum was horrified.

Another girl who was often chosen for ads with me was Louise Nurding, the singer, one-time member of the girl group Eternal and now also known as the Liverpool football star Jamie Redknapp's wife. I was friends with Louise all the way through Italia Conti and we're still mates now. In fact, as you will discover later, Louise provided a place for me to stay when things weren't going quite as well as they did at Conti's.

Because I was olive-skinned with dark hair I tended to do a lot of advertisements that were to be shown in places such as Saudi Arabia, the Middle East, Italy and France. In the

Arabian ads I had to do some crazy things such as sing in
Arabic about chocolate mini-rolls and Mickey Mouse
hamburgers. The mini-rolls ad was absolutely barking! I had
to be dressed in a Hawaiian outfit, do a Hawaiian dance and
then sing about the virtues of mini-rolls in Arabic! I have no
idea what I was singing but I can still remember the chorus.
We may have been kids but we certainly had to earn our
crust.

Bullying seems to go on at every school, and Italia Conti was
no exception. Even though I was older now, I still found
myself a target. This time it was my success that was causing
the problem. There were rumours going round at Conti's
that some parents were paying agencies cash to get their little
ones jobs. One girl came up to me and said that she'd heard
a rumour that my Mum was paying the Italia Conti agency
to get me work.

'You're having a laugh, aren't you?' I said. 'Look at you,
little rich girl, with your Italian-label clothes. We've got a settee at home with no legs and we can't afford anything better,
so don't tell me we're paying an agency. The only way I pay
an agency is by being talented and doing what I do. If you
don't like it because I get jobs, then tough titty.'

That shut her up! It's always been my attitude to face up
to people like that and by now I was used to people having
the odd pop at me. Some of it was jealousy at the fact that
I got quite a lot of work. The bottom line, though, was that
I wasn't going to have some mouthy girl telling me the way
things were. My Mum didn't give a toss whether I did an
advert for the Dixons electrical-goods chain, Kool Aid or
whoever. All the money I earned went straight into my own
account, so that if I wanted to leave the school tomorrow

I could. Mum had nothing to gain from bunging agents.

I never got teased for being poor at Italia Conti, which was quite surprising, since so many of the kids were from really well-off families. The bullying thing really boiled down to who you were friendly with and who you saw as rivals. I'd always thought that a girl called Dionne Compton was great. She was very beautiful with long blonde hair, olive skin and piercing blue eyes. She was very similar in looks to the movie star Uma Thurman. If anything, she looked much more stunning in real life than in photos. I wouldn't say she was classically beautiful, but she definitely had something about her. She was tall, maybe five foot eight by the time she stopped growing, with gorgeous long legs and a wonderful athletic build. What's more, she always picked up the dance routines quickly and had a great figure. I had a good figure at school, too, like a ballerina's, and I think people looked at us with green eyes. They'd think the pair of us were a little bit too cliquey, but they were wrong. I think Dionne and I were each other's equal. We would never be horrible to each other and we tended to stick together through everything.

We had other mates in our class, too, such as Victoria Smith. She was a bit of a Patsy Palmer character. She had loads of ginger hair and was a bit of a loony – and very funny with it. She made everyone laugh all the time. I also particularly remember a guy called Giuseppe Pelluso. He was Italian and he too was hilarious and was good mates with a boy called James Hart. We girls used to tease the two boys mercilessly at a time when sex was on almost everyone's mind. At least talking about it was. When the boys were in ballet class and wearing tights we girls would sit together, point at their crotches, and tease: 'Oh look at Giuseppe, his pouch is getting bigger and bigger!'

I was a late developer physically and never really had that

much close contact with men, particularly during my years at Italia Conti. Singing, acting and dancing were my priorities and everything else came second. I was always told, 'Boys will come and go but if you work on your career you'll get back what you put into it.' With men you could never guarantee that. What's more, at Conti's there were a lot of gay men in the making. It wasn't like attending an ordinary school in that respect.

My first television job came up after I'd been at Italia Conti for only a few months. I landed a part in a children's series called *Bluebirds*, in which I was to meet someone who would eventually become my mother-in-law – well, in *EastEnders*, anyway. Her name, of course, was Barbara Windsor. The series was all about these kids who wanted to clean up their estate but got into all sorts of trouble in the process. It also starred Lance Percival, who'd been in lots of *Carry On* films too; Sean Blowers, who went on later to star as the fireman John Hallam in *London's Burning*; and Isabelle Lucas, a very gentle, lovely West Indian actress. I played Mandy, the lead girl. I was the only girl in a gang of boys.

Bluebirds, which ran for six weeks on BBC1, was great fun to do and I adored hanging out with Barbara, whose career – and she'd be the first to admit this – wasn't quite as buoyant back then as it is today. It's funny, because at that time she appeared a lot more distant than she is now. I think she always expected kids, whether they were six, twelve or twenty-three years old, to be professionals, and so it was good to work with her, as she was professionally demanding. I watched her closely and I learned quite a lot from seeing her at work. I saw how she had developed this character of Barbara Windsor – you know, everything from her personality and her laugh to her general demeanour. The real Barbara was the complete opposite of the dizzy blonde sex-bomb character she had created. Barbara is an intelligent and sophisticated woman who is always on top of her game. There's no fooling her. It's amazing to watch her step in front of a camera and see how seamlessly she changes into a totally switched-on person as soon as the director calls 'Action!'

We had a bit of a soft spot for each other even then and she'd help me during filming by telling me where to stand and things like that. One day after filming we went down to this little shop where I bought her a scented make-up bag as a sign of my heartfelt appreciation. That's how much I liked her. The other thing I remember about Barbara was that she never felt the cold. Weird or what? I'd be freezing, wrapped up in a thick coat, while she would be walking about outside in a thin little top and a pair of trousers, teetering around on her high heels as if it were a summer's day.

Talking of summer, once *Bluebirds* was out of the way, Mum took me for a special treat to see one of my heroes live in concert: Mick Hucknall and his band, Simply Red. The very first time I clapped eyes on Mick Hucknall was in the video for the Simply Red hit 'Holding Back the Years' in 1986. I was only ten then but I remember thinking what an amazing voice the flame-haired singer had. He is truly blessed.

Two years were to pass before I got to see Mick and his band in concert. Mum had managed to get two tickets for us to go and catch Mick on the New Flame tour in Docklands. We didn't have great seats but when Mick sang 'Holding Back The Years' solo, with just an acoustic guitar to accompany him, he brought the house down. I may have been a pre-pubescent schoolgirl but he reduced me to tears with that one. Even now I shiver as I remember it and would regard that night as the best concert I've ever been to. At the end of the show I turned to my Mum and just went, 'Wow! Wow! What a top star.'

When we got home Mum teased me over the tears. 'Mart, you were crying,' she giggled, but I wasn't embarrassed in the slightest.

'I know,' I said, 'but I've just got this overwhelming feeling that I'm going to know him one day. I want to put posters of him up everywhere but I'll allow myself only one, because I know I'm going to know him one day and I don't want to embarrass myself by having to tell him I wallpapered my room with Simply Red posters.'

So a solitary poster of Mick went up on my wall, as he took his place next to Frank Sinatra, Marilyn Monroe and Kylie Minogue.

That autumn I got a big boost of confidence at school when I threw a Hallowe'en party at home and invited loads of people from Conti's. In the days leading up to the bash, I started wondering what would happen if only a few of them turned up or if they felt we were too humble to be worth a visit – but turn up they did, as zombies, skeletons, witches, every nightmarish creature imaginable. What Mum must have thought when she went down into the cellar and saw thirty kids dressed up for Hallowe'en, dancing away to 'Bad' by Michael Jackson, I don't know! It must have been a bizarre, not to say slightly ghoulish, sight. Even better, everyone loved the party, which made me feel much more a part of things at school.

When you're at school and find out what the other kids do at the weekends or see what cars their families pick them up in each evening, you soon learn who's got what in terms of money. You soon find out whose parents are loaded and whose are just scraping by. There was a girl called Alison who went to my school and she'd always have to pay for any school trips or fees in cash, because her Mum and Dad didn't like to use cheques! Some of the kids used to be dropped off in Rolls Royces. It was great. Gangsters' kids went to my school, too, as well as a lot of 'old money', because Italia Conti was considered to be *the* traditional stage school.

This period coincided with my transition into woman-hood, and yet, other than hanging out with classmates such as Giuseppe and James, boys didn't really figure in my life at all. I had no interest in them whatsoever. If someone told me 'So-and-so fancies you' I'd be mortified with embarrassment. 'Oh no, that makes me feel ill,' I'd say. Some girls at school were already getting into boys by then and one girl, I recall, always used to have love bites down her neck. She was terrible, absolutely terrible, and was always getting up to something.

In your early teens friendships can be volatile things, but my relationship with Claudia Hill was rock solid throughout our time at Conti's, and it paid dividends, too. I remember landing one job thanks almost entirely to Claudia, which doubled up as a dream holiday. Claudia was with this other agency, not connected to the school, called Little Boats, and had gone for an audition for a Kaye's catalogue photoshoot, which was to take place in Tenerife. Up to that point I'd been abroad only once before, to Spain, with my Mum, who wanted to cross the Channel before she turned thirty. Anyway, I went with Claudia to her audition and got a job on the shoot even though I wasn't registered with Little Boats. Even more embarrassing – though she took it in her stride – Claudia didn't. I had to sign up with Little Boats double quick, because the agency soon wanted to know who on earth this Martine McCutcheon was.

Compared with our first holiday abroad, when we went all the way to Lloret del Mar by coach because we couldn't afford to fly, this was something else. I had to sneak off school to do the job, since it wasn't through Italia Conti's own agency. You weren't allowed to do any other work outside of Conti. They got quite stroppy about that.

But it was worth it. Tenerife was great, absolutely great. I went with Mum and was there for a couple of weeks to do the modelling shots and, although it was quite demanding work, there was also time to catch some sun. My favourite memory of that trip was a woman called Diane, who was the mother of one of the other kids on the shoot. Diane, it turned out, was the first woman I'd met who'd had a boob job. I remember thinking, Oh my God – look at them! Mum was intrigued, too, and in the end she went up to her and said, 'I'm sorry, love, I've got to ask you about your boobs. Natural tits just don't stick up like that when you lie down sunbathing – have you had 'em done?'

Diane was quite open about it and didn't seem to mind Mum asking. 'Yes, I've had them done.'

There was no stopping Mum now. 'Where are your scars?' she asked her.

'Oh, I had them put in my armpits.'

'What?' my Mum shrieked, because at that time we didn't know where the implants went.

I said to her, 'What do you mean – they put your boobs in your armpits?' And then she showed me these little scars underneath where she'd had the silicone put in. She also told us how she'd felt so much better in herself since she'd had them done.

That was the first time I realised the power of boobs. It was hard to miss their effects, really, as all these men on the black sand beach kept looking at Diane's chest. Well, not so much looking as gawping. First of all I wondered what they were staring at, and then it dawned on me: 'Oh – her boobs!' I remember wondering if I'd have ever have a pair like that – but that was before I grew them myself!

Puberty can be a horrible time for kids but I seemed to have it pretty easy. In fact I was very lucky. I never had spots; in fact I never had trouble with anything like that. I think I got my first period when I was fourteen, though my boobs didn't grow properly until I was sixteen. I never wanted big ones because I was brought up believing that the best figure in the world was that of a ballerina. You didn't want boobs and you didn't want hips, but then, almost as soon as I left school, I got curves. I suppose a similar thing happens to gymnasts who quit the sport. You train your body hard to be a certain way for years and then, when you stop, you know slowly but surely that the natural things you've been suppressing will suddenly burst forth.

Apart from experience with Dad making it hard for me to trust men, a girl at school called Gemma Flanders, who at fifteen was two years older than me, almost put me off boys for life! She'd tell me about her boyfriends and what their willies were like, how big they were and that kind of thing. I was absolutely terrified. Gemma was blonde and buxom and all the blokes used to look at her on the train in her uniform, because she looked, well, like a woman. She had a heaving bosom barely contained by her school uniform, and I can remember sitting next to her thinking to myself, God, everyone looks at Gemma.

Of course, I liked it if people looked at me, too, but at that time I wasn't really sexually attractive, because even when I was a couple of years older, say fifteen, I was still very waiflike.

There was little of me when I was at school. Gemma, though, was very Kim Wilde, loved a slash of red lipstick and would always wear black tights, hitching up her skirt to show more leg than she really should. She was a great character but she put me off men for ages. She hailed from Norfolk and, when she returned from seeing her mates there, she'd start telling me about her adventures, of rolling in the hay, all delivered in a country-bumpkin accent.

Back to Tenerife. It was there that Mum was introduced to the tarot, a hobby she still practises today – and one, I have to say, that she's alarmingly good at. Another mum on the trip, called Kim, was a bit of a bohemian. Her daughter went by the name of Star and used to go to Italia Conti on Saturdays. Star's family was very wealthy and very trendy, to boot. Kim got on really well with my Mum and read her tarot cards one evening. Mum picked it up quickly and then read Kim's. Kim couldn't believe how good she was and said, 'Jenny, you really should get some cards when you get home.'

Many years later the tarot cards told me something about life I almost didn't want to know, but it was something I had to act on. I'm not a superstitious type but I definitely believe in the power of the tarot and have had a few goes myself. Mum and I share an interest in the supernatural, or what we call witchy-poo. We're both a little witchy-poo – I used to see auras, haloes of coloured light, around people throughout my teens, and still do when I meet some people now. Then there are premonitions, little things like, 'Oh, I think the phone's going to ring', only for it to do just that a few seconds later.

When I was twelve I had auditioned for my first big show. It was a production of *Stop the World (I Want To Get Off)*, written by and starring the late Anthony Newley, at the

Churchill Theatre in Bromley. It's a musical about a guy who goes through his life doing what he wants, womanising and generally being incredibly selfish. He goes out with lots of women until he finally falls in love with one, played in this production by Rhonda Burchmore, a redhead Australian actress who had appeared in the musical *Sugar Baby* with Mickey Rooney.

When we arrived for the audition and walked into the auditorium we could barely believe our eyes. There were so many kids there that my heart sank as I looked around. There's no way, I thought, that I'm going to get picked with this many kids here – though it wasn't as bad as it looked. Children are not allowed to work consecutive nights at theatres so producers needed to choose two teams to work alternate evenings. They needed two girls for each team and they'd already selected the first girl for the A-team. I hadn't met her before. She was a pretty blonde girl with a big grin and bundles of energy. Her name was Denise Outen, though she's now known to millions as the television star Denise Van Outen.

I'll never forget seeing her in action. Denise walked in with a mass of blonde hair and a fringe. Mum narked me a bit when she remarked what a nice figure that blonde girl had. I remember thinking I was looking really cool in a cycling-shorts outfit from Marks and Spencer. Well, I did until *she* walked in! Denise was going to another stage school, Sylvia Young's, at the time and she must have been about fifteen.

Happily, our paths were destined to cross many more times in the future. When I was in the pop group Milan a couple of years later, Denise was fronting a TV show called *The Edge*. I remember her telling me then that she really wanted to be a TV presenter. She's always been determined and very ambitious but not in an in-your-face way. She certainly fulfilled her ambition because, when I was playing Tiffany Mitchell in *EastEnders*, Denise was the big-star presenter on Channel 4's *The Big Breakfast*. Whenever I went on the show, Denise would always insist on interviewing me, which was very sweet.

Mum had brought me and Louise Nurding along to the audition and the pair of us had to go up and sing a piece. I sang 'Honey Bun' from *South Pacific*. I think Mum was much more nervous than I was – so much so that she had to go downstairs and lock herself in the toilet in case her jitters rubbed off on me. Her last words before she headed to the loo were, 'You go for it' – and off she went to hide. What she didn't realise was that the theatre had loudspeakers down in the toilets. So there was Mum, sitting in the toilet, and then suddenly she could hear me belting out 'Honey Bun'.

Afterwards, I went off stage and walked back down to where Mum – now back from the loo – and Louise were sitting. 'That was amazing,' Mum told me. Apparently one of the other mums had said to her that I'd been hysterical to watch, because I was doing all these arm actions and had had people in fits of laughter. We then sat through dozens of other kids doing their pieces while I was getting more and more nervous as time ticked by.

Eventually they called every child back on to the stage. Tony Newley thanked everyone and said we'd all done well and then he said, 'I'm going to call out some names and I'd like those kids to take a step back.' He began to reel off the names and suddenly I heard him say mine. I thought, Oh, that's it, then, and felt pretty gutted. Then he called the others to the front and he said to them, 'Thank you very much for your time, but you've been unsuccessful this time.'

I and the other girls at the back just looked at each other as it suddenly dawned on us that we hadn't been asked to stand at the back because we were being rejected: we'd been asked to stand there because we'd been picked for the show – and, of all the people I could have been teamed up with, I was put with Denise. She was to play Jane and I was to play her sister Susan. We were both thrilled.

I've never forgotten the costume fitting for the show, because I was left utterly deflated after Denise got to wear all black, whereas I had to wear pink. Denise had a wonderful figure. She suffered with her skin, though, while mine was as smooth as a baby's bum. Denise kept commenting on my skin while I'd look at her, feeling green with envy at her remarkable frame and poise. Anything she put on looked great, so I told her, 'Surely, out of the two of us, I should be the one to be wearing black and you should be wearing pink. I can't believe they're making me wear pink!'

We were signed up for a six-week run at Bromley, doing every other night, and we earned about £70 a week, whatever the Equity rate was.

Denise and I played Anthony Newley's daughters. Strangely, I played the elder one, while Denise was the younger. My character was Tony's character's favourite, because she was supposed to have reminded him of the love of his life. She has a right old time and in the story gets pregnant at thirteen and then gets married. I had to have my hair corkscrew-curled, and I just looked awful.

After Bromley the show transferred to the Lyric Theatre in Shaftsbury Avenue, London. This was to be my first appearance in the West End. The first night fell on Anthony Newley's birthday. It was very exciting. Joan Collins, who had been married to Anthony, was there, as were the singer Frankie Vaughan and a whole load of other stars. Mum was there, too, of course, with John, and she brought one of those small cameras that take little cartridges of film. She kept trying to take my picture next to the stars, bless her. She even had the nerve to ask Joan Collins if she'd mind being photographed with me. Joan, being Joan, was really lovely and said I looked fantastic in my horrible stage gear, before happily posing for a photo with me. Afterwards Mum was really naughty and kept trying to have a sneaky look behind Joan's ears to see if she'd had any cosmetic surgery done, while I was acting as a decoy by talking to her. I wanted to die! Later Mum walked past me and whispered, 'No, I didn't find none. She looks great but I had to check.'

If there's one thing for which the West End run was unforgettable for me it was a highly amusing episode – although at the time it felt like the worst moment of my life. It was the day I was nearly sacked. We were backstage one night waiting for the second half to start, and I thought that, rather than go to my dressing room, I'd just wait in the wings and have a chat with members of the crew and the wardrobe girls, with whom I got on really well, until my call for the second half. So there I was chatting away, listening to the orchestra getting started, building up to my cue.

I wandered to the back of the stage, where a pair of doors led on to the stage itself. That was where the actors met up each night before the second half. Curiously, no one was there, so I walked back round to see Dee, one of the technicians, again. A few minutes later, with the orchestra still playing, I walked back to the entrance doors again. Funny, I thought, where's Denise and Tony? Slightly perturbed, I again walked back towards my dressing room and carried on yakking to the wardrobe girls. I kept hearing the music building to our cue but none of the cast seemed to be ready. 'Never mind,' I told the wardrobe girls. 'I'm sure they'll come for me before the curtains are pulled back.'

The next thing I knew, Dee, dressed all in black, came running round to me with a worried look on her face. 'Martine,' she said. 'Tony Newley's about to explode! They can't find you and they're about to postpone the second half of the show!'

At that very moment the music stopped. Tony was on stage, walking towards the front, and the auditorium was filled with people. Dee literally grabbed me and pulled me round to the doors leading on to the stage where everyone was supposed to wait before going on. I was in a complete fluster, made even worse when I spotted Denise laughing her head off at me. Rhonda was also there and in her finest Australian twang told me, 'Go on, mate, you betta get on stage – Tone's about to explode!' And, with that, Dee just pushed me on to the stage, where Tony – I still can't believe this happened – was standing with one hand raised, telling the audience that the second half had to be postponed, because they had lost one of the child actors – me!

Midway through his explanation, Tony realised I was behind him. He turned his head away from the audience towards me. 'Where have you been?' he spat, barely able to contain his rage.

I told him straight, 'Tony, before you shout at me, I want you to know I've been in the wings waiting.'

'What the hell do you mean?' he demanded. 'We've been playing this piece of music for ten minutes and it's only scored for two.' Then, facing the audience again, Tony, rather theatrically, asked me again, 'Where have you been? On the toilet?'

'No,' I said. 'I haven't been on the toilet. I've been sat in the wing over there. You know Buffy the wardrobe girl? Well, I was sitting there with . . .'

But he interrupted me gruffly: 'I don't want to hear this . . .'

But I'd started and wasn't going to stop until he and the audience knew what I'd been up to, that I hadn't acted unprofessionally. 'No,' I told him adamantly. 'I'm going to tell you exactly what happened. I was sat at the side talking to Buffy . . .'

Those on stage or in the wings at the Lyric must have been amazed at the sight of a legendary performer desperately trying to read the riot act to a twelve-year-old girl who was having absolutely none of it. God knows what they must have thought! Tony then apologised for the delay and said the second half of the show would begin in a matter of moments. The curtains came down and we all returned to our starting positions behind the double door.

Once there, Tony let all his anger out. Maybe he thought I'd been trying to upstage him in front of the audience just now, but I was still determined not to be blamed for something I hadn't done. 'Tony,' I continued, speaking more slowly now in an effort to get the man to understand. 'I was sat at the side talking to Buffy. I came round and checked the stage a couple of times but no one was there. Then, the next thing I know, I get in trouble and I'm pushed on stage by Dee.'

By now I was getting really worried as Anthony's face was getting redder and redder. 'You know you could be fired for this?' he shouted.

'No, don't fire me,' I said, my voice wavering as the tears started to flow. 'You can't fire me!'

'What are you trying to do?' he raged. 'What are you trying to do? This is my show. How dare you?'

'I know it's your show,' I said. 'I didn't want to be late and you're making me cry.'

By now tears were streaming down my cheeks, which, I suppose, took some of the fire out of Tony's anger, as he then said, quite softly, 'Now don't cry. Don't start crying. We've got to go on with the show.'

'You hate me,' I sobbed. 'You're going to fire me.' All the while Denise was bending over in fits of laughter. She had a wicked sense of humour even then and used to take the piss out of me, because hair was beginning to grow on my legs as puberty arrived. It was a little more obvious on me than on someone fair like Denise, and she'd never miss the chance to point that out, saying things like, 'Oi, Hairy Legs, shave 'em' in front of everyone at rehearsals.

I would feebly stammer back, 'But they've only just started growing.'

'Just started growing? You want to get 'em shaved, girl.'

I was so embarrassed I wanted to die. After all, I was only twelve going on thirteen and I was embarrassed by things like that – what twelve-year-old wouldn't be humiliated by being told in public to shave her legs? Denise, meanwhile, thought it was all very hilarious and continued cackling her head off.

Denise was always a really attractive girl, though. She used to dye her hair even when she was just in her teens. Mind you, look who's talking! I used to have a corkscrew perm. We both thought we looked the cat's whiskers, whereas I suspect we actually both looked quite hideous.

Looking back on it now, I think Tony, God rest him, probably did find the whole episode of my missed cue quite funny, because, after the curtain came down that night, he pulled me to one side. 'Listen, Martine,' he said. 'I know that we've had our differences but I think you're going to go a long way.' I suppose it was his way of apologising for shouting at me. He sometimes said that I reminded him of Joan, which I thought was a nice compliment.

I had another strange experience with a legendary star while doing *Stop the World*, although I never actually met the man concerned. After the performances at the Lyric I'd wait in my dressing room with my chaperone until Mum arrived to take me home. One evening, just as we were leaving, I asked her if she knew who Peter O'Toole was.

'Yes,' she said. 'He's dead famous. He's an actor who was in the film *Lawrence of Arabia* and lots of other things. Why?'

'Because I think he's got a problem,' I said.

'Why do you say that?'

'Have a look,' I said, pointing at the open window. She looked out and there was Peter O'Toole almost hanging out of a dressing room window of a nearby theatre where he was performing in a one-man show. 'He's always drunk,' I said. And he was, too. Anyway, I can remember him regularly leaning out of the window and bellowing at the top of his voice, 'I hate fuckin' London.'

After *Stop the World* I started getting lots of work. In fact I was getting more work than I was allowed by law to take on. As I said, there are restrictions on how many days children are permitted to work professionally – this is to prevent them from being exploited – and sometimes I'd go to an audition and get the job, only for Gaynor Seward to phone Mum and tell her that I'd run out of days on my licence and I couldn't do it. Otherwise I might have been working non-stop. It didn't mean I was rolling in money, though, as kids don't get paid that much.

Over the next three years I did three episodes on ITV's *The Bill*, a series that used to have a strict policy that you had to wait at least a year between appearances if you were to come back as a different character. My third episode was a real plum role. I was fifteen by then and I played the part of a girl called Mandy, who accused PC George Garfield, played by Huw Higginson, of raping her.

CHAPTER 7

Milan

I WAS FOURTEEN when I spotted an ad in *The Stage and Television Today*, the weekly show-business newspaper that carries adverts for all sorts of jobs. This particular ad had been placed by a music production company called Reproduction. They were looking for a solo singer aged sixteen, it said. I phoned the number, but knowing that I was too young – I was fourteen but must have looked about eleven – I realised they wouldn't even consider seeing me on my own. Quick as a flash I asked if they would like to see a group of girls together, thinking I could get my mates Claudia Hill, Dionne Compton and Julia Jones – who was from up North but was boarding at my house at the time – to muck in with me.

It was a time when record companies were just starting to form all-girl bands, though it would be another six years before the Spice Girls were launched. Even well-known boy bands such as East 17 and Take That were only just beginning to make their mark.

'You do know that we're looking for singers of sixteen and over?' the voice on the other end of the phone told me when I rang.

'Yeah, yeah, I know,' I replied. 'But I'm in a group. We just want to come along and show you what we can do.' My bluff must have worked, because the voice suddenly sounded quite enthusiastic and agreed to meet us.

As I mentioned earlier, I'd first met Claudia, who was two years younger than me, at Conti's Saturday school and we met again later when we both used to attend the same auditions. She and I often used to come across other young hopefuls from Sylvia Young's, a rival stage school. Kids from the Sylvia Young School were all in a very particular mould. It was quite remarkable how similar they appeared when you saw them at auditions. They were all very confident, very loud and very much in your face. They weren't so hot on the training at Sylvia Young's as at Conti's, but they were very hot on personality. You could always spot a Sylvia Young kid at an audition – they all acted like stereotypical stage-school brats.

Having said that, I can't knock them, because her kids kept getting work. Sylvia's system definitely worked. My Mum, though, would always say to me, 'Thank God you ain't like them lot, Martine – you'd drive me mad. I mean you drive me mad as it is, but thank God you ain't like them!'

One of the other big stage schools was Arts Educational in West London. The kids who went there were again very easy to pick out. Arts Ed was a much stricter place than Italia Conti and a good deal tougher than Sylvia Young's. It was all about discipline in the classical sense at Arts Ed. The academic teachers there, I recall, used to walk around with their hair held up in neatly done buns. I was always rather glad that I didn't go there. While Arts Ed pupils could all out-dance the Sylvia Young lot technically, their personalities seemed to suffer. They were the kids who always seemed to be standing quietly in the corner at auditions.

As for the Conti lot, we were quite loud, yes, but nowhere near as brash as the kids from Sylvia Young's. If anything, we were in the middle compared with the other two schools. At Conti's we were all very into our training and were good at auditions on our own, but at the same time I know we also felt a bit threatened by Sylvia's lot. The first time I had ever come across them had been at an audition when I was maybe eleven years old, and they were downstairs singing scales. It seemed so pretentious even then, so showy. Even I didn't think people like that really existed. Everyone hears about the bratty stage-school types, with larger-than-life personalities, but to see a group of them en masse is a real eye opener and, even though you would see the same girls over and over again at subsequent auditions and screen tests and come to know them quite well, it was still a daunting and rather intimidating experience. Even at such a tender age, there was intense competition between us and we'd see each other very much as rivals.

There was a girl called Kelly Bright, who later found fame on *The Upper Hand* and as a character in *The Archers*; and there was Lyanne Compton – Dionne's older sister – who always used to go for a lot of the same jobs as I did, probably because we had very similar colouring. Whenever I saw them I always thought, Oh, no! because I used to feel threatened by them all, especially Lyanne, who was, in essence, a louder, more outrageous version of me.

I'd found out at the beginning of my second year that Dionne was going to join me at Conti's. Not only that, I was told she was going to be in my class. I was quite put out by the thought at first: 'Oh no,' I said to myself. 'Dionne's going to be just like Lyanne – and she's not going to like me, because me and Lyanne always go for the same auditions.' I couldn't have been more wrong. Dionne and I got on like a house on fire and we ended up being best mates, though Milan would almost finish our friendship. However, I'm getting ahead of myself.

Dionne was great, a real inspiration for me on so many different levels. We bonded immediately and ended up doing so much together. She came from a far wealthier family than mine and encouraged me to indulge myself a little more. She was the first person to take me around the West End shopping, to places like Carnaby Street, which was far trendier then than it is now. It's more of a tourist trap these days. Dionne was the person who took me to all the popular shops and got me into things like nice Levi's, as opposed to any other sort of denim jeans, and into dance-influenced clothes from Pineapple, which was about the trendiest, coolest dance studio complex in the universe. Dionne had a huge influence on me and taught me so much about girlie things such as Clarins skin-care products and Clinique make-up. None of it cheap, of course, but you could feel the quality on your skin.

I was never jealous of Dionne, but was impressed by her. They had this massive house in Epping, north-east London, complete with sweeping driveway. I'd never seen anything like it in my life. Her Mum and Dad, like their kids, were good-looking as well as rich. They had a Golf convertible and a Jag in the driveway. Their whole set-up was like something from a fantasy for me.

As soon as I put the phone down after blagging our audition, I got on the case with the other girls. Claudia and Dionne were up for it, of course, as was my friend Julia, the lodger. Our first audition had been set up at the Danceworks studio just off Bond Street in Mayfair, and we had a couple of days to polish up our act. As we'd often sing and dance together anyway, it didn't seem too much of a problem. The day of the audition clashed with school, so we arranged to go to Danceworks first, so that we could do our thing and still make it to school without anyone there knowing what we had been up to. As the audition had nothing to do with Conti's, we all knew they wouldn't be too thrilled to find out about our little scam.

At Danceworks we met some of the Reproductions people: Brian Harris, who ran the management side of things with Anna and Mark Jolly through their company Jolly Harris Jolly, and Teresa Wolf, who would be looking after whoever they signed up from the audition. Teresa was married to a guy called Steve Wolf, or Wolfie, as he was known, who was a big-shot player in the record business at the time. They all seemed OK – they certainly didn't bat an eyelid when they saw the four of us walk in aged thirteen to sixteen and plastered in make-up.

Our audition routine was made up of some of our favourite songs. We did '1, 2, 3' by Gloria Estefan, the Bangles' hit 'Eternal Flame', and Beverley Craven's ballad 'Promise Me'. We rounded it off with another hit of the day, called 'Hippiechick' by Soho. As always at the end of a turn, they said they'd let us know. Still, I thought, we must have fared better than a lot of the other contenders, who seemed to be mainly women in their thirties with backcombed hair, desperately pretending to be sixteen.

What we hadn't bargained for was their saying they didn't want all four of us. When they came back to us about three weeks later – they called my Mum first – they said they were interested in taking us on but, while Julia was great, they didn't want her. They felt that Julia was too much of a ballerina who just stood with her feet in various ballet positions. Julia's Mum, Elaine, was quite a pushy lady and had been a professional dancer herself. Elaine had big plans for Julia, who had a graceful, athletic figure but perhaps wasn't funky enough to fit into a pop group like ours. Reproduction felt she was just too straight. 'Listen,' they told us. 'You know we want you to see some record companies. We think we can get you off the ground but I'm afraid we don't want Julia. Can you deal with that?'

That put me in a very difficult position, as, apart from the fact that I was Julia's mate, she was also boarding with me. At the same time, the school encouraged us all to be professionals, a very important lesson young performers have to take on board, and so I knew we had the very unpleasant task of telling Julia she was out. I did consider kissing the job goodbye to try to save the friendship, but that would have meant jeopardising all our careers by passing up this chance.

It was a horrendous position to be in, all the same. I remember I talked it over quietly with my Mum first and I persuaded her to talk it over with Julia's mum. The fact that Julia lived with us made it doubly tough. She was really upset, of course, but there was nothing we could do about it. After all, work is work and there would have been no point in the rest of us turning the job down simply because they didn't want all of us.

This was the first time I'd found myself in such a difficult situation, of having to be brutal with someone by telling them something they really didn't want to hear. It must have been a crushing blow for the girl and I certainly didn't enjoy doing it. But Julia was brilliant about it and didn't seem to mind at all. It certainly didn't affect our friendship, though I'm not sure her mother saw it the same way! Anyway, the management company thought we remaining three girls had potential, and, once the uneasiness concerning Julia's rejection was over, we were taken round to meet various record company executives. Every time we went to a new record company we'd have to perform for them and let them see what we could do – all of it done behind the backs of our teachers at school.

After a few weeks Brian Harris, on the management side, came back to us and said that he had some good news – he'd got us a deal. He said it was a three-single deal – which sounded great at the time but was, we were to learn, something we should probably have walked away from.

'It's with Polydor,' Brian enthused. 'They want you to be the new big girl band.'

We couldn't believe it. We thought it was great that we'd got a deal, although we didn't realise what a small one it was compared with others: they didn't even offer us an album, which in retrospect meant we obviously weren't going to be a priority for a record company. We didn't realise that we were probably going to be flogged to death for virtually nothing. To three young girls the words 'record contract' sounded as if we were on our way to the top of the charts and nothing was going to stand in our way. Oh, the naïveté!

At this stage, we didn't even have a name for the group, but since we now had a contract we had to dream up a catchy name. The three of us would spend all our breaks at school trying to come up with a good name and in the process went through loads of really stupid, stupid ideas. I can remember asking the other two, 'Why don't we call ourselves Meat and Two Veg?' We were so overexcited at the prospect of becoming pop stars it all seemed unreal. In the end one of us, I can't remember who, came up with the idea of Milan. It turned out that we all loved Milan in Italy, even though I hadn't been there (it just sounded so glamorous to me), and so Milan it was.

Within weeks we were packed off to a recording studio for the first time to start laying down our first tracks. Only then did I develop my first reservations about the project. I could sense that Anna was more interested in Claudia than in Dionne and me. When it came to my turn to sing, I'd go into the studio and get only a couple of shots at laying down my part. I'd barely warmed up my voice before one of the technicians would tell me through my headphones, 'Thanks, Martine, that's fine.' Claudia, on the other hand, got to sing her parts over and over again. The parts got bigger and I started to sense that Anna wanted to make Claudia the star and relegate Dionne and me to the role of backing singers. I knew I couldn't, or wouldn't, be a backing vocalist. I was too ambitious and felt very much that this was my own project, because I had got the band together in the first place – but at that telling moment in the studio I merely thought, Oh well, maybe things will be different on the next single.

The first track we recorded was a cover of 'Is It Love You're After?' by Rose Royce, followed by a dancy number called 'Affectionately Mine'. The third song we cut – the best in my opinion – was called 'Lead Me On'. All three were heavily dance-influenced tunes, less poppy than I had envisaged, but that was what the management and production companies had in mind for us. They knew that dance didn't make much money, that it had to cross over into chart territory to do that; but if Milan were judged solely on that basis, then we were pretty successful, as we had loads of dance hits. We were top ten in the dance charts with all three singles but, as that meant we were just popular with DJs and were getting well played in clubs, it didn't automatically mean we were selling a lot of records, which in turn meant we weren't automatically making any money. To promote ourselves and our music we toured and played club gigs around the country. Obviously, *somebody* was getting paid, somewhere along the line, for all our work – but it wasn't us. Meanwhile we were working as hard as dogs, missing home and feeling more and more disheartened with it all.

By the time recording was complete Italia Conti had cottoned on to what we were up to, and they were not impressed one bit. Gaynor knew the record industry well and she wasn't sure we were going to be well treated or chaperoned or looked after properly. She appeared quite concerned about what we'd got ourselves into. At the time, it was hard to know whether her feelings were genuine, because our parents were always suspicious that, if the school didn't broker the deal, and therefore didn't get a percentage out of it themselves, then they would invariably raise an objection.

We managed to stay on at school and somehow persuaded Gaynor to release us to continue with Milan, even though she made it clear she thought the band wouldn't get anywhere. When I look back on it now, I think she did have my best interests at heart, because she knew me as an individual and perhaps had an idea that I wouldn't work too well within a group, that I had too much of a singular talent to be happy sharing the limelight.

At the same time, despite our being free to pursue the band, there was a lot of wrangling between Polydor and our management, which took what felt like forever to get sorted out. Months went by, maybe a year, before we could get things moving with the band, by which time I had just turned sixteen and had to sit my GCSEs.

*

There had been other, albeit nicer, distractions in my life. Just before my sixteenth birthday Mum delivered a bombshell. She told me she was pregnant, which was doubly surprising considering she had been told by doctors that she would never be able to have another baby after she'd given birth to me. My reaction to her news was very strange. I couldn't get my head round the fact that there was going to be another human being walking around in our house, another human being who was going to call my Mum 'Mum'.

As you can probably tell from my story so far, Mum and I had an astonishingly close relationship, but in some ways we were occasionally too close for comfort. We loved each other so much that each of us spent almost too much time worrying about how the other was faring. We would end up doing everything together (except when I was working) to make sure neither of us was feeling left out. When she told me she was pregnant, my first reaction was one of jealousy. 'Mum,' I said, 'you can't have this baby!'

'What do you mean?' she replied, understandably gobsmacked by my outburst.

'Well you just can't,' I continued sulkily. 'It's just not right. I'm still fifteen and there's too much of an age gap, and I didn't think you could have kids, anyway. What were you thinking about?'

My Mum was furious. 'Stop being so bloody selfish,' she said. 'Stop sitting there and thinking about yourself and start thinking about me. It wasn't planned, but you weren't planned, either, and you were the best thing that ever happened to me. I'm hoping it'll happen again and hopefully it'll make me and your Dad a lot stronger,' she added.

That last comment spoke volumes to me, because that's what a lot of women make the mistake of thinking. Mum realised her error almost as soon as it had passed her lips and backtracked immediately.

'Then again it might not,' she said. 'Because it didn't do me or your Dad any favours when we had you. Anyway, Martine, I was told I couldn't ever have kids again after I had you, yet it's happened and I think it's happened for a reason.'

I realise now that I was such a cow about it, yet Laurence's arrival six months later, just after I'd got back from holiday with my Uncle Laurence in Ibiza, was one of the best things that has ever happened to me. When I first saw him I immediately went all gooey. I've got a little brother, I thought to myself, and only then realised how much I'd always wanted somebody else in the family. Only then did I appreciate how very alone I'd felt until that moment. Having a brother, someone to share my mother's love with, gave me some space at just the right time. I might have had difficulty in finding it without him. To an extent, Laurence's birth released me a little from my mother's bosom. We both sort of let each other go a little. Without that space I think I would have struggled to develop a proper relationship with a man.

That's not to say that my brother's birth was a magical cure-all for our family's problems. Money was still very tight and it was obvious even to my youthful eyes that things weren't going great with my Mum and my stepdad. John was still very keen on Mum, as far as I could tell, but his old-fashioned values and black-and-white view of the world didn't seem to fit with hers.

Somehow, despite all the distractions at home and with Milan, I managed to study and ended up passing nine of my exams, including getting an A for drama, a B for English and history and a C for art. With my exams out of the way, I was ready to give Milan my full commitment. We were ready to take on the world.

Everyone thinks working in showbiz is always fun and games, an easy life, but being in a band is anything but. Although Claudia, Dionne and I got on well, stresses, strains, rivalries and jealousy inevitably exist in any band. All three of us began to feel this as the months went by. I felt frustrated because I wasn't getting to sing any lead vocals, even though I knew I had a good voice. Dionne felt frustrated because she lacked confidence in the studio, and I think she eventually realised that, just maybe, a pop career wasn't for her after all. Although she lacked confidence, she definitely looked the part, and the men loved her. She was an important part of the group and a great dancer, too. Claudia was in the hardest position of all, because she could do the dancing and manage the whole singing thing as well – but she found it gruelling juggling all that with school. She was only thirteen when we first started and had a hell of a lot on her plate. By the time we found ourselves shooting videos, gigging and doing personal appearances, Dionne and I were free of school. Claudia, though, still had two years of Italia Conti ahead of her and had to try to cram in her studies wherever she could.

At the same time the frustrations that we harboured when we first started recording were growing into something bigger. We were spending an unhealthy amount of time together and rifts were beginning to develop. I always felt different from Dionne and Claudia, primarily because they both came from wealthy families and had money, whereas I never did. It sounds simple, but when you're all teenagers those kinds of differences really can start to tear relationships apart. Sometimes they'd go out in the evening together, to clubs and other venues, but would never invite me along. They'd just say, 'We didn't think you had the money,' or, 'Oh, sorry, Martine, we forgot' – or even, 'Oh, do you want to come?' Whatever they said or whichever excuse they used, the effect was always the same: I felt left out. Perhaps I wasn't popular with Dionne and Claudia because I was always the first to complain if things were not right. I'd rant and scream, 'Why am I not being given a fair chance to sing? I don't understand why I'm not being given a fair crack.'

For some reason the management, as I say, always preferred Claudia to do lead vocals. I felt increasingly sidelined and neglected. I thought it was unfair, since I was the one who had got everyone off their arses to go for it and it was always me who ensured we rehearsed properly. I was the one who was truly dedicated to all of this. Yet more and more I found myself reduced to the role of backing vocalist. I felt I wasn't considered as sexy as Dionne, because she was blonde and gorgeous, while my voice lacked that deep clubby feel that Claudia's had. I still had some confidence. I knew I had a good voice, looked good and could dance, and even my figure wasn't half bad. The music business is full of sycophantic idiots and sometimes I could overhear them soft-soaping Claudia, gushing to her face about how she was going to be the star of the group. Then the very same people would come over to me, pull me to one side and start the same bullshit: 'Martine, you're the star of the group – you're the one that'll go on to do great things!' I always used to think, You arseholes! But in the pop business you find there are always loads of people like that.

At the time of Milan, a girl group like ours was quite a rarity. Bananarama had had their day and the Spice Girls were years away. Maybe Milan happened too early, or perhaps we could have been marketed and managed better, but I do truly believe that if things had been right we could have been as big as the Spice Girls. They were lucky, though, to have got the money, hype and advertising deals they signed. They were tremendously focused, too, but lots of influential people believed in them and helped make them the biggest thing on the planet. It was a different story with Milan. Even before our records came out I knew we all had our own separate agendas. I had one dream for the band. I wanted to use it as a springboard to something else, such as movie acting. The other two girls used to say, 'You can't want that!'

'Why not?' I'd scream back. 'Why can't I be honest and say out loud that we ain't going to be able to be a little girl group forever? One day, not now, but later on, I'd love to do films.'

I think a lot of people thought I was bolshy and up my own arse, because I'd always say exactly what I thought and the truth sometimes hurts people. When I voiced my complaints about our record deal or the management company, the other two would get annoyed. They felt we should all be grateful for our deal.

That was the way they saw it and I understand why, but that didn't make me hold my tongue: 'Well, hang on, girls,' I'd say, 'I ain't got to be grateful for a contract because these people believe in me. They're not doing all this for their health, you know. They're not doing it because they love us and want to look after us. It's because we're earning them money and ultimately they want to look after themselves, so if I think something's not going to do me any good then why can't I say there's something not right with it?' The more problems I voiced, the more the atmosphere between me and the other two girls deteriorated.

We never had proper fights but the rows led to some really

nasty tension. Now that it's all ancient history I can say, hand on heart, that I think I was right to kick up a fuss. I feel quite strongly that no one had a long-term plan for us, that we were just there to be exploited, as we discovered to our cost when we started touring. Just thinking about those days is like reliving a nightmare.

Louise Nurding had formed her own girl group, Eternal, and their managers spent years carefully preparing and grooming them before launching them to the public. We would even bump into them at various studios. The Eternal girls would be trying on rack after rack of fabulous clothes while Milan would be trying on a handful of unsuitable outfits – clobber without class.

Kylie Minogue was, as you know, one of my heroines at the time – I loved the way she moved from TV actress to pop star so effortlessly – and if we had an image at all it was vaguely Kylie-esque, with the emphasis on 'vaguely'.

Milan had been together for a long time, perhaps two years, before we went on the road for a proper – now that's a laugh – tour. Almost as soon as we hit the road I realised we were not one of the record company's priority acts. On the tour we must have played every dingy club there is to play in England. We weren't getting any radio play, and we weren't getting any decent TV spots other than an appearance on *The Big Breakfast* and a few other pop programmes. I started wondering if the only reason Milan had been brought into existence in the first place was so that somebody at Polydor could say in their weekly meeting, 'Oh, yeah, the girls are in Doncaster tonight,' which made them look busy.

Talking of Doncaster, just thinking of that place makes me shudder. Without doubt the worst gig we ever did was in that South Yorkshire town. It was so horrendous that even now I dread the thought of going back there. That night we all got dressed up as usual. I was wearing tiny hot pants with boots and a little cropped top. We warmed for the show by jigging away backstage. Then we took a gulp of breath and went out there, totally unprepared for what was about to hit us.

The first thing we realised almost as soon as we stepped on stage was that someone somewhere had made a dreadful mistake. They'd obviously booked us for the wrong night at this club. Instead of a dance evening, as we'd been told, we found ourselves performing on Grunge Night and there we were dressed up like three mini Kylie Minogues. It was about nine o'clock when we hit the stage and, as I looked out into the crowd, I could only see a man and a woman standing there, one with black hair and the other with blue hair. The guy with the black hair had a ring through his nose and a chain from there to his ear. He stood there, no word of a lie, with his dog on a piece of string.

I had to go out and sing Rose Royce's 'Is It Love You're After?' As soon as we'd finished that song Teresa Wolf came up to the side of the stage and shouted out, 'Just go for it, girls. Imagine it's a rehearsal for Wembley!'

'A rehearsal for Wembley?' I screamed back. 'A rehearsal for Wembley? You're having a laugh! There's two people out there, a pair of crusties with a dog on a bit of string. Are you serious?'

Dionne and Claudia immediately went on the defensive. 'Oh, Martine, please don't start, please don't start.'

'Please don't start?' I retorted. 'I'm getting paid a hundred pounds a week to do this. Look at it out there!'

While Doncaster was undoubtedly the worst gig I've ever played, all the venues we visited were on the seedy side. More often than not we had to get changed in the backs of these clubs, which invariably were decorated with pictures ripped out of porno calendars. You would get guys trying it on with you too, saying things like, 'Hello, gorgeous, we can help you get another gig here and pay you cash if you sort us out.' Their idea of being sorted out had nothing to do with our singing abilities and everything to do with our young and innocent bodies. We were so vulnerable – I was nudging sixteen while Claudia was little more than fourteen – and we didn't have anyone to protect us from that kind of stuff. There would be three of us squashed into a toilet that doubled up as our dressing room and stank of piss. Sometimes, when we were on tour, we'd have to do two clubs in one night, every night of the week.

We were driven round mostly by Teresa Wolf from the production company, or occasionally by our tour manager, whom we never knew very well. Claudia used to try and do her school work during the day on the coach or in the car while Dionne, who was a real Brain of Britain, very bright, would help. We travelled round in a people carrier most of the time with Dionne and Claudia always sitting at the front. They'd always sit together. Sometimes we used to take turns sitting in the back, but most of the time I'd end up there, as they agreed on more things and were happy to go along with the charade. There were times when even Dionne and Claudia wouldn't be on talking terms. We just overdosed on each other, spending day in, day out in each other's pockets, stuck in a horrible van.

On trips further from our homes in London we stayed in hotels that I didn't even know existed. They were more like fleapits. 'Surely we're not staying *here*,' I used to protest on arrival. In one place all three of us had to share one tiny room where the three beds were pulled down from the wall, and the bathroom only had freezing cold water. The bedroom was so small that we had to hop over the beds to get to the bathroom.

Those sorts of conditions didn't help matters within the band and the bickering grew to an unbelievable level. I would ring Mum and whinge about what a nightmare we were having and how I was beginning to miss having Dionne as my best friend. I felt like I was losing her as well as my dream of making it big. Dream? Milan was slowly becoming a living nightmare. Everything was feeling out of control – I could feel it all just sliding away from under me and there was nothing I could do to stop it.

There were some good moments of course (though not many), such as the time we toured with East 17, Brian Harvey's band, for three or four shows as their support band. This was after the Doncaster fiasco. All the fans at the East 17 shows used to hate us, because they thought we were all getting-off with the band backstage, so they would throw mints at us. The girls would break their Polo mints in half, because they said that if you snapped a Polo in half you got two shots at trying to hit Milan. That was how far we had sunk by then.

The first gig at which we were showered with mints was in Sheffield. I'll never forget that. Tom Watkins, East 17's manager, absolutely hated us, because he didn't want his boys – Brian, Tony Mortimer, Terry Coldwell and John Hendy – having any female distractions around them. Tom tried to keep us apart but it was ridiculous, since we used to see each other backstage in the changing rooms regardless. There we'd have a chat and a laugh. Dionne, I recall, always got on really well with John and they became firm friends.

I also got to meet one of my idols, Luke Goss, one third of Bros, not long after their band had disintegrated into a gloomy financial mess. Luke later recorded the rise and fall of one of Britain's best-known boy bands in his book *I Owe You Nothing*. We met at a radio roadshow, where Milan, as usual, were somewhere at the bottom of the bill. Luke, now solo after the collapse of Bros, went on stage to do some stuff and I remember thinking that he didn't seem happy. I was quite shocked, because Bros, to my mind, had kicked off the whole modern boy-band thing and I couldn't understand how someone as famous as Luke could look so miserable. His blond locks were longer than in Bros days, yet he still looked as handsome as ever. Like millions of other girls I always considered the Bros twins to be stunningly handsome men. We didn't speak much that afternoon but years later, after I had been in *EastEnders* for a while, I got to know Luke's brother Matt extremely well and I can now consider both twins to be good friends.

Another laugh at that time was the money, which, even though it was only peanuts, was the first regular income any of us had received. We'd never earned proper money before but because it was such hard work being in Milan I still got the feeling we were being exploited. Anything I earned used to go into my Woolwich building society account, looked after by my Mum. With money being so tight at home, most of what I saved from Milan went to pay for my next year's school uniform. My stepdad John was now working as an industrial window cleaner. My Uncle Laurence had set him up with the job, which involved cleaning all kinds of buildings, including the House of Commons and various tower blocks, in those frightening-looking hoist things.

By the start of 1994, when I was seventeen, it was becoming clear that Milan was not long for this world and even the other two girls were beginning to see that. Like mine, their patience with the whole situation was beginning to wear thin. At the same time there were a lot of changes going on at Polydor, which is one reason I think we were given no direction. They would send us out on the road and just forget about us for a while. Nobody from the label was coming to see us, nobody was interested in Milan and we could kid ourselves for only so long. I think Dionne and Claudia began to realise that some of what I'd been saying was true. It was the beginning of the end.

A couple of months before my eighteenth birthday, I went away with Dionne for my first holiday abroad without my Mum. Dionne had lined herself up with two weeks in Tenerife. She had no one to go with and was desperate to get away from Milan. With our friendship all but on the rocks, because of the constant bickering on the road, I suggested that I join her on holiday. I really wanted to see if we could patch things up. We went away, had a great time and a few holiday snogs each, and things felt normal again between us. Unfortunately, almost as soon as we returned for what turned out to be the last hurrah for Milan, things fell apart again. The band was destroying our lives, and I still sensed that I was the one who was being blamed for most of our troubles.

It may have been that in some ways I was a bit too hard on the management, but, as far as I was concerned, they were in control of our lives. As I say, I think that by now even the other two had started to see that things weren't happening the way they ought to be, that we were kidding ourselves if we thought Milan was going to make it to the top of the pops. It was a bad time all round, but there was one bright spot on the horizon for me.

I'd met this lovely man called Gareth Cooke. Ironically I'd never have met him if it hadn't been for Milan – so something good *did* come out of the band after all.

CHAPTER 8

Gareth

MUCH LATER IN my life I met a clairvoyant who told me, quite convincingly, that I was a very spiritual person. Perhaps that explains why the first time I met Gareth Cooke I sensed that he would play an important part in my life. It may sound odd, a little far-fetched even, but it's true.

I was seventeen, going on eighteen, still singing with Milan, and had never had a boyfriend in my life, when I went out for an evening to Hollywoods nightclub in Romford with friends. I'd just come back from that holiday in Tenerife with Dionne and was looking forward to partying on familiar territory. The holiday had lifted my spirits – this was about eight months before Milan finally called it a day – and I was up for a good time.

Ironically, it wasn't me who spotted Gareth first: it was Dionne. We were both standing by the bar, dressed to the nines, when she suddenly nudged me. 'Look,' she said, nodding towards the DJ in a booth in the middle of the dance floor. 'It's John Louis.' John was a DJ we'd met in

Tenerife, a great guy, and the three of us had got on well during that sun-soaked holiday. It was obvious that Dionne fancied him, because she was almost beside herself with excitement. 'We can go and chat to him about all the good times we had out there,' she gushed, urging me on, but I wasn't so sure.

As my eyes focused more on the figure behind the turntables, I began to have my doubts that Dionne had her sights on the right bloke. 'You know, I don't think it is John,' I told her. 'But he's rather nice all the same.' We giggled as only girls in nightclubs do, until Dionne could wait no longer and took control of the situation.

'We'll go and talk to him anyway,' she insisted.

'I can't,' I said. Zeroing in on a man and chatting him up has never been my style – although a few moments later, spurred on by Dionne, I decided I could just about summon up the courage to speak to him. I thought if I approached the DJ booth and requested a record – there was a song I loved at the time called 'Excited' by M People – it wouldn't be as obvious as just chatting him up cold. So I sauntered over, a bundle of nerves, and asked this good-looking man, who most certainly wasn't John, to give it a spin. I actually asked for the Judge Jules remix of the song, which had a Latin, Spanish flavour and was a vast improvement on the original. As not everyone knows all the different mixes that are performed on a particular song, I could tell the DJ was impressed by my request, that I even knew the mix existed. I could see he was several years older than me, but to my surprise I found I rather liked that.

'How do you know it?' he asked in a public school accent, which again, I liked.

Blushing, I told him, 'I'm really into my music.'

Stilted our conversation may have been, but we could both

sense that something more was going on between us. There was a lot of eye contact; indeed, we didn't seem to be able to take our eyes off each other. I thought he was lovely.

From the minute we met there was this instant chemistry, the kind of thing that happens only a couple of times in your life if you're lucky. It was weird – I had this overwhelming feeling about him, one of the most powerful feelings I've ever had, right from the off. I just knew that one day I'd know him in such an intimate way and that he would play a big part in my life. My emotions were rushing over me like the steamy water in a power shower. I was intrigued by him, fascinated by him. There was real electricity between us.

'My name's Martine,' I said as I turned on my heels and headed back towards my spot at the bar next to Dionne.

'And I'm Gareth . . .' his voice called after me. With all this stuff sizzling away unspoken between us, I made it my mission to return to that club every Friday night without fail to see what would unfold.

I got back to where Dionne was waiting for me. 'I was right,' I said, desperately trying to keep a lid on my feelings. 'It's not John. It's a guy called Gareth, but he's absolutely gorgeous.' I knew Dionne could tell something had changed with me, but no more was said on the matter. We went home that night, and I had butterflies dancing in my stomach, the kind you get when you meet someone special. I'd be lying if I said I didn't think about Gareth quite a lot during the week that followed.

I mentioned to Mum that I'd met this bloke, which prompted her to pull out the tarot she had bought after that holiday a couple of years earlier, when she had first been introduced to them. I think she did it more for a laugh than anything, but the results were uncanny. Using the cards,

Mum described Gareth, his short, neat hair and chiselled features, and gave me a few useful tips.

'You know,' she said, 'you've got to let this man know you're around and are interested but at the same time you need to back off a bit and not appear too keen. Just say, "I'm here if you want me, I'm your friend, but that's it."' It was good advice, as it turned out.

The following Friday we returned and I got chatting to Gareth again. He seemed to know that I was in a band, which made me think he may be interested in me, too, as he'd obviously gone to the trouble of asking people about me. I learned a lot more about him that evening, too, though not all of it good. He told me how he had quit a job in the City as a money broker to work at Hollywoods. He explained that he didn't want to be a money broker, because it made him feel old before his time. His real passion was music, and so he'd decided to chuck in his career and have a go at doing what he liked best, which was clubbing and DJ-ing. I suppose he'd been quite brave, giving up a well-paid job to do whatever he wanted to do.

And he seemed to be doing it well. He and his friend, another DJ called Tony Grimley, had persuaded the owners of Hollywoods to launch a new night that they would promote called Culture Shock. The idea was that they would play more new tunes than the usual Friday-night fodder, which was mainly pop and dance cuts from the eighties. Culture Shock became a popular night almost immediately and Gareth, Tony and the club made a lot of money from it.

Another bit of news wasn't so good as far as I was concerned. It turned out that Gareth was dating a girl called Vicky Morely, who, at sixteen, was a year younger than I was and eight years younger than Gareth. That revelation hit me like a bombshell, and I would go home that night feeling gutted: I'd met a lovely, bright, attractive guy – but he already had a girlfriend. Just my luck, I thought.

The girls and I left Hollywoods in the early hours and went back to Dionne's house, where we were all staying the night. We sat up until it was almost light, chatting and eating loads of toast, which we'd dip in tomato sauce. Dionne did her best to take the sting out of my discovery and encouraged me to put a brave face on the situation. Part of the problem was my relative innocence and naïveté.

Of course, I'd already been out on the odd date – 'odd' being the operative word – but I'd never had a proper boyfriend. There had been a boy called Scott, whom I'd met at an under-eighteens night at Hollywoods. I had been to that club night a couple of times with my girlfriends. It had all been very innocent. The furthest I'd ever got with a boy at this time was a first kiss, and that had been with Scott the Grott, as I used to call him after we'd gone our separate ways. Scott and I got to grips with each other – quite literally – at a bus stop next to Hollywoods. Needless to say, it wasn't very classy.

He had walked me out of the club to the bus stop, where Dad – that's John McCutcheon – was due to come and pick me up. Dad was still working as an industrial window cleaner and would usually come to get me in his van, with all the mops and buckets in the back. That night was no different, except that Dad had got my cousin Mark, my Auntie Pam's son, with him. Mark was sitting in the passenger seat as the van approached us and had seen Scott make his move to kiss me. Mark knew what Dad was like and did his best to keep him distracted from the spectacle unfolding at the bus shelter. He knew John would go mad if he saw his little girl kissing this guy, so Mark kept talking enthusiastically to John about anything that came to mind.

I saw the van just as my mouth locked with Scott's and recoiled immediately. At least I *tried* to recoil. I couldn't move. Somehow my top lip had got caught on the railway-track bit of Scott's dental brace. The pain as I tried to pull away was unbelievable. Mark was a real hero as he managed to keep Dad distracted just long enough for me to wrestle the remains of my top lip free. I could feel it bleeding, I'd obviously left part of it behind with Scott. The remainder throbbed and hurt like hell.

I got into the back of the van, clambering over buckets and mops to do so. 'Are you all right, Martine?' Dad asked.

'I'm fine, thanks,' I lied, my words coming out a little strangely because of my busted lip. Mark nearly gave the game away as he almost pissed himself with laughter.

'What's the joke?' Dad snapped – because he thought Mark was laughing at him and had come over all insecure. As we've seen, John was quite a simple man who saw things very much in black and white.

'Oh, no, Dad, it's nothing to do with you. Everything's fine,' I fibbed.

Despite the memory of that painful lip, I somehow allowed myself to be talked into going out on another date with Scott. He'd said that he'd like to see me again as I disentangled myself from his brace that night and I'd foolishly agreed. I even gave him my phone number before hopping into Dad's van.

Scott's family ran a few stalls in Romford Market and I remember thinking that he may have ambitions above that or a passion to make something of himself. I had big dreams for myself and even then thought, I can't be a movie star with a greengrocer for a boyfriend!

Scott had brown hair that was quite long and usually tied back in a ponytail. Even though long hair was quite fashionable at the time – the whole rave thing was very in back then – and he used to wear polo shirts and jeans, Scott really wasn't my type. Yet I still went for him. Why? Because just about everyone else I knew had at least had a kiss with a boy, including the other girls in Milan, and Claudia was a couple of years younger than me!

Scott rang the next day and suggested we go shopping in the West End for our next date. We agreed to meet at Romford Station. I got there first. When Scott arrived, the first thing I did was look at his hands. They were filthy. He had dirt caked on his fingers and under his nails.

'Why didn't you wash your hands?' I asked him irritably.

'Oh, that's because I've been working on my Dad's fruit-and-veg stall this morning and came straight here,' Scott explained.

Later on the date, as we rode the tube into town, I asked him what he wanted to be when he was older. He told me, 'I want to be the best fruit-and-veg man there is.'

Oh, I thought, and suddenly felt all peculiar and panic-stricken. My mind started racing: Oh no! What am I *doing* with him? Get him *away* from me! Looking back now, I realise that my reaction sounds a bit mean. After all, the poor bloke only wanted to make an honest buck. But even then I was ambitious and was desperate to be something, to fulfil my dreams.

Anyway, the date was shaping up to be a real disaster by the time we hit the West End. I had bought one of those massive Coca-Cola bottles from a stall in Oxford Street which you use to put your small change in, like a giant moneybox. It cost only a pound or so. When we got on the tube to go back home Scott asked me if I was coming back to Romford.

'Oh, no,' I lied. 'There's a party, you know, in Hackney.

I've got to go, as my Mum's said they're having a barbecue. I'm sorry I forgot to tell you earlier that I was supposed to go . . .'

It was a little white lie, as Mum was indeed going to a barbecue. It was just that *I* hadn't actually been invited. But I needed to get away from Scott, because I felt sick of the sight of him. He'd embarrassed me earlier in the day by going up to people in the street, mainly tourists and complete strangers, saying stupid things like, 'Oi, you. I'm English, I'm a nutter.' His antics were probably quite normal for a teenage boy but, after my education at Italia Conti, I was quite the little snob.

By now we were sitting on a tube on the Central Line and I'd wedged this giant Coke-bottle moneybox between us. I can remember even today looking at Scott through the bottle and seeing his face distorted by the plastic. He kept trying to keep the long-dead date alive by rabbiting on at me about this and that, but all I did was shriek, 'I can't hear you! I can't hear you!' The noise of my cries, combined with the thundering of the train, all but drowned out his cheesy chat-up lines.

When the train reached Bethnal Green, I gave him a quick kiss on the cheek and scarpered. That was the last I saw of Scott the Grott. I took the moneybox with me, though. When I caught up with Mum she fired a string of questions at me about the date.

'Mum, I don't like him,' I responded. 'He makes me feel sick.'

She replied by telling me she knew our romance would last only two minutes. 'The second you told me his family were greengrocers, I knew it wouldn't last,' she laughed. My Mum was always the first to say what a snob I could be.

Before meeting Gareth I'd had only one other run-in with

the opposite sex. One night, three months or so before meeting my dishy DJ at Hollywoods, I had bumped into Sean Maguire while out doing a PA (personal appearance) with Milan. At that time Sean, a dishy, outgoing Irish boy with a real gift of the gab, was making quite a name for himself in *EastEnders*, playing Aidan Brosnan. He was at the same PA, saying hello to fans, when we got chatting about the current number-one single, 'Dreams', the first hit released by Gabrielle, which we both adored. The conversation led on to Nicola Stapleton, who was also in *EastEnders*, playing Aidan's girlfriend Mandy, and whom we both knew. Out of the blue Sean suggested that we all meet up and have a drink. I agreed. Sean was, and is, lovely, a real sweetheart, but even as the words came out of my mouth I regretted uttering them. I was still very innocent and, no doubt as a result of my childhood, still quite nervous of boys. Yet, at the same time, I was thinking, I've *got* to get a boyfriend. I was succumbing to peer pressure and was beginning to wonder if there was something wrong with me, as teenage girls often do if they haven't got a fella. Everyone else seemed well ahead of me as far as boys were concerned. Dionne had already lost her virginity and although Claudia hadn't she was certainly having a good time getting to know guys.

So I gave Sean my number, and a few days later he called, inviting me over to his home in Ilford. My Mum eagerly offered to drive me over there in John's window-cleaning van, filled with damp mops and half a dozen buckets, which I tripped over as I tried to get out on arrival. Sean's mother opened the door.

Sean's family are Irish and when I went inside I found just about every relative he had was there waiting to meet his hot date. As well as the grown-ups, there were kids running about everywhere. I was introduced to all of them: close family, aunts, uncles, cousins, nephews, nieces, everyone. Talk about nerve-wracking.

I felt under an enormous amount of pressure, a situation not helped when some of Sean's family spilled outside the house and on to the street to wave us off for our date. It was a Saturday night and Sean had fixed for us to go for a Chinese meal and then on to Hollywoods, which was never much fun on a Saturday. That night I positively loathed the place. Sean can dance and was really exerting himself on the floor, but I wasn't in the mood. Then, when he tried to kiss me, I simply couldn't cope.

'I've got to go, Sean, I'm sorry. I've just got to go.'

He looked upset and I felt incredibly guilty, because he was a good-looking, fun guy to be with. I just wasn't willing or ready to go out with him as a girlfriend.

'But, Martine, what's wrong?' he asked gently. 'I'd love to take you out, you know. Perhaps another time?'

'That sounds lovely, Sean,' I fibbed. 'But we'll have to see what happens.'

Again, Mum was all too keen to hear the gory details – or lack of them – when I woke up on Sunday morning. I told her everything and then went on to say how I felt I didn't really want to have a boyfriend.

'Then you've got to tell him that you don't want a boyfriend,' Mum reasoned. 'It's as simple as that. Tell him that you like him as a friend but you don't want a boyfriend.'

I was in a real state about what I'd do when Sean rang, and to compound it all Mum was cooking Brussels sprouts for the Sunday roast. I could smell them in the kitchen and the odour made me want to retch. 'Mum, those Brussels are making me feel sick,' I wailed. 'I feel sick anyway and they're making me feel even worse. Are you doing this to me on purpose?'

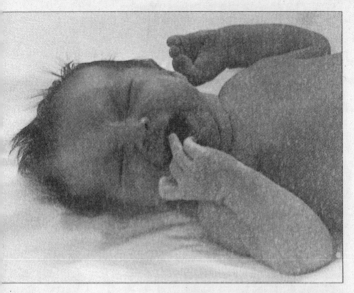

The photograph that launched the 1976 Labour Party campaign: me, aged six weeks. It's hard to believe I've been in this business nearly 25 years!

Mum and Dad in 1974 – the start of a stormy relationship.

Mum, aged nineteen, struggling through the heat wave of 1976, three weeks before I was born

Mum and me, aged two days. After a long labour I finally arrived in the world.

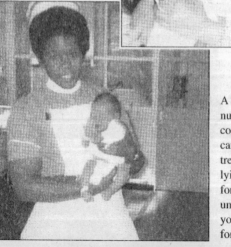

A Salvation Army staff nurse and me after coming out of special care where I had been treated for jaundice. After lying under bright lights for two days I emerge unscathed. Even at a young age I was destined for the spotlight!

Me, aged sixteen months, on our first holiday away – I loved that duck rubber ring!

Me, aged two. Always smile on your birthday!

Me, aged two and a half. Quite a serious pose for a child that age!

Me and my cousin, Yasmin – the two of us shared a passion for pink pyjamas and bacon-flavoured crisps!

Right: Mum, Uncle Chrissy and my cousin, Carrine. I adore this photo, as I adored my Uncle Chrissy – everyone said we were so alike.

Me, aged four. I adored Christmas and still do.

Me, aged five. A little bucket to wash a big car!

Me and Nanny Hemmings. Nanny always took me to school while mum worked.

Me with Marc and Martyn Paris. The three mouseketeers – we were the original blues brothers and sister!

Above: Me, preparing for the police disco-dance championships. I never lied about the green flock wallpaper, and managed to win the competition three years running.

Top right: Me and my dance tutor, Mark, at the Wendy Foley School of Dance where it all started.

Right: Me, aged seven. A stream of modelling work kept me busy.

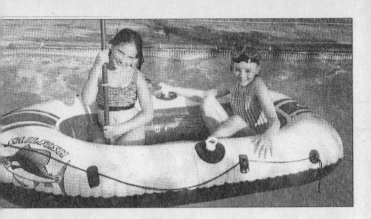

Me and Leila Birch.
I became Tiffany
and Leila became
Teresa Di Marco.
Who would have
thought we'd both
become a part of
the *EastEnders*
family?

Me, aged ten. I was
so proud of those
teeth when they
came through!

Me in bed. Beautiful room, Patrick Swayze on the wall, boiled egg and soldiers for breakfast – shame I had the flu!

Me, aged ten, dressed in my Italia Conti uniform. This is one of the first photos I smiled in because my front teeth had come through at last!

'Of course I'm not,' came her calm reply. 'I just fancied sprouts today, that's all.'

After lunch, the phone rang. 'Do you want me to say you're not here if it's Sean?' she asked. I nodded, thinking what a great Mum I'd got. She picked up the receiver.

'Hello? Oh, hello, Sean . . . Yeah, I'm fine thank you . . . Do you want Martine? . . . Yes, she's here . . .'

How could she *do* this to me? First sprouts, now this. Silently seething, I snatched the phone away from her.

'Hello, Martine, how are you? I just wanted to know if you fancied coming out to the pictures . . .'

I didn't give him a chance to finish. 'Well the thing is, Sean,' I said, trying to control the tremble in my voice. 'The thing is, it doesn't feel right. I'm sorry, but it's been going round and round in my head. It's all a bit too much for me, Sean. I'm a bit scared. I get a bit scared of boys, you see. Can we just be friends?'

Sean was very brave. Apart from an initial 'Whhaaaat?' he remained calm. 'Yeah, sure we can be friends,' he said finally, and with that he put the phone down.

'I think I've upset him,' I told Mum.

'No you haven't, I'm certain of that, Doughnut, but he probably thinks you're weird.'

And so, with such a dismal record as regards men in my past, you can only imagine my disappointment when I learned that Gareth was a taken man. But all was not lost. I had an ally at Hollywoods in the shape of Gordon Phillips, one of the club's managers. We were good mates and I recall he always used to go on about how I reminded him of one of his ex-girlfriends. Gordon was always very sweet to me. He knew I was a bit strapped for cash and used to let me into the club for nothing, not to mention sorting me out with free drinks.

Gordon was also a good friend of Gareth's and would often regale the DJ with his thoughts on little Martine, the wannabe pop star. He'd tell him the same things he would tell me: 'You're seventeen, you're a baby and you've got a future ahead of you like you wouldn't believe, Martine. You've got something special.' Gordon was one of the first people to say he saw something special in me. 'You're not the most beautiful girl in the world,' he'd argue with no small degree of charm. 'But you've got something that makes heads turn. I've got a feeling you're going to make it.'

After five or six weeks hanging out, gawping at Gareth on Friday nights at Hollywoods, he made his first move, getting me to swap numbers with him. He was very subtle about it. I was chatting to him as usual at the DJ booth when he suddenly said, 'Listen, I'd like to give you my number but if anybody asks what I'm doing just say you were asking me to get you that mix of "Excited" you want. Now give me your number,' he said, 'and I'll let you know when I get the record.'

The following week I saw him again. 'I didn't manage to get the record,' Gareth grinned. 'But I've still got your number.'

We used to flirt subtly with each other at Hollywoods but, because the DJ stand was right in the middle of the dance floor, everyone would look on wondering what on earth Martine thought she was up to with this DJ who already had a girlfriend. They weren't the only ones. I couldn't explain my behaviour even to myself. I felt guilty as hell but unable to stop myself from catching Gareth's eye. I would even do it when Vicky was in the club, which was quite often. I tried to stop myself but I simply couldn't and would make out I didn't know he had a steady girlfriend if anyone confronted me about it. I needed to know what the score was regarding Gareth's feelings for me, so one night I quizzed him face to face over his relationship with Vicky.

It took a lot for me to ask but I was so into Gareth by then I simply didn't care – and Mum's tarot reading had given me a boost.

'Yeah, we're seeing each other,' he answered. 'We've been seeing each other for about six months. It's a very casual relationship but I'm having a good time.' Then he added, 'But I do think you're lovely, Martine. I think you're absolutely lovely and, you know, I'd love to go out with you. The trouble is, I can't. I can't do that to Vicky because we work together. She's here at the club during the week and helps me promote Culture Shock. I'm sorry, babe, but I couldn't do it to her.'

It may have been a bit of predicament for Gareth but after that conversation he nevertheless started phoning me frequently. If I was away with the band and he called – which he did quite often – I'd answer quite coldly. 'Hello, how are you? How's Vicky?' I used to ask him that all the time, because I didn't know what he wanted from me. If he asked me out, I'd refuse. 'No, Gareth, because you've already got a girlfriend.'

I must have known Gareth for about two-and-a-half months when he called me at Mum's and tried again. 'We're going to a night club called Club Raw on the Charing Cross Road. Judge Jules, who did the mix of "Excited", is going to be there, and no doubt he'll play it, Martine. You'll *have* to come down.'

'Is Vicky going to be there?' I asked sweetly. He said she wasn't. 'OK,' I said. 'I'll meet you there. We'll have a good time, see how we get on and that way we're not upsetting anybody, we're not doing anything wrong. Then, if we don't get on that well . . .' I put the phone down. My heart was going nineteen to the dozen.

Every time the phone rang at home the next day my first thought was, It's Gareth – he's calling to cancel.

'What's the matter with you?' Mum would ask before urging me to get a grip and calm down.

I spent ages rummaging through my things looking for something to wear. I ended up picking out this glittery seventies-style navy halter-neck top with flashes of silver running through it. It was done up with thin little ties and showed a lot of flesh. It went perfectly with a long, blue, velvet skirt I had with a daring slit up the side and these trendy boots. It was a very clubby – dare I say tarty? – look and totally in keeping with the style of clubs like Billion Dollar Babes, which was *the* place at the time.

I wasn't going to go alone, of that I was certain. Dionne couldn't make it – she already had a date – so I persuaded her sister Lyanne to come along with me. As fate would have it, the evening was a disaster right from the off, and I often wonder now if a higher force tried to stop me meeting Gareth that night.

We tried to get a train into town but the trains were going only so far that night for some reason, so we had to get off, walk to another station and catch another. When it arrived we got on, only to be told that the loco had broken down. Off we got again, back on the street to catch a bus. It was the right bus. The trouble was it was going in the wrong direction. We hopped off at the next stop, crossed the road, waited ages and caught one going the right way. Problem solved? Not quite. The bus had the wrong sign up and stopped before it reached our destination. We ended up walking most of the way to the club.

When we finally got there it was gone 1.30 a.m. I was going

on three hours late. Lyanne and I tried to do a sneaky and blag the doormen, saying our names were on the guest list – but they were having none of it so we faced the humiliation of paying to get in. How uncool! Even worse, Lyanne, who liked to watch her pennies, was moaning by now. 'I can't believe I'm spending all this money for you, Martine. This is ridiculous,' she complained

In my heart of hearts as we wandered downstairs I assumed Gareth would have probably left the club already, thinking that I'd stood him up. Once I was inside the first people I spotted were Danniella Westbrook and Brian Harvey from East 17, who were going out together at the time.

'Are you all right, Mart?' Brian asked me. 'You look a bit lost.'

'Yeah, I'm trying to find somebody and I can't see them.'

'Is his name Gareth? 'Cause he came up to me earlier and asked if I'd seen you. I presume he asked me because he knew that you supported us on tour. Anyway, there's me going on, I'm sorry . . . He's still here, somewhere.'

Squeezing through the frenetic clubbers I soon found one of Gareth's mates, a guy called Paul, who ran a gym. 'Am I glad to see you,' he said. 'Gareth's here. I think he must have been quite nervous about meeting up with you, because, er, he's drunk too much and is in a bit of a state. In fact he's absolutely lagging drunk, Martine. He's in a bad way. He thought you'd stood him up.'

I hurriedly explained to Paul about my nightmare journey as he walked me over to where Gareth was sitting, nursing a bottle of beer. I explained the reason for my tardiness a second time, got Gareth on his feet, dragged him to the dance floor – he pulled himself together pretty quickly – had a bit of a bop and then, well, by then it was time to leave. So much for our great first date.

We shared a taxi home, stopping at my house first. Gareth made to kiss me. 'No,' I said firmly. 'I can't do that, because you've already got a girlfriend and to be honest with you I'm feeling a bit dehydrated and I so wanted our first kiss to be a nice one.'

Gareth persisted but in a nice, non-pushy way. 'Well why don't we just have a little one?'

I could hold out no longer. I was in seventh heaven as I hopped out of the taxi and bounced indoors. I'm in love, I thought. I'm in love.

My heart told me Gareth felt the same way. He certainly couldn't wait to call again: the phone rang early the next day. He wanted to see me. We needed to talk, he said. We arranged to me at Pizza Express in Brentwood for dinner. I was rapidly running out of outfits to dazzle him with and that, combined with butterflies, my feverish imagination and my thudding heart, must have affected my judgement when it came to choosing the best of what was left. Oh, Martine, what were you thinking of? I ended up in trousers that were too big around the waist, which I then hitched up too far so the bottoms were half-way round my ankles. I grabbed a white, slim-fitting T-shirt and then searched for a jacket. The one that went with the trousers was at the cleaner's and nothing else matched. I ended up slipping on this huge woollen cardigan instead. I reckon I looked a bit like Frank Spencer gone wrong.

I wasn't far off the mark because I remember that when Gareth came to pick me up he gave me a look that said, 'Christ, what on earth are you wearing?' Gareth's dress sense, on the other hand, was always good. He was never an in-your-face designer-label man, though he did wear a few upmarket items but always quite plain, classy threads. His favourite combinations were black moleskin trousers matched with a slim-fitting T-shirt or a nice big baggy jumper with a pair of dark denim jeans. He liked a little bit of silver jewellery, too. He was very normal, really – you wouldn't point him out in a crowd and say what an amazing-looking guy he was – but he had a sexiness about him that a lot of girls liked. He had beautiful green eyes with long lashes, which I adored from the moment I saw them. But it was more than Gareth's looks that attracted me. He had an air about him that was everything I wasn't. He was very calm and had a quiet confidence about him, verging on arrogance at times, but then I quite liked the fact that he seemed so secure within himself.

Dinner was quite difficult. 'I don't think I can eat – I'm quite nervous, you know,' I told him at the start, but as we talked about the night before and our feelings for each other my nerves vanished almost as quickly as my pizza. As he paid the bill Gareth looked at my empty plate and smiled. 'I reckon you're OK now, aren't you?' OK? I was on cloud nine. He did act strangely, however, when I put my arm through his as we walked back to his car, a red Fiat Uno, and was surprised to feel him flinch. I'm a tactile person and like to walk arm in arm even with friends. Gareth was different in that respect and I can remember being quite surprised by his reaction. I could sense he was about to tell me what he needed to talk about.

We drove back to my place without saying much and pulled up by these flats next door. 'Listen,' Gareth said. My heart froze. 'I think you're really lovely, Martine, but I really feel bad about Vicky. You see I've got no reason to be unhappy with her other than that you and I have, well, been out a couple of times and get on, you know? All the same I think I'm going to find it quite difficult to justify myself to her, even though nothing's happened between us. Oh, I don't know,' he stammered. 'I want to finish with her but at the same time I don't want her to think that . . .' Gareth was trying to tell me he was confused, I suppose, but I knew that already. 'I think perhaps we should just be friends,' he said finally, perhaps expecting me to register a look of enormous disappointment on my face.

If he did then it was his turn to feel let down as I kept my cool. 'OK, we'll be friends,' I echoed calmly.

The facts were that I didn't want somebody who didn't want me. I could easily accept we were to be nothing more than mates even if my heart wanted more. I was a little bit upset, sure, but did my best to conceal that so, when it came to saying goodbye and Gareth asked for a kiss, I allowed him a peck on my cheek, no more.

'Can't I have a kiss on the lips?' he asked.

'No, because friends don't kiss goodbye on the lips.'

'Oh, come on,' he persisted.

How could I resist? Except my head overruled my heart at that very moment and I kissed, drawing short of a full-on snog. However, as our lips parted, I told him straight, 'We can't see each other if you're seeing Vicky and that's for definite. I've never had a boyfriend before and I want it to be right and it can't be right if you're seeing somebody else.'

I think Gareth felt guilty for enjoying another female's time when he had a steady girlfriend. He seemed overawed by it all and was quite messed up. Ah, that's love for you. As it was, circumstances meant that I wouldn't see him for another month after our pizza date as I was away for my last spot of touring with Milan. He phoned me on my mobile a couple of times during that period but I wasn't going to change my mind. As far as I was concerned we couldn't go out until he was single and that was that.

On the last night of the tour in London Dionne and I

decided to celebrate by going straight to Hollywoods after the gig. We were still togged up in our Milan outfits – these little red velvet trouser-suits – and I saw Gareth almost as soon as I got to the club.

'You know I've really missed you – it's so lovely to see you,' he said, giving me a huge hug. We went into a quiet corner for a chat and I told him that my eighteenth birthday was coming up the following week. 'I was wondering, maybe, could you DJ for us, for the party I'm planning?' I asked. He went one better and offered me the club's VIP room for the do. 'It's local, I know it's not London,' he apologised, 'but all your family are near here so why not?'

As it turned out Gareth couldn't DJ at the party, he'd got a booking elsewhere – his name was becoming increasingly respected in club circles – but that conversation between us must have had some impact on his life because the very next day he finished with his girlfriend.

CHAPTER 9

Mum, I Feel Like a Woman

YOU WON'T BE surprised to learn that only a couple of days after my eighteenth birthday Gareth and I became an item officially. He even came round to meet my parents before whisking me off for a night on the town. True to form, the date was another a disaster, but this time the blame was fairly and squarely on his shoulders.

'I'll be there at about nine o'clock or something like that,' he promised. By 10 p.m. I was beginning to feel embarrassed by his tardiness, especially with Mum and Dad staring at me. By 11 p.m. it was beyond embarrassing and Dad was steaming with the rage. Gareth, I knew, had an important meeting with the boss of Hollywoods that evening so I knew he might run a *little* late. I also knew that Vicky would be there, which didn't exactly help put my mind at ease. As it turned out there'd been a bit of barney between them and she'd said things that weren't very nice about me, but I didn't know that at the time because we were all sitting at home, waiting for him to show. Dad was beside himself and kept ranting on about how it was poor form not to ring and explain himself. Mum was getting agitated, too, but told Dad to calm down as he was only making matters worse by banging on.

Finally, just after 11 p.m., the doorbell rang. Dad opened the door. 'Who the fuck are you?' he said, barely able to restrain his temper.

And this little voice went, 'I'm Gareth, I'm taking Martine out tonight.'

'You're one-and-a-half hours late. Don't fucking do it again!'

I was absolutely mortified. Dad wouldn't even let him in the door at first.

'I'm so sorry I'm late,' Gareth said when Mum finally got John to let him pass. 'I'm *so* sorry. If you want to say you don't want to come out with me I'll completely understand. I know it's very late but it's up to you if you want to come.'

Before I got a chance to say I'd love to go out, Dad butted in again: 'No you're not fucking taking my daughter out. We've been sat round here waiting more than two hours for you to show . . .'

'John, *John*,' Mum shrieked. 'Let her make her own fucking mind up. She's eighteen and if she wants to go out she can.'

'Thanks, Mrs McCutcheon. I promise I can explain everything,' Gareth said, the very model of politeness – unlike my folks. And with that we slipped out for dinner alone.

A couple of weeks later Gareth was invited round for dinner *chez* McCutcheon. Not surprisingly, he arrived on time as I don't think he fancied a repeat performance from Dad, who was particularly protective of me after all the business with Keith. He would have probably been the same with any prospective boyfriend. My little brother Laurence, or LJ as we call him, was about two years old at the time and quite a character. He'd suffered badly as a baby after receiving his jabs and has had a problem with his speech ever since, though thanks to brilliant speech therapy these days you'd never know. Despite LJ's problems, he's always great fun and that evening was no exception. At one point he clambered on to Gareth's shoulders and sat there like a giant, grinning parrot. Then he sneezed and a dollop of snot shot out of his little nose and landed all over Gareth's hair! Surprisingly, even that didn't put me off him and we started seeing each other every day we could.

We were madly in love. I knew that I'd found the right man at last, a person I felt attracted to and loved by. I felt safe in his hands and knew that our relationship could progress until I became a woman in my own right. We were going to be together forever, I thought – and occasionally dreamed. I loved him. He was my Romeo, I was his Juliet. When I was daydreaming I would fantasise about our future together: he'd be a record producer and a DJ and I'd be a top actress. We'd have children, lots of money and live happily ever after. I was open to everything and a hundred per cent in love. I had no inhibitions about my feelings.

Considering that Gareth had had a few past break-ups and was older than me, he was amazingly romantic and open. We idolised each other and I really thought I'd met my equal. He was always game for a laugh. If he wasn't as loud and boisterous as I was, then he was certainly funnier and both Mum and Dad adored him, too. I remember once watching *My Fair Lady* on video with Mum and Dad when Gareth suddenly got up and started tap dancing and singing 'Wouldn't It Be Lovely?' He was very intelligent and great to talk to. I admired him for leaving the stable business of stockbroking to pursue music, his passion. My knowledge of music today is mainly thanks to his influence. His flat was full of records in purpose-built racks. He used to say he loved the smell of new vinyl.

As my relationship with Gareth went from good to better, Milan went from bad to worse until it was finally time to call an end to the fiasco. There was lots of to-ing and fro-ing with management and the record company about what our third single – the last of the contract – would be. We'd also decided to stop touring. There seemed no point if the record company wasn't going to support us with proper promotion and we told them so.

Anyway our third single, 'Lead Me On', came out to no fanfares and no publicity, and generated no real interest from anyone, even though I thought it was the best track we'd done. The trouble was we'd all lost heart by then. Somehow 'Lead Me On' got to something like number forty in the charts, which was frankly amazing as it had received such dismal support from radio and the media.

The girls and I decided about four months after my eighteenth birthday – and 'Lead Me On' had all but flopped – that it was time to call it a day. We'd all had enough by then. Brian was the first to bring it up, in the back of the car that was ferrying us away from what turned out to be our last radio interview, at Capital Radio, if my memory serves me correctly.

'It's pretty much up to you,' he said, drawing short of mentioning the 'split' word.

Claudia didn't hesitate. 'I think it's time to end.'

'I don't mind – whatever,' Dionne added.

For my part I just nodded. I thought, I don't want to be in a group where I'm not getting on with the girls any more and

I'm losing my friends because of it. I don't want to be in a group that's not working and I don't want to keep earning this little money for working so hard. That said, I was still very grateful for our weekly handouts.

I was exhausted from the touring and gutted about the way my dreams of pop stardom had failed. On top of that I was desperately sad about how my relationship with Dionne had gone downhill. I'd never had a best friend like her before, and I've always believed that for quite a few women losing a best mate can be like breaking up with a husband or partner. We'd gone through everything together; we'd grown up together and shared each other's dreams; yet now we had almost lost respect for each other. It was horrible, truly horrible. Despite my happiness with Gareth the whole time was rather ghastly.

We still went out together for a while after Milan broke up but not for long. I had always sensed Dionne was more popular than I was. She had a way with people and I always knew she'd end up all right. When Milan finally broke up she went back to Tenerife, where she stayed for quite a while, getting into the whole clubby/party scene that was developing over there. I reckon that must have helped her get over Milan, because I heard she came back as something of a new woman. Over the years we bumped into each other quite a few times and I knew that she still thought about me and asked after me from time to time.

Astonishingly, just as I was finishing this book, completely out of the blue, Dionne rang me and we met up and I was thrilled to see that, like me, she had put Milan behind her and had got on with her life. We were both really nervous when we met up, more than six years after the end of Milan. Instead of being wild and clubby, Dionne was very holistic and healthy, into organic food and detox diets. She's left music behind and moved into film, working behind the camera as a first assistant director. Her long hair was cut short into a neat bob that really suited her and she wore only a little mascara. Instead of pop music and boys we talked about healthy eating and the environment. I sometimes feel I must have known her in another life.

There are only a couple of women who keep coming into my life and she's definitely one of them. I was surprised at how comfortable I felt in her company. Women, after all, should be friends, not enemies. When I look back on my life I realise I've had a problem with a lot of women, especially those who are too insecure, as they invariably find me a threat, but that's certainly not the case with Dionne.

Abandoning Milan was a bad time, that's for sure, but being with Gareth certainly cushioned the blow. I went from being a budding pop star one minute to, well, to taking a job in Knickerbox – one of the smaller units in the giant Lakeside shopping centre in Essex – at £1.50 an hour! I knew, of course, that I had to make some money somehow – but it was a crushing blow to the old ego, nonetheless. I also realised that I needed to get back into acting if I was ever to escape from the joys of hanging up panties. By then I had an agent, a lovely lady called Joelle Martin, who ran the Creative Talent agency.

Great, I thought, I'll call her, but she rang me first. 'Martine,' she said rather sadly after I finished giving her my tale of woe. 'I've decided to leave the agency because I want to start a family.'

That news just added to my worries. Oh God, I thought, I've got no agent, I've got no record deal, there's no possibility of my acting happening now. I've got no money – this isn't what I trained for. What am I going to do about it?

Money was a big worry. I'd saved only a little from what I

earned with Milan. I knew that Mum and Dad didn't have any and I didn't want to take money from Gareth. I wanted to make my own way in life and earn my own money, so it was goodbye to new clothes and fancy boutiques and hello to charity shops. It was important to my self-confidence that I felt good and looked attractive and I found some great stuff in those shops. Properly attired, I then tried to find a new agent.

Gareth would drive me to all these different agencies and sit outside doing his work on the mobile phone while I'd be inside seeing different people. I always introduced myself in person because if you phoned in advance they'd say, 'Just send us your CV,' and never get back in touch. Everywhere I went I drew a blank. I felt like a complete failure. Nothing was working out.

Then Mark Devene, who used to work for Joelle, rang up to say he was keeping the agency open, going alone without Joelle. My heart leaped. 'As we already know what you do I wondered if you wanted to stay with us.' That was the news I'd be waiting for. I was thrilled. 'I'll see what I can get you – you sound desperate,' Mark added before ringing off.

Safe in the knowledge that Mark was looking out for me, I felt happier than ever hanging out with Gareth, whose own career was picking up no end. At the weekend he would be DJ-ing at various clubs and more often than not I'd go with him. During the week he'd work during the day, badgering people on the phone and getting bookings, and in the evenings he would come round to my parents' for dinner or I'd go over to his place. They were brilliant times and I got to meet many fascinating people through Gareth's clubland connections. It was a fun, exciting world though Mum couldn't conceal her concern about the amount of drugs that were circulating in nightclubs.

Hers was a completely understandable and rational fear especially after the death of my Uncle Chris. But I didn't do any drugs – never have done and never will – not that I didn't see their effects all around me. Indeed, throughout my life, whether I was gigging with Milan, clubbing with Gareth or at *EastEnders*, drugs were always around. There was always someone you'd see who seemed to have lost the plot from doing too many drugs. I'd seen how people who got heavily involved in drugs, whether with cocaine or ecstasy or whatever, would age so badly. They didn't seem to get very far with their lives, which seemed to stand still for as long as they were using chemicals. Some people, I suppose, just want to have a laugh all the time and not think about real life. They would find their escape route in drugs but never saw where that path led them. Without drugs they would be completely soulless and devoid of personality.

Funnily enough, soulless and devoid of personality was pretty much how I was finding life during the day at Knickerbox. The job was not my cup of tea at all. I spent hour after hour trying to hang up knickers on little rails, which was not as easy as it sounds. There was a real knack to it, which I simply didn't have. I was much better at clearing the place up, making sure the knickers were in line and the sizes were in the right order. I did all that beautifully and I was a very good wrapper, too.

Selling was my strongest attribute and if I'd worked on commission I could have done quite well. Guys would come in and say things like, 'I need a black underwear set for my wife,' and I'd say, 'What size is she?' and they'd say, 'I'm not sure . . .' So I'd ask them, 'Well, is she my sort of size or like that girl over there?' By this point most men would be either dribbling or glowing red with embarrassment. It was great fun and was one of the upsides to the job. The downside was the terrible pay, which meant I could afford to eat only a few biscuits for lunch rather than the nice sandwiches they sold at Marks & Spencer.

The other girls I used to work with didn't exactly help. Whether out of jealousy or disbelief, they used to taunt me over my past. 'You're a liar, Martine,' they'd bitch. 'You say you've been in this group, Milan? Well, we've never heard of them.' Not that I was surprised about that.

After my lunch of a couple of biscuits and a while spent window-shopping, gazing at all the things I couldn't afford – just about everything – I'd come back. 'You're a minute late,' the manageress would moan. 'You'll have to stay behind, shut up shop and count the takings.' Cinderella's ugly sisters seemed almost charming by comparison.

To add to my growing sense of shame and disappointment I found quite a few of my friends shopped at Lakeside and used to hate selling them underwear. I also felt that I'd let Mum down because she'd invested so much time and energy in helping me get to Italia Conti and make something of myself and there I was at Knickerbox, not earning real money and being a complete misery to live with. Gareth was the only bright spot and I'd spend all day counting down the hours until he would come and pick me up. He knew how unhappy I was and was very sweet about it.

One day when I was particularly fed up he said manfully, 'You know you don't have to do this. I can help you out.' But I was having none of it, even if Gareth could have afforded to keep me, which I doubt. I was determined to maintain my independence.

He was kind and thoughtful and seemed as smitten with me as I was with him, whether we were grabbing a TV dinner or visiting his family in Wales. Everything just fitted together perfectly for us. I had no insecurities as far as past relationships were concerned because I'd never had a proper boyfriend before. I had no worries of being hurt because I'd never known what it was like to be hurt – at least, not by a boyfriend.

Gareth was more sceptical. 'You're so young and you've got so much ahead of you,' he'd say. 'It worries me that one day you'll grow out of me. You know I'm right for you now but, whatever it is, you've got it. And when you get what you want, what about me? Those thoughts do frighten me.' I couldn't see what he was driving at because I felt so secure in his arms.

Gareth lived in Dartford, Kent, sharing a flat with his friend Mark Westhenry, who was also a good DJ. He worked with computers, too, and I always thought he was quite posh. Mark loved the whole thing of being a lad, sharing a flat with Gareth and chatting about girls and stuff just like the boys in the TV sitcom, *Men Behaving Badly*. Then I came along and ruined it all! To his credit, Mark never showed any resentment.

'Gareth's very much in love with you and talks about you all the time,' he confided once when we were alone. I couldn't believe it. Here was I, a gushing eighteen-year-old, and I'd made this lovely man with gorgeous green eyes go potty over me. Career-wise my life may have been in the doldrums but it still felt as if I was having the happiest time of my life.

They may have wanted to live the lads' life but the two men were also quite house-proud. Mark and Gareth both had double bedrooms, which were always tidy, just like the kitchen and the little bathroom. Gareth also got me into lovely bath products from Neutralia. He loved everything smelling nice and clean and the Neutralia gave the place a lovely clinical feel. We used to use tons of the stuff in the bath because it smelled so gorgeous. There was a Futon in the living room and a cat called Cat because they couldn't be bothered to give it a name.

After we'd been going out for a while, a couple of months or so, I began to stay with Gareth at night. And as time went on I trusted him more and more until I felt the time was right to lose my virginity. Perhaps because I waited, or I chose the right man, I remember it as a wonderful and enjoyable experience, everything it should be.

There was a lovely, relaxed build-up. That evening, a Saturday, we went to Greenwich for something to eat before going back to Gareth's place. For some reason, even though nothing was said, I just knew that this was going to be the night. Gareth had never pressured me into sleeping with him and he knew I was a virgin. Apparently Gordon at the club used to lean over his shoulder, telling him to take double care of me: 'You look after her, mate,' he'd say. 'She might go clubbing and she might hang out with all you grown-ups but she's a young girl at heart and she's, you know . . .'

'What?' Gareth would ask. 'She's, "you know", what?'

'She's a virgin.'

To his credit I think Gareth had probably already sussed that out for himself. I think he quite liked the fact that I'd never had a boyfriend before.

We had all the time in the world. We both revelled in the romance of it all and, when we did talk about sex, we both agreed that when the time came we'd know it. We'd have kisses and cuddles and nothing more when I first used to stay overnight and then, as time went on, I became more confident and ready in myself. Throughout what must have been a frustrating time for Gareth, he was never anything but the perfect gentleman. I know it must have been really hard for him, especially as I knew he was as attracted to me as I was to him. I had all the feelings and emotions but didn't know what to do with them. He did, and that night I discovered what all the fuss was about.

On Sunday morning I woke up and couldn't wait to get back and tell Mum. I walked in the front door and bounded over to her. 'Do you notice anything different about me?' I asked her teasingly.

'No.'

'You must be able to tell something's happened. I thought most mothers could tell. There's a glaze in my eyes, isn't there? And my hair's ruffled.'

'What the fuck is she going on about now?' Mum said, feigning ignorance.

'Mum,' I cried. 'I've become a woman!'

'I suppose you'd better have a bacon sandwich, then, you must be starving.'

We both howled with laughter.

After eating my sarnie we both kicked back on the sofa for a proper natter and I remember watching her as she lit a fag.

'You know, Mum, everybody does that, don't they, after they've made love?'

'What, dear?'

'You know, have a cigarette after sex.'

'You do that and I'll fucking kill you,' she said firmly. I'd had a few chest infections when I was much younger and used to have to take Ventolin. She was always worried that smoking could bring my chest problems back.

It was just before Christmas 1994 and I'd been slaving away at Knickerbox for about four months when I got a call from Mark Devene.

'Wonderful news, darling: there's an audition for *EastEnders* coming up. They're looking for someone to play a character called Tiffany.'

You'd have thought I'd have been grateful but pride got the better of me. 'I don't want any soaps,' I told him firmly, but Mark, who was very camp and devastatingly funny with it, must have been reading my mind.

'Frankly, my dear, I don't really think we're in a position to be picky. Aren't you hanging up knickers for a living, love?'

'But Mark, I don't want to look dreadful all the time,' I whinged. 'I want to look beautiful. Everyone looks terrible on *EastEnders*. It all looks a bit muddy and dreary to me. I want to be a star – I don't want to look like somebody that works on a market stall. It's just not me. It's just not what I want to do. It's not at all starry being in *EastEnders* is it?'

'Actually, Martine, this character *is* very glam and she's going to be the new big thing on the Square. She's a little bit tarty, very funny and quick-witted. I really think if you threw yourself into it you could play her really well.'

Mark was over-egging the custard, but then that's what most agents do if they're faced with a reluctant client – not, I should imagine, that there are many reluctant clients around. The truth was I loved watching *EastEnders* on the telly and was already quite excited at the prospect of going for a job on the BBC's biggest show.

What I didn't know, because Mark hadn't told me, was that Tiffany was not certain to stay in Albert Square. She had been scheduled to appear in only seventeen episodes to cover for the temporary departure of Natalie, alias the actress Lucy Speed, so it was hardly a job for life. 'OK, all right, then, I'll read for it,' I said and went back to my knickers.

The date for the audition was set for the middle of the first week of December. I booked a day off from Knickerbox, which was a laugh in itself because the manageress couldn't believe it when I said I was going for a part in *EastEnders*. It finally dawned on the silly cow that I hadn't been making up fairy stories about being in a pop group. I was also given a couple of pages of background notes about Tiffany Raymond – stuff like how her Mum and Dad had parted after her Dad's business collapsed, that she had a brother, that she went to work in Spain as a beauty consultant for a while. They were quite detailed notes that helped you see what sort of character she was.

As it turned out, the first audition was hardly a life-changing experience. I read a few scenes, met a few of the executives and was sent home with hardly the most encouraging of comments. Jane Deach, the woman in charge of casting people in *EastEnders*, thought I didn't look right and told me that I should come back for a second audition but this time dressed as Tiffany.

I booked another day off from Knickerbox and started working on what Tiffany would wear for the second audition the following Tuesday. I borrowed bits and pieces from various people – miniskirts and fishnets – and found these ridiculously long false nails, more like talons really. All the accessories were tacky and coloured gold. I reckoned I'd look like a right little tart.

The day of the audition dawned and things were not looking bright. I felt ill. I had been battling some bug or other over the weekend. Mum had even booked me an appointment at the doctor's for the following afternoon. I was thinking about that and feeling distinctly below par as John drove me to Elstree in full Tiff costume because Gareth was busy. At Elstree the first person I bumped into was the actor Sid Owen who played Ricky Butcher. I ran into him in a lift. He looked at me as if I was a hooker!

The BBC people waiting for me seemed unusually enthusiastic. Carolyn Weinstein, one of the senior execs essentially in charge of the smooth running of *EastEnders*, who was to become a good friend of mine, did a great job soothing my nerves: 'Just go in there and do your best.'

I did exactly what she suggested. The audition in a nondescript beige-painted typical BBC room seemed to go well, even if all I did was sit down and read from a script – you don't move around when you read for big TV shows. I could tell it had gone well because various people tipped me the wink when I'd finished. 'We've only got a couple more people to see,' one of the producers told me. 'But we think you're the one, although we're not really allowed to say that in case we do see somebody that's the even more "the one". That said, we don't think we will.' The audition over, I jumped back into John's car, still togged up as Tiff the tart, and headed home, feeling confident, but not *that* confident.

The following day I woke up feeling a little tired and depressed because of the bug and wasn't exactly looking forward to whatever awaited me at the doctor's. I walked down to the surgery and announced myself to the receptionist, and some time later left the surgery feeling sick and miserable. The audition the previous day felt like ancient history and I wasn't exactly overjoyed at the prospect of spending the rest of Christmas, not to mention New Year, slaving away in Knickerbox. On top of that it was a miserable, rainy, cold day. By the time I got home I was totally pissed off with my lot.

Mum was in, sitting down, and I remember clearly noticing that her hand was spread across the arm of the chair, gripping the sides as if her life depended on it. Her knuckles were white and her eyes were wide open.

'What's the matter with you? You look like a loony,' I said with as much sympathy as I could muster. Mum didn't answer. Instead, she asked me how I'd got on at the doctor's surgery. 'Fine,' I lied. I asked her again, 'What's the matter with you? What's the matter with your hand? You look like there's something wrong with you?'

Still gripping the chair for dear life, she told me to ring Mark.

'What?'

'Ring Mark Devene, *ring Mark Devene.*' She was almost squealing by now.

'All right, I'll ring him in a minute. Give us a chance to make a cup of tea.'

'No, no, no. Ring him now.'

'Mum, is there something you're not telling me? You're acting really weird. What is it?'

'Oh, nothing. He's just got to go through some work and bits and bobs with you.'

Seeing that she was in such a state and making no sense, I agreed. I thought maybe she'd had an argument with John or something and wasn't telling me. Astonishing as it may seem the penny hadn't dropped – it really didn't occur to me, in my black mood, that I'd got the part.

I picked up the phone and called Mark but I wasn't in the mood for exchanging camp pleasantries. 'Mark,' I said sternly. 'What's going on? What do you need me for? I've had a right miserable day and . . .'

'I'm glad you rang. I just wanted to let you know that you didn't get that commercial we were talking about. And the film audition, the one I mentioned? Well, that's not happening now, either.'

I was beginning to wonder whether my lot could get any worse when Mark piped up with, 'Oh, by the way, darling, you've got *EastEnders.*'

'What?'

'You've got *EastEnders* – they love you!' he squealed.

I looked at Mum. She was now leaping up and down in her chair screaming, 'Yes! Yes! Yes!' over and over, rather like Meg Ryan in the fake-orgasm scene in *When Harry Met Sally.* 'That's right, Martine,' my Mum cried. 'That was what I was trying to tell you, but I didn't want to spoil the surprise.'

CHAPTER 10

EastEnders

TO SAY I was a nervous wreck at the start of my first day on *EastEnders* – just before New Year's Day 1995 – would be a huge understatement. I was in pieces. For starters, three years had passed since my last TV acting venture, which was a small role in ITV's *The Bill*, and I was feeling badly out of practice. My confidence was virtually nonexistent and my heart was thudding uncontrollably as we drove round the North Circular from the East End to Elstree, Herts, where the BBC1 soap has been based since its launch in February 1985.

EastEnders may have launched in the mid-eighties but, from the dilapidated, old-fashioned feel of the place, I'd guess that Elstree last had some major investment breathed into it at the end of the sixties. It looks and feels badly dated, like those civic buildings that sprang up at the same time as concrete tower blocks.

When you first arrive you're greeted by the security men at the front gate. Saying hello to them each day makes you feel as if you are in a French and Saunders sketch, because these guards are totally surreal. Every single day, no matter if you've been there five weeks or five years, they would make out that they had never seen you before in their lives. 'What's your name and where are you going?' they'd ask.

Well, on my first day they really didn't know who I was and so, after a few minutes spent checking that I was legit, they let me through.

On the right as you go in there's a bit of grass and then an old-fashioned rectangular building that serves as the canteen and on-set pub. It's where all the *Top of the Pops* people go and hang out when they're not filming so you can often spot a few stars there. On the left are the studios, all set in a sort of Legoland environment with loads of little zebra-crossings dotted everywhere. The further into the area on the left you venture, the stranger it becomes. All the *EastEnders* sets are stacked up on giant trolleys. They seem so lifeless propped up like that, like a load of wooden planks, until all of a sudden you catch sight of a banner saying 'Kathy and Phil's house' or 'Sanjay's stall'. A little further and you see all these rundown Portakabin-type buildings decorated with photos of *EastEnders*.

You are now in the middle of *EastEnders*-land. There's a little seating area where everybody hangs out while they're waiting to go on set. Walk in a little further still and on your right is the runners' room, the runners being the people at the bottom of the production career ladder, who give you your scripts and your fan mail as well as taking your messages. They also give you your filming schedules and highlight all the scenes you're in.

My nerves did not steady. This was the first TV production I'd ever worked on as an adult and my first experience of a rolling drama series such as a soap. I had worked in TV before, sure, but it's hard to impress on someone quite how frenetic *EastEnders* was. I didn't have a clue about how such a big show was made. The runners handed me a script and I remember that my first thought was, Why's everyone else got a smaller script than me? The next was, Why are all their lines highlighted with a fluorescent pen?

I asked to borrow a highlighting pen and set to work with it, not having any idea what I was supposed to be doing. I was highlighting lines left, right and centre because the truth was I didn't know which lines you were supposed to highlight and which you weren't. Everyone was in such a rush, off to Studio D or Stage 1 or wherever – you used to have to film all over the place at Elstree – so no one had any time to explain things to me. When people began drifting off for lunch I didn't know where to go, so I just followed them back to the canteen. Aargh! It felt as if it was my first day at school but with added complications because there was so much more to worry about.

Dean Gaffney, who plays Robbie Jackson, and Howard Antony, who played his dad, Alan, were both knights in shining armour as far as I was concerned when they came over to rescue me. Howard, in particular, was a real hero because for my first few days on set I didn't have a bean. The wages at Knickerbox had hardly set me up for life. In fact I had only £3 to my name on my first day. As I browsed the canteen for lunch I had to keep lifting up the little plastic plaques on top of the various dishes to find out how much they were. I remember I was wearing Gareth's white Levi's and a big navy polo-neck jumper and a pair of Gareth's shoes, because I didn't have enough money to get my own boots. I was utterly skint.

Howard must have spotted me looking lost because he

came over and asked if I was OK. We had already been introduced and he was really sweet right from the off. I noticed he had chicken Kiev and carrots, a nice dinner, and I looked enviously over at his Kiev, even though I knew I couldn't afford it.

'Why don't you get the same?' he asked.

'I can't lie to you, Howard,' I replied. 'But I haven't really got much money on me today.' Oh, the shame of it!

'I'll get you it, that's no problem,' he said. 'Are you a bit skint? Well, don't worry.'

There were a few times in the days after that when Howard gave me a fiver here and there. Considering how wary the cast of *EastEnders* can be with strangers – they have suffered plenty in the press thanks to a few dodgy characters leaking stories about people being sacked or taking drugs, that kind of thing – Howard proved himself a great friend right from the start. New people come and go all the time in *EastEnders* and most actors and actresses are pretty thick-skinned – they have to be. They just come and do what they've got to on the show and that's it. But I couldn't pretend to be so tough. I just felt lonely and vulnerable that first day. Dean Gaffney then came and sat with me just as I was finishing lunch. I'd seen him a couple of times before at the odd party when the Italia Conti and Sylvia Young kids would get together. He was also a regular at dos thrown by the Pickard brothers, Nick, John and Mark, at their pub in Ladbroke Grove, which is now called the Chilled Eskimo. We ended up chatting for quite a while, which helped put me a little more at ease, but I was still glad when the day came to an end. Glad? Over the moon more like.

By then I had also spent a lot of time thinking about Tiff and the kind of girl she was. I didn't really see much of myself in her, but I did see a lot of my Mum – her unhappy childhood, failed relationships, working in a pub.

Gareth came to pick me up that night. I saw him sitting in his car waiting for me. 'How did it go, Mart?' he asked.

'I hated it. I don't ever want to go back. Nobody's very friendly apart from Dean and Howard. I just don't feel like I can do it, Gareth. Everything's so fast. They're all talking about Lot This and Stage 1 That. They film it all out of sequence. I don't know what I'm doing. I've got more script paper than lines.'

Gareth handled this hysterical mess of emotions with finesse. 'You've got to come back tomorrow, Martine, and you'll see everything will be fine.'

I told him of my day's adventures, how all I had to do was hang about in the lot, which doubles as the market and Albert Square, in a black cocktail dress. 'All I did was freeze my tits off,' I babbled. 'But other than that I didn't have to do anything. Tomorrow I have got some actual scenes, though,' I went on, adding meekly, 'And they're in the studio, inside, so I should be a bit warmer. At least that's something.'

It was the same story when Gareth dropped me off at my Mum's. She was all excited and bombarded me with questions I didn't want to answer. Obviously she could tell I'd had a bit of day and did her best to reassure me everything would be fine.

'It'll take you time to settle in, Angel. There's a lot of people there you've got to meet. You're not going to be bosom buddies with everyone. It takes time.'

I went to bed that night with the hump, feeling disappointed and still wondering whether I really could hack it. The trouble was that it was all so different from what I'd imagined. I thought that, as it was such a big show, there'd be people there whose job it was to make you feel at home, but there was none of that.

I went in the next day, stopping off first for hair and make-up – they didn't half slap it on – and thinking to myself that working at Elstree was like entering a different planet, a mini-world. It was a place where everyone went to play someone else, a weird place. At least that day I had something to contribute: my first scene. It wasn't the first scene of mine to go out on the television, of course, but a scene shown sometime later as everything was filmed back to front.

My character, Tiffany Raymond, had to go into the fish-and-chip shop with Bianca, her friend, played by Patsy Palmer.

The two of us had to clap eyes on Ricky, Bianca's other half, played by Patsy's real-life mate Sid Owen, which then prompts Bianca to suggest we all go out together. Tiff responds by saying she thinks Ricky's a bit of a drip. 'We fancied playing Scrabble,' Tiff pipes up. 'But I didn't think you'd cope, Ricky, so that's you out for tonight.' Oh, miaow!

I remember I was wearing black Oasis moleskin trousers, a little cream top with a gold chain belt, a blue leather flying jacket with a fur collar and a pair of black patent loafers. The trousers were really tight and I had my hair in a ponytail. Tiff, in those early days, was the tart-with-the-heart type, but I was still worried about the wardrobe department going over the top with my costumes.

Everything moved so fast when it came to recording a scene. Instead of playing to one camera, almost everything is shot on two simultaneously at *EastEnders*, so people had to keep moving me in the right direction to make sure both cameras got me. You soon learned that if somebody was blocking you, you had to move a little bit to get in front of the camera otherwise the director would call for the shot to be redone and it would hold everything up. I was definitely out of my depth but did my best to bluff my way through.

I winged it through the whole first month, if I'm honest, and my nerves and anxiety came out through my mouth, which just went on talking whether my brain was engaged or not. I'd chat away for Britain and keep yakking even when I wasn't getting very much back.

The shooting routine at *EastEnders* is confusing, no doubt about it, but you soon get the hang of it. Outside scenes shot in the lot were filmed the week before the corresponding studio scenes. You had three different scripts on the go at any one time.

Of course there was a huge buzz to be had from being in *EastEnders*, at first anyway, which I'm sure contributed to my nerves. It's a great kick to find yourself having a drink in the Queen Vic when you've seen it on telly for the past ten years. But, after you've done something ridiculous like twenty-two scenes in there in one day, the novelty soon wears off. The workload was incredible. Those guys in the soaps really earn their money and I'm sure it's the same in *Coronation Street* or *Brookside* or *Emmerdale*. I remember Mum taught me how to pull a pint. She told me to lean forward, show a bit of cleavage – but not too much – give the punter a smile and say, 'Anything you fancy?' If you did it right, apparently, you might even get a tip!

It's hardly the most glamorous of jobs, either, when you're actually there. Take my dressing room, for instance. When they first start, most people share a room. Luckily I had my own from the off. I think I took over that of June Brown, who plays Dot Cotton. She's taken a couple of breaks from Albert Square in her time. It was in a newish area of the site, an area that had been given over to cope with the expanding cast, a result of the soap increasing from two to three episodes a week a couple of years earlier. A lot of the older cast members were holed up at the other end of the set. All the dressing rooms were essentially subdivisions of this great big Portakabin and were all quite small. There was a tiny little bed/settee in each, a toilet, a small shower, a wardrobe and a big mirror, but that was about it.

A lot of regulars did their best to make their dressing rooms feel like home by bringing in pictures and photos, maybe a portable stereo. I also used to have a little duvet inside mine. It sounds nice but when you first walk into the dressing room area it looks like a borstal!

Everything appears very basic and quite rough. Mine had dingy cream walls and a royal-blue carpet. Everything is done to a minimum budget in the finest traditions of the BBC, you see, but you do your best to make it as nice as you can. The other thing about the dressing rooms I should mention was the little gold-coloured plaque on each door – or in my case, in those early days, the lack of one. The regulars all had these brass plaques with 'London Borough of Walford' stamped on them and their name above it. When you first join the show you get only a sticker on your door with your name typed on it. I knew I was there to stay when my gold-coloured plaque arrived some six months later. I kept that plaque when I left. Steve McFadden, who played my brother-in-law Phil Mitchell, unscrewed it for me on my last day. 'There you go, girl, you've got to keep that gold plaque to remind you of everything.' But I'm getting ahead of myself again.

At this time I was still a big Kylie Minogue fan. I am even today, but back then she was huge and had just undergone this complete makeover. She'd gone really trendy for 'Confide In Me'. I said to Gareth one night – I was still technically living with Mum and Dad at the time but staying most nights with him – that I needed something to brighten up the main wall in my dressing room.

'I feel like I'm in a mental asylum,' I said before switching out the light and going to sleep.

Quick as you like he said, 'Oh, I've got something that will do, I think.'

He got up, opened a cupboard and brought out this massive poster of Kylie that was big enough to cover the entire wall. I was there for ages the following day, on my lunch break, putting on enough Blu-Tack to keep her in place. That wasn't my only personal touch. I took in a little stereo that I'd had for years. It had a bit of paint on it where I'd been decorating once but that didn't matter. It worked a treat so I just plugged it in on the side. Quite a few cuddly toys that people had sent to congratulate me on getting the part made the journey to Elstree and moved into my dressing room. A couple of flyers bearing my beloved Gareth's name and dates where he'd done really well at clubs such as the Ministry got the Blu-Tack treatment as well. I surrounded the frame of my mirror with photographs of family and friends, not to mention Polaroids of me in my first Tiffany outfit or with Patsy Palmer or Danniella Westbrook – Sam Butcher in the programmes.

Danniella and I have been mates for years. She's a very sweet and pretty girl who had the world at her feet, but I'm afraid there were people around her who were destroying her by offering her drugs. She had too much too young. There's so much pressure when you're young and in a show like *EastEnders*, pressure I had yet to experience. Eventually I did understand how some people would take drugs to escape from it all, to escape from living in the shadow of their TV character. There was a constant expectation to be perfect, which Danniella, like others, found hard to tolerate. Later, when things turned badly for her and she left the show I asked her to come and stay with me in my flat. She declined for her own reasons but sent me a little teddy bear saying,

'Thank you so much for all your support – you've been my life line. I love you lots. Danniella.' She knows that if ever she needs me I'm there for her.

Even her departure from *EastEnders* wasn't without drama. She learned she was going to be out, a few months after I joined, after swiping an advance script. There's a script called the blue script, which make-up people would have so they could order in the appropriate supplies. The blue scripts were a couple of months ahead of the actors' white scripts. Anyway, Danniella got hold of a blue script by pinching it out of a make-up room. She read it and saw that her character was off 'travelling' again. She was gutted – especially as no one had bothered to inform her of this.

Back to my dressing room. My Mum had made this patchwork quilt and seeing that it was never used at home I nabbed it for my room along with a little pillow. The perfect combination to catch a mid-afternoon kip! I used to go to sleep snuggling up in that quilt, gazing up at a postcard of Marilyn Monroe that I'd stuck on my wardrobe, Marilyn looking out of a window in a white dressing gown. Marilyn, I've mentioned before, was something of an icon to me. I caught her in *Gentlemen Prefer Blondes* when I was about ten and was impressed by her tragic life story. I've always admired sexy, glamorous, feminine women, which I suppose relates back to the days when I wanted to be a stripper. I even remember thinking Marilyn and I were inextricably linked in some way as we both had the same initials. That was until Mum pointed out that my original surname, the one on my birth certificate, says Ponting!

Even though I'd already filmed three proper scenes with dialogue and had those in the can, the first the public ever saw of Tiffany Mitchell was when I waltzed into Bianca's house where she was having a party. 'Hello, Bianca,' Tiff says. 'I've just got back from Spain.' The woman who directed that scene was called Audrey Cook. She had no time to see that I was nervous and I had no choice but to get on with it.

As I got used to the manic chaos of life in *EastEnders* and the way people stared at me on set, I started picking up on some of the scams the other actors were carrying out. I quickly realised that some people had not always mastered their own scripts, let alone taken an intelligent and logical interest in those of the other actors. Instead they would tuck them underneath their seat in the Vic or underneath a settee if they were supposed to be in someone's home. Everyone was at it and I soon twigged that I could do likewise.

My first meeting with Ross Kemp, who was destined to play my future husband Grant Mitchell, was less than encouraging. I went into the wardrobe department one day early on and saw him there. He was obviously very preoccupied, going over his lines, washing his hands, when I said, 'Hello, Ross, I'm Martine and I'm playing Tiffany, Tiffany Raymond. I just wanted to say hello.' He said hello back but when I put my hand out to shake his he didn't respond as he was still drying his hands off. It was an awkward moment. I thought to myself, Oh, he's scary; I can't do this, and went on my way. I seemed to have a knack for catching Ross off-guard. He was always the consummate professional. All his lines would be neatly laid out on index cards so he could learn them perhaps a week or two in advance. Me? I just had a natural way of picking them up, my lines and everyone else's. My casual approach to learning lines used to give Ross a major headache as he was always worried I would forget a crucial bit of dialogue. I never did though, did I, Ross?

EastEnders is filmed six to eight weeks ahead of transmission so it was almost two months before the public, not to mention Mum, John and Gareth, got to see Yours Truly doing her stuff. My own thoughts when I finally got to see my first episode were typically girlie. I thought I looked a stone bigger than I was, a common but unwanted side effect of TV cameras. 'Oh, my God,' I cried aloud. 'I want to kill myself!' Melodramas aside, I was with Mum and Gareth when the big night came up. We all just sat there on the settee in utter silence for the whole half-hour. No one said a word until the theme music came up at the end, when my Mum, cool as a cucumber, sighed, 'That's my girl,' but that was about it. It wasn't until the next day that I got some gauge of what life in *EastEnders* was going to be like.

I wasn't working the day after my screen debut. Instead I was spending the day with Gareth and my little brother Laurence. We'd hit the road quite early and were getting peckish come breakfast time so we pulled off for a meal in a Little Chef restaurant not far from home. The newspapers, it turned out, had all run pictures of Tiffany's arrival in Walford, but I wasn't aware of this as we walked in, although I do remember clocking a woman who was flicking through one of the tabloids as we took our seats. The woman, I noticed, kept glancing at the paper and then looking at me. Gareth noticed, too, and elbowed me after a while.

'I think you've just been recognised, Martine,' he said quietly.

'I know,' I whispered. 'Isn't it brilliant?'

I wasn't used to being recognised at all. Milan hadn't exactly put my face on the map, and I can remember being quite unnerved by this woman until Gareth brought it up. Each time she looked over I thought she could see something on my face. I even asked Gareth if I had a bogey hanging off the end of my nose!

While I enjoyed having days off like that I was also getting increasingly involved in *EastEnders* as my initial nervousness dissipated. I would start sticking my nose in a little more, particularly concerning the producers' plans for Tiffany, who already seemed to have scored a hit with the public and the press. I also realised there was a definite hierarchy among the cast. Your position was dictated by how you handled yourself on set, how big your part was, how attractive you were – all the usual things that would affect your position in a normal office job. I can remember there was one table in the canteen that always had seated around it the same group of cast members. People such Barbara Windsor, Ross and Steve McFadden. In those early days I'd often wonder whether I would one day sit there, too. In reality the hierarchy was made up of those actors who had the biggest scenes, the ones that would be given major storylines. I was aching for Tiffany to get her first big break.

In truth it wasn't long before I got a well-meaning-but-not-official nod of approval from the powers that be – though it didn't come from a fellow cast member. About two months after joining the show a guy called Tony, one of the scriptwriters, called me in for a chat, very informally. The conversation went along these lines: 'Martine, you do realise life's not going to be the same for you any more? You do realise that as time goes on and more of these episodes are transmitted you're not going to be able to walk around Safeway's any more? In fact you're not going to be able to walk around anywhere any more. You're going to dread getting out of the car to fill up with petrol.

'This character's going to be massive,' Tony continued, his voice rising in tune with his enthusiasm, a combination that had my heart racing. I liked what I was hearing. 'Tiffany's going to be pretty much one of the biggest things on this show. Can you cope with the workload? Can you cope with the press?'

'Yeah,' I said coolly, doing my best to keep a lid on my emotions. 'I can cope.'

This was the first time anybody at *EastEnders* had ever addressed the celebrity side of the job with me. Those first few months had been an intoxicating mix of fear and a growing sense of self-confidence – I hadn't really thought or felt anything else as far as the show was concerned. But the truth, especially in my early days, was that one was not very protected by the public-relations people at *EastEnders*. The publicity department was there purely to talk about what's happening on *EastEnders* – without giving too much away, of course. Looking back, I really believe that they ought to have someone there whose job is to show the cast the ropes, point out the pitfalls and save them from doing anything in public they might regret later. I understand that we all have to make our own mistakes but it would surely be helpful to be given a few tips about how the press operates. You need to know what they want from you and equally importantly what you want from them.

'How do you think it's going?' Tony asked me flatly.

I told him I thought things were great. 'I think there's lots of things that could happen to her. People seem to believe Tiffany. They seem to believe the way she is, her personality. She's quite proud, quite bubbly and a bit feisty. She's a bit OTT sometimes, especially when she first appeared – the little pink fluffy coats and miniskirts, the fishnets and those strappy, disgusting plastic shoes – but people seem to've taken to her and accepted her.'

I wasn't exaggerating, either. There was a real vibe about Tiffany. I could feel it. It wasn't just what the press were saying: you could also feel it with the public. People were always going, 'Oh, you're great and so funny. You and Bianca are hilarious together, but don't you go giving that Ricky a hard time. You're really horrible but I can't stop laughing.'

I could see what they meant. Tiffany had quite a mouth in the early days and used to come out with the sharpest, truly wicked one-liners. Full credit to the writers: they produced some great stuff just for her.

It felt only natural for me to want more for Tiff. They had tried to get her involved with Steve, the guy who worked in the café, for a while. But it was obvious it was never going to develop into anything serious. But it did give Tiff the chance to show what a flirt she could be.

'That was just a warm-up to see how things went,' Tony said, adding equally calmly, 'They've just told us Letitia Dean's leaving so, er, we need to sort you out with somebody.'

I didn't take so much as a microsecond to proclaim who I thought Tiff should get involved with. Well, if Sharon – I mean Letitia, who I didn't really know – was leaving, that meant Grant – sorry, I mean Ross – would be all on his own. 'I think she'd be fantastic with Grant,' I said without hesitation. 'I think Grant needs somebody to bounce about with, someone more his match. I think Tiff and Grant would be brilliant together.'

'That's good,' Tony said. 'We've already sort of planned what's going to happen to Tiffany some six months ahead. It's going to change your life. Not many people ever get to tell anyone this,' he said gravely. 'But your life will change forever. This show will be with you forever.'

'Yeah I know,' I said, making to go. It was only when I was outside again that I let the first wave of excitement rush over me. You're on to a winner, here, Martine, I thought to myself as I all but skipped back to my dressing room. You're on to a good one, here.

Once I was back in my sanctuary my brain shifted up a gear and thoughts started racing round my head. Most of what Tony told me thrilled me to the core. But that bit about the show being with me forever had got under my skin. I want my career to last forever, I thought, and if some people keep bringing up Tiffany fair enough. But I'm going to do other things, I vowed silently. I'm going to be doing films. I'm going to be doing records, I'm going to show all the people that treated me badly that I can be this massive star. I am going to push Tiffany to the maximum – but only so that I can go on and do what I really want to do.

As far as Tony's warning about the media was concerned, I didn't really take much of it in. In my own naïve little way, I thought there wasn't much the press could ever find out about me, other than my Dad, and I reckoned I was quite prepared for that by this time. I'd had only one boyfriend. If I'd had loads of affairs then I would have appreciated the fact that people might crawl out of the woodwork and boast about their twenty-four-hour sex sessions with Martine. But, as I hadn't, I thought there was nothing worth worrying about.

Meeting Tony had changed my entire outlook on life. I had a new contract. My agent Mark Devene called to tell me I was now on a three-month contract with a three-month option, which meant at the end of three months I had the option of walking away or staying for another three as long as *EastEnders* still wanted me – and it sounded like they would. It felt like job security to me and it was a damn sight more appealing than working back at Knickerbox.

I'd even begun taking driving lessons and was desperate to pass my test before the summer was out. I had to use a bit of money my Uncle Laurence had given me and what I could scrape together from work – which was never enough – and my instructor finally recommended that I have a go. Even now the memory of my first driving test makes me shudder. I know loads of people fail but I doubt many have done so in such spectacular fashion.

I decided to do the manual test in Brentwood, Essex, which in retrospect I don't think was a great decision, because it's very hilly, which makes clutch control a nightmare. More importantly, I was nervous. Nervous? I was shaking like a leaf when I woke up that day. I felt sick, giddy and faint all at the same time. I must have been a right old state because I decided to take some Kalms pills, which I had once tried for auditions, before the test. I think I must have taken one too many. My body is very sensitive to medicines anyway – half a Junior Disprol and I run around like a hyperactive loon – but the Kalms really got to me. I started sweating first, then falling asleep.

I must have nodded off in the waiting room because the examiner apparently called my name three times before I responded. I managed to get into the car but was still a total zombie. I tried talking to keep myself alert as we proceeded with the test and turned into this narrow little road, but I was talking so nervously I was driving the examiner mad. 'Will you shut up?' he barked. 'Will you please shut up?'

I crumbled. 'I'm sorry,' I babbled, 'but I've got to keep talking because I've taken two pills to try to calm myself and now I just feel like I'm going to fall asleep at the wheel.'

Amazingly I still thought I had a chance of passing, but just then a teenager pulled out of a side road in a Renault Clio and I nearly ran straight into the side of him. In fact I would have done had the examiner not grabbed the steering wheel and pointed us to safety.

'Well, in case you haven't noticed, Miss McCutcheon,' he said, his face ashen, 'you have failed.' He scrabbled out of the passenger seat and virtually ran round to my side. 'I'm taking you back to the driving school,' he snapped. 'You've made me a nervous wreck.'

I decided after that nightmare that cars with gears weren't for me and opted for the automatic test, as it would be easier, especially in London, and also because I needed to drive as quickly as possible to save Gareth a lot of grief ferrying me to and from *EastEnders* all the time. I had a lovely guy called Jim teaching me and I remember just before the second test he shouted out, 'Don't you take no Kalms pills. I don't want you giving the examiner a heart attack.' He told me later that I had been the talk of Brentwood for quite a while after my first test.

The second, I'm pleased to say, was more successful. With the test behind me I bought myself a Fiat Punto, a black one, M-reg. Loved it. It had electric windows and a sun roof. I thought I was the bollocks.

The newspapers and magazines started fuelling that feeling, too, as I was being turned into some sort of sex symbol in print. I started getting fan mail from men, as well as from little girls, nans, vicars and nutters. It was all kicking off. People were starting to ask me to do photo shoots, which hadn't happened before, either. The publicity department at the BBC broached the subject with me first.

'Listen,' they said. 'We don't stop hearing from men's magazines and that kind of thing asking you for photo shoots, and we don't think it would be a bad thing necessarily. Do you want to go and do a couple?' They said there was this page called 'Most Wanted' in *Loaded*.

A relatively new lads' mag, *Loaded* was at that time the big thing. I didn't think about it long.

'Well, yeah,' I said. 'I don't mind doing it. I've never done anything like that before.'

Even though I was eighteen, I was a baby really – but I decided to give it a go all the same. I told Gareth, adding that I wasn't exactly sure if it was the right thing to do. But he was impressed. '"Most Wanted", Mart? That's brilliant!'

Jane March, who'd done the film *The Lover*, had done it already, he said, and so had my old friend Louise Nurding.

I went along to the studio thinking somebody from the BBC would meet me but, as they didn't consider the shoot to be bona fide BBC work, nobody, it turned out, was dispatched to look after me.

There was nothing overtly unpleasant about the situation and I don't suppose every girl would have felt as uncomfortable about it as I did. I met the photographer at a hotel. Rather worryingly, there wasn't a phone working in the place that day for some reason. I'd done only one photoshoot before, for a *News of the World* piece and that photographer made me look absolutely beautiful. I thought 'Most Wanted' would be a similar kind of thing: sexy but beautiful. And initially that was the way it seemed to be going.

We had to do my shots in the bathroom. I knew that Catherine Zeta Jones, by coincidence, was coming over later that day, too, for a shoot. This somehow helped me to feel largely untroubled by the proceedings at first. 'I'll just shout out if I need you to do anything,' the photographer said, merrily clicking away. 'Just straddle your legs a little bit further apart, Martine,' he said as the shoot dragged on. 'Good. Now just put your hand . . . like . . . in the top of your knickers, there's a good girl.'

'To be honest with you,' I said curtly. 'I'm not quite sure I want to do that. I really don't fancy doing —'

'No, no, no, Martine,' he argued. 'All the girls do it. It'll be fine. We'll check it with you before it goes in the mag, darling. Please don't worry.'

He was very persuasive, that was his job – and he was obviously good at it. I said OK, that we could do one shot like that – just one. Even before the flash gun went off, I was already regretting going along with it. But the frame, as they say, by now was in the bag. Did I get to see it before it went in the magazine? Did I hell! That single picture went just about everywhere and I was utterly devastated as a result.

Loaded is a great magazine but I was in a vulnerable position. I had nobody there to stick up for me and say, 'She's eighteen and she's never done anything like this before. Why has she got to have her hand down her knickers?' I've got nothing against women baring all. I'm a big believer in freedom of choice. If you've got a great figure and you can capitalise on it – and you're not bothered about it – then do. Great. But if you don't feel completely in control of the situation, if you feel beholden because you're grateful to be there, or a bit out of control because there's nobody there in the room trying to advise or defend you, then don't make the mistake I did. Make an excuse, go to the loo – that's how I'd deal with it now. I wouldn't make a big fuss, but at the time I just felt like crying, I just wanted to get out of there. I hated it, hated every minute of it.

I knew everyone on the show was bound to see it and, being the new girl, I dreaded their reaction. The more I thought about it, the more I felt let down by the BBC. Someone should have been there to guide me through and protect me when I felt uncomfortable. They had approved the idea in the first place, after all.

I was with Gareth when I saw the picture. I'd bought the magazine from a newsagent's shop and opened it as we drove back from Elstree. My initial reaction was a weepy one. I burst out crying. Until that moment I had still naïvely believed or at least hoped that they wouldn't use the hand-in-knickers shot and that the mag would instead treat me as some kind of glamorous pin-up. I was actually excited about seeing the pictures.

'I feel dirty, I feel so dirty,' I wailed as I chucked the magazine on the floor – only for Gareth to retrieve it. He was great about it, if not a little shocked.

'It's a horny picture, Martine, it's a very horny picture.' But his words failed to stem my tears. 'It's just one picture, Mart, it's something to remember yourself by,' he continued. 'One day you'll look back on it and think how young and sexy you were, how you had the oomph to do it. OK, it's not the biggest thing to be proud of in the world but at least you've gone and done it. You've been there, you've done it, now move on. Forget about it.'

My Mum was just as cool when she saw it. 'Mart, it's the nineties, for heaven's sake! I'm not being funny, darling, but there are a lot worse pictures about than that. So what if you've got the tips of your fingers down your knickers? It's no big deal these days. It's nothing nobody's seen before. Oh, and by the way, your tits look fantastic.'

With that she just laughed and encouraged me to do likewise. I couldn't bring myself to have a giggle but she did make me feel a lot better. But I still had to face *EastEnders*.

The next day, almost as soon as I got through the gates at Elstree, the publicity department asked to have a word with me. I should have guessed their reaction. 'You shouldn't be doing photo shoots like this,' they said, winding up to a full-blown bollocking. I told them how it was their idea in the first place, how it was going to be great publicity for Tiff and how, at the end of the day, the only person who'd got really upset about it so far was me. As I left the office I vowed not to let them take control again. I'd be better off sorting myself out in the publicity department, I reckoned.

Worse was still to come. I bumped into a fellow cast member in the wardrobe department. I considered naming names here but decided I wouldn't give this particular individual the privilege as they weren't nice about my appearance in *Loaded* at all.

The gist of the conversation as I entered the room was about the so-called curse of *Hello!* magazine, how it was considered bad luck to let the glossy mag cover your wedding, since a lot of celebrities such as the Rolling Stone Bill Wyman and the model Mandy Smith, who did get *Hello!* on board, ended up getting divorced shortly afterwards.

'You what?' I said nonchalantly as I walked in. 'You can't say there's a curse on *Hello!* magazine so far as weddings go —'

I was interrupted by this person who burst out with, 'What would you be worried about appearing in *Hello!*? You've shown everything you've got already. Who do you think you are? You've only been here a few months . . .'

Now it was my turn to interrupt. I turned to face my critic. 'Have you got a problem with me?'

Silence. I asked again: 'Have you got a problem with me?' But they carried on regardless, saying how everyone had seen the picture and implying that most found it beyond the pale.

Steve McFadden did his best to shut this person up, saying: 'Come on, aren't you being a little hard on Martine? It's not your place to say . . .' But I was furious and stormed out.

We bumped into each other again later that day when my harshest critic had the audacity to ask me what time we were supposed to be on set. 'Find out yourself,' I snapped before launching into a big one. 'If, in future, you've got a bone to pick with me you pick it by yourself and to my face because, while you might have been here quite a long time and I haven't, I intend to be around some yet.' The row was far from over and lingered for another six months before this person finally apologised and we cleared the air. After that we got rid of a lot of unpleasantness. Indeed everything felt very good again, though I still maintain that *Loaded* has a lot to answer for.

I'm a great one for counting my blessings – and I've had plenty to count over the years. With the exception of the *Loaded* fiasco and my nervous first few days, my first year at *EastEnders* was a blinding one. But the best was yet to come – the Christmas party.

Now as Christmas parties go, the *EastEnders* bash has – until recent times anyway – always been a good one. Past years have seen the odd casualty. Quite literally people have ended up going to hospital as a result of overindulgence. My first wasn't quite as debauched as that but it was a wild old do, nonetheless. People work really hard on the show, more so than the general public could ever imagine, and when Christmas comes around they invariably, and quite understandably, want to let their hair down a bit, and unless they're really out of order the BBC's top brass seem to turn a blind eye.

We had a great time at the *EastEnders* Christmas party 1995. I'd had only a couple of drinks at Elstree's not particularly glamorous Stakis Hotel but was already feeling quite tipsy – I'm a right lightweight as far as alcohol is concerned – when Michelle Collins, who played Adam Woodyatt's scheming screen wife Cindy Beale, dragged me to the loos. I always looked up to Michelle when I was there. She was always quite glamorous and outgoing but largely kept herself to herself about her private life, although she's a real girlie and was great to have a chat and a gossip with between scenes. I was very impressed with the fact that she lived in Chelsea and wore designer clothes and I remember thinking to myself, I'd like to be like that one day if Tiff ever takes off.

Michelle was the complete opposite to her screen husband. Adam, by the way, is a *very* normal man, not showbizzy at all. Indeed he's the last person in the world I would ever expect to be an actor. He's got no ego and will happily let someone punch him if it's in the script, which a lot of other male actors might object to, in case they look a little weak.

Michelle and I had been boogying down most of the evening and were having a right giggle when we went into the ladies'. There was already quite a gathering of girls there and for some reason – and I really can't remember why – Michelle suggested we have a boob-comparing competition. Lindsey Coulson, who played Carol Jackson, was there and a couple of others including one of our producers, Jane Harris. We were having a scream, talking about boobs, complaining, being complete women. Gradually the loo party trundled back out to the disco leaving me and Jane behind. I was in a chatty mood and starting talking to her about Tiffany. After my chat with Tony I was feeling impatient, I suppose, for something to happen to Tiff and started telling Jane how I felt the character was worth more than just pulling pints and being one half of a double act. I tipsily asked Jane when I'd be getting some meaty storylines.

Jane listened intently, despite the unusual location, and as I went yakking on she even took the weight off her pins by hoisting herself up on to the sink. Well, Jane was a powerful woman in all senses of the word, and I soon clocked that she looked uncomfortable perched like that. The laugh came when she tried to get down and she realised she couldn't. The sinks were tiny and Jane was, er, quite well rounded at the rear. What started as a semi-serious, alcohol-fuelled conversation had now descended to high farce as I watched the producer try to pull herself clear of the hand basin. It was hilarious.

When she eventually freed herself, I got back to Tiff. I balanced my complaints by acknowledging that I had no right to say such things, but I was charged, *really* enthusiastic. 'You see, the thing is, Jane, I've learned my way round the cameras and taken loads of the different technical issues on board. I just want to get my teeth into something.'

Her response made my Christmas. 'Don't worry,' she said. 'You won't be wasted, Martine, please believe me. You will not be wasted . . .' There was a pause as she dried her hands. 'I think I can tell you this much: you're going to be one of the main characters pretty soon . . .'

I cut her off. 'You've got to tell me more, Jane. Go on, I've got to know, you can't leave it hanging in the air like that,' I pleaded with her.

'I'm not telling you any more,' she said. 'But you said you wanted to get your teeth into something juicy. Believe me, it'll happen.'

And with that she walked back to the party.

CHAPTER 11

East End Tales

A WEEK AFTER our chat in the loo I was summoned to see Jane Harris officially but didn't have a clue what the meeting would actually be about. It was only when I went into her office that I discovered the show's top executive producer, Corinne Hollingsworth, was leaving, and that Jane was getting her job. Jane wanted to let me know that she fully intended to carry out all the things she'd said to me that night at the Christmas do. 'You will have a great storyline,' she said. 'We're thinking of getting you together with Grant.'

I said, 'Oh, that'd be brilliant, I think that'd be great – the public will love it.'

'Well, we'll soon see – there'll be a few changes. We're going to bring you a brother into the Square.' She went on to tell me all about how I was going to date Tony, a drug dealer, who would later drop me for my gay brother, Simon. Tiff was to get pregnant but have no idea who the father was due to a one-night stand with Grant Mitchell. I walked out of the meeting buzzing. Yes! I thought to myself. Here we go. It was a brilliant feeling.

I was getting more established at *EastEnders* and making some good friends. Barbara Windsor has always been great to me, and I'll never forget the way she greeted me when I first saw her at *EastEnders*. It had been something like seven years since we'd last met on the set of the TV series *Bluebirds*, but she still remembered me.

I walked in to wardrobe one day and she said, 'Well my, my! I think you've become a beautiful young lady.' I thanked her. 'You're not a scraggy little girl any more – you look lovely, really well.'

I thanked her again. Then I said, 'To tell you the truth, I'm very nervous.' She smiled again and said, 'I understand. I was really nervous, too, when I started here. I've been lucky because the boys' – she meant Steve McFadden and Ross Kemp – 'have looked after me so well. Playing their Mum has big advantages.'

I could see that. As Barbara was playing their mother, she had a link to Ross and Steve: they had something to talk about, whereas I had no roots as Tiff and no relationships with anyone to discuss at length. As I said I felt very lonely during that first year, but that soon changed. I became really close with Howard after he was so sweet to me on my first day and I grew much closer to Patsy. Patsy had been very close to Lucy Speed, now known to fans as the long-suffering Natalie Evans, who left the show for quite a while not long after I joined. I knew Patsy missed her and I was very conscious about not being seen as some kind of replacement for her in Patsy's affections, but we did get on well.

I continued to be very intimidated by Ross, though. He was good for work because even when it came down to our first snog he was very businesslike in his approach, which made it more funny than embarrassing. The kiss itself was fine. It was the way he talked about it beforehand that was funny, especially as I kept giggling every time I thought, Ooh, in a minute I'm going to be kissing Ross!

The kiss itself had to be filmed from just the right angle, which isn't as easy as it sounds. What's more, just for the record, we didn't use tongues! Tongues never get used in *EastEnders*, in fact they're not usually used on camera unless the director calls for them. When you see actors kissing on screen you might bear in mind that they're both probably dreading that moment when the director shouts 'Tongues!' Anyway, after the kiss, everyone said we'd done very well. Ross seemed pleased. I think he was warming to me as time went on. When Tiff first had the affair with Grant and the producers told him that Grant was going to be linked with Tiffany full-time six months or so later, I think he thought – and Ross would be the first to admit it – that I wouldn't be able to handle the intensity of the scenes they were plotting.

In fact a few people thought the same and there were rumours flying round all over the place. Rumours and question marks. The view among some of the cast was that Martine was too young and inexperienced to hack it. The rumours reached my ears and I have a good idea who was saying what. That wasn't my concern, though. I was more concerned that the rumours might reach the producers and that they might then give the storyline a second thought. I thought the best thing to do would be to see Jane and tell her what I was hearing.

She was happy to see me and listened as I explained how, under no circumstances, did I want to lose the opportunity of a major storyline just because of what other people were saying. 'I can do this,' I assured her. 'And nobody else's opinion is going to affect this, is it?'

'No,' she said. 'I've made up my mind. There are rumours flying about everywhere, Martine, but there always are – and always will be.'

Then she gave me one very good piece of advice – and sort of told me off at the same time. 'If you listen to rumours within any industry, or any office, you'll be an insecure, nervous wreck. You should just get on with your job, let them get on with theirs and I'll get on with mine.'

I said, 'OK.'

She'd put me in my place in a gentle but firm way but I felt better for seeing her anyway and went back to my dressing room feeling much happier.

I'd learned a lesson – but also made my point. I didn't want anybody telling me I couldn't do something. As far as I was concerned it was an amazing opportunity for me, because up until that point I hadn't done anything of substance. I'd just been cheeky, chirpy Tiff and the spur for everyone else to have their big dramas.

I'd been in *EastEnders* for just over a year and was beginning to feel more relaxed on the show. At home, too, things were great as I'd bought this lovely house in Brentwood, Essex. While it was a charming old place, I nevertheless decided to get the builders in to totally revamp it for me and Gareth. I wanted it to be *perfect*. The property itself I bought for £117,000 in my name, but Gareth and I planned to share the mortgage. It was set back from the main road and had a lovely sweeping drive and ivy growing all around it. I wanted to make this Georgian cottage feel more Italian, Tuscan, and romantic, and got workmen into transform the place. It ended up with a stainless-steel kitchen, a very airy Tuscan living room and a four-poster bed with white muslin hangings in the bedroom – but that all came later. The next big thing to happen in my life was totally unexpected, a real bolt from the blue.

Gareth's Dad, Haydn, was down from his home in Wales and was planning to get engaged to his girlfriend, Christine. He had divorced Gareth's Mum, Sylvia, a while before. Haydn invited us to join him in Hatton Garden in London, where there are loads of jewellers, to help him look for a suitable ring.

We walked along looking in all the windows, staring at one fabulous trinket after another until I spotted this ring – a gold one with beautiful aquamarine stones. Gareth knew aquamarine was my favourite colour for an engagement ring because I'd told him a few months earlier about a dream I'd had about a ring *just* that colour. Honest, I did! Anyway, Gareth caught me gazing wide-eyed at this beautiful jewel.

'That's the ring you were talking about, the one you saw in your dream, isn't it?'

I nodded and felt a bit embarrassed. 'But we're here to look for your Dad and his fiancée,' I explained and urged him to keep up with Haydn. We walked past it again a little later after his Dad was done and then sneaked into the shop together.

We both knew how we felt about each other. We shared the same dream of getting married one day, but that was only talk. I was quite freaked when Gareth asked the jeweller to bring the ring out of the window. 'Go on, Martine, try it on,' said Gareth. I put it on my engagement finger and it fitted like a glove.

It wasn't a hugely expensive ring, but money isn't what buying an engagement ring is all about. I adored the stone and the style and, more to the point, it was just the ring I wanted. Gareth looked on as I tried it on. When he saw it was a perfect fit he looked me in the eye and said, 'I know that you're too young to get engaged but at the same time . . .' He took a breath and began again. 'You know, I've never, ever been in love with anyone like I'm in love with you and so, I was thinking, if you don't want to call it an engagement ring then we won't but I want to marry you one day and I want us to be committed to each other. I want to get you this ring to show you that I love you.'

I just screamed and jumped up and down and gave him a big cuddle and a big kiss. It felt like a scene in a film. Then he dashed off to the nearest branch of Abbey National to get some money. He was back in minutes, paid for the ring, waited while they put it in a lovely box with a ribbon round it, then we went home to my parents where I told Mum what had happened.

She took a sharp intake of breath when I'd finished. 'Are you sure, Mart?' she said, clearly stunned by the news. 'It's a bit soon, darling, you're only nineteen. I had you when I was nineteen and when I look back now I was so young, you know? I know you love him and I know he loves you, and if you're happy then I'm happy, but just think about it first.'

'I know, I know, Mum,' I said excitedly. 'Gareth said it's like an engagement ring or a commitment ring. It's a ring to say "I love you" and one day we would like to get married. We're not going to get married tomorrow or anything like that, not in the near future.'

A few days later, however, the story of our getting *engaged* was in the papers and then *OK!* magazine called up and asked if the pair of us would like a weekend away in Paris at their expense to celebrate. That suited us fine, although Gareth hated one aspect of the idea: he didn't think he was photogenic enough!

'I never look good in photos and I hate them,' he said.

But we had an amazing couple of days there and ended up on the front cover of the magazine a few weeks later in March.

Happy at home, I was happy at *EastEnders*, too, especially after my chat with Jane. I felt more confident in myself and found I was really starting to get to know people. Wendy Richard was a real revelation. On screen you see her as dowdy Pauline Fowler, one of the few faces to have lived on the Square since day one. She's been an *EastEnder* for years and knows the whole place inside out and back to front. She's seen everyone come and go, act like the star and move on, either successfully or unsuccessfully. She's also got a fantastically dry sense of humour. Even though I never got to know her that well I still laugh when I think of some of the things she used to say and do.

She's a very honest person who does and says what she thinks. There were times when she'd be sitting in the bar and would say something thing like, 'Oh, for fuck's sake – that director's driving me mad today,' or, 'How long is it going to be? You told us we'd be done in an hour.' She'd always speak her mind and would say all the things I'd want to say but didn't have the nerve. She had the guts, the experience and, more importantly, she had the respect to be able to say it.

I'd always admired Barbara Windsor, who has the most incredible energy especially for a woman of her age. She's got more energy than I have, and that's a fact. She's a workaholic and totally professional. During all the years I've known her I've never, ever, heard of her being late. She's just on the ball all the time and always interested in anything that goes on in my life. I think Barbara sort of saw me as her little protégée sometimes – and I'd be very flattered if she did.

Barbara would be the first to tell you that she was never an ambitious person but she is a workaholic who dotes on her work. She's a romantic, Barbara, but at the same time she's become wiser for taking a few knocks here and there. She reminds me a little of myself in some ways, in that we're both full of contradictions: everything we love we also somehow hate, everything we hate we love.

She'd say to me sometimes, 'Don't make the same mistakes I made. I mean it's good that you're a together girl, it's good to be focused. When I was young I used to go, "Oh, no, I can't do this part," and I'd talk myself out of the role. People would be saying, "What are you talking yourself out of the part for? You're supposed to *want* the part."' Barbara has real charisma and a real aura about her, and even now when she walks into the room, she's there. Straight away people notice. She may be small but she's got a huge presence about her.

At times she was really good for me and would give me the occasional kick up the arse when I needed it. If I was fed up she'd say, 'Oi, don't get down on your luck. What are you all depressed for? You're in a top show, you've got a top part, you're beautiful, you're talented. What have you got to moan about?'

'But I'm really down, I feel really depressed,' I'd moan, and later, when I split up from Gareth, Babs wouldn't stand for any self-pity. 'We've all had it,' she would say. 'We've all been there. I've bought the T-shirt, love. I've got the T-shirt and worn it again and again and again. Move on, let go, toughen up, you can't let it affect you.' She was brilliant. There were times that I needed that, and Barbara was always there for me. She's a tough woman, for sure, but she's also very sensitive and absorbs everything. I'd be in a bit of a mood and she'd click her fingers, and go, 'Oi, snap out of it!' Even now, Barbara and I are on the phone all the time. She likes to keep track of what I'm doing and if she's got some useful advice she will give it to me. Back in those days at *EastEnders* it was like having another Mum with me.

Carol Harrison, who played my treacherous mother Louise, was also incredibly supportive. She used to say she saw me as the daughter she never had, which was quite a compliment. I've become really close with her. We're very similar in lots of ways. We're both into glamour and she pouts her lips like me. When I left *EastEnders* she got terribly upset at my leaving do and started crying.

The set of *EastEnders* was full of characters. What can a girl say about Mike Reid? There's so much more to Mike than the public realise. He's a comic, a writer, an actor and a TV presenter. He's also had more than his fair share of personal trauma and tragedy – but that's for him to tell you about, not me. He has a huge personality, absolutely huge, and a razor-sharp wit. Woe betide anyone who tries to outsmart him, as I discovered to my cost.

One day he came in to do his first scene with me and I noticed he was wearing the naffest pair of trainers you've ever seen, complete with brilliant-white, unwashed laces done up in big, beautiful, immaculate bows. The shoes themselves were a tasteful combination of beige and baby blue. I introduced myself to him and said hello, adding, 'Oh, by the way – nice trainers!' Quick as flash Mike hit back: 'Yeah – and you've got nice tits.' All the crew burst out laughing and Mike turned round and said to them, deadpan, 'And I see you boys have already noticed that.' I went bright red. He put me in my place, all right, and I never again said anything that would slightly challenge Mike Reid.

Pam St Clement was another funny one but in a

completely different way. She turned up for a work in a tracksuit, with not a scrap of make-up on and with her hair everywhere. Then she would go into wardrobe and make-up and slowly transform herself into Pat Evans. She'd put on these massive chandelier earrings and, almost as soon as they were sorted, her voice would change from dead posh to, well, Pat's voice. She truly *transforms* herself into Pat.

Pam's completely different in real life. She's beautifully spoken with a dry sense of humour and is quite serious. It's not until you meet her that you realise what a great actress she is simply because she and Pat are poles apart.

Different people were helpful to me in different ways. At the time Patsy was going through a lot of changes in her own life with regard to her then boyfriend Nick Love. She married him a couple of years later, but that was one relationship that wasn't destined to last. At this time, they were having more than a few problems. In theory I don't think Patsy and I would ever have become friends if it hadn't been for the fact that we worked day in, day out together. Even now I'd never say Patsy and I were really compatible as people. We were best mates on screen, of course, and great confidantes off camera. I could talk to Patsy in ways that I would be able to do with a very best friend. If I want to be understood and I want to talk to somebody I'll always know I can talk to her, and vice versa. It's that kind of relationship. We're not too close but we're never too far away, either. In a competitive industry like acting there's another plus in never being best friends with a fellow actor, because it can be tough when you both find yourselves going for the same auditions.

With everything looking so bright I suppose it was almost inevitable that something bad was going to happen – and, sure enough, it did, that spring, when Keith crawled out of the woodwork. Mum and I had always assumed that he'd find it impossible to resist the temptation of taking money from newspapers at some point in return for his story of life with the pair of us. If there was anything surprising about his move it was the fact that he had waited so long. His story appeared sixteen months after I'd been in Walford, on 21 April 1996, and was splashed across several pages of a Sunday newspaper. It was no big shock.

In fact just a few weeks earlier Mum and I had had a conversation about the likelihood of his doing it. I remember sitting down in the house when Mum said, 'I can't believe that Keith hasn't crawled out from under a stone yet. In a way it's quite nice that ever since we went to court, other than the odd "Happy Birthday" tune down the phone or a card, it's seems he's left you alone. Maybe finally he's letting you get on. But it would never surprise me if he did make a reappearance or go to the papers.'

I first caught wind of it after finishing filming one day when Alex, a runner, came over. 'Listen,' he said. 'I didn't want to worry you while you were filming but we've had this message . . .' I'll never forget – Alex had this Post-It pad in his hand. 'A guy's been calling the switchboard all day today and for the last couple of days,' he went on. 'He just said to tell you that your real Dad has called.'

Alex had underlined 'Real Dad' on the pad. 'Does that make any sense to you?' he asked. It did. I stood there for a moment, trying not to show how upset and frightened I was. Everything came flashing back from my past. I'd thought I was safe from all of that, and everything was going great at that time. Even though I might have imagined I was prepared for this, I burst out crying in the runners' room and Alex must have wondered what on earth was going on.

The story appeared a few days later. I read it with waves of anger rising up inside. My reaction? I just thought, You are so full of shit. You've been no father to me! How dare you!

It was a pack of lies from start to finish. A load of twisted rubbish. He even said all this stuff about Mum brainwashing me against him. I thought, The man's lost his mind. After all, I'd been there. I had seen so much of what went on, how he treated my Mum, and, believe me, you don't forget things like that. At least now he had made his move. I refused his requests to call him, put his revolting deed behind me, and got on with my life.

There was more aggro in the shape of my first serious stalker, a man called Reece. Like so many people in the public eye, I've had unwanted attention from stalkers dating right back to my early days on *EastEnders*. I'd even had a death threat from a guy in prison, but Reece was far scarier than any of those, a right case. He started hassling me not long after I bought the house in Brentwood with Gareth. His sick campaign began with some strange fan mail which my Mum dealt with: she deals with all my mail. However, his letters became increasingly frequent and grew weirder every time. He needed personal advice, he wrote, and wanted to speak to me on the phone.

I wasn't aware of a lot of it because Mum kept his more deranged ramblings away from me, as she knew that I wouldn't be able to get on with my job properly if I thought I had a loony on my case. Reece was very angry with Gareth for touching what he considered to be his 'precious thing'. More worrying still, his later letters mentioned certain times and places where he had seen us, even down to what we were wearing. Scary.

One night I was over at Brentwood with the actor John Pickard and Mum. Gareth was away working. We were in the kitchen when John said he saw torchlight in the garden.

'Don't say that,' I told him. 'You're going to freak me out and it isn't funny'.

'I'm not mucking about,' he said sternly.

Mum got straight on the phone to the police, who had installed an emergency telephone line because of Reece's letters. They arrived, checked the garden and reported that someone had indeed been outside. Things went quiet again after that. For a while, anyway.

People have this idea that filming television is really glamorous and fun. Nutters aside, I suppose to a degree it is, but it's also very technical. It's not necessarily easy pulling pints as though you'd been a real barmaid for years while getting your lines out right – it certainly wasn't easy in my early days. In fact doing the drinks was really hard, especially as the optics sometimes used to stiffen where the drink would get in overnight. Now, much as some people might like the drinks at the Queen Vic to be real, they're not. Perhaps that was why the optics would be so tricky. All I know is that it was a right rigmarole having to serve a round if a few of the characters wanted gin and tonic. Like the Rover's Return, I guess, the Vic is the pub with no beer and the one where no one ever talks about last night's football or TV. Amazing that the actors and technicians keep creating exactly the opposite impression.

One day we were all having a bad day at the Vic and Barbara and I were moaning and groaning because the cameramen kept changing the shots. Then, the next thing I knew, I had to get a G & T for someone. I already had a reputation for being a bit clumsy, especially when I got nervous. Ross used to joke that if someone tripped or fell over a box it was always me he'd see lying spread-eagled on the deck. 'Oh, she's at it again,' he'd laugh. 'She's fallen over again! 'Ere, Martine, we're trying to get some work done here. Will you stop falling over!'

Anyway, on that particular day I'd come round the bar and was saying my lines – yak, yak, yak, yak – and, as I pushed the optic up with the glass, the gin bottle came completely out of its bracket and smashed me on the head. I stood there for a moment and can remember hearing Patsy down the other end of the bar asking me if I was all right. 'Yeah, yeah, ha, ha, ha,' I said, apparently, before bursting out laughing. Then I started to feel dizzy.

Patsy could see I wasn't OK but by the time she said, 'She's not all right, Martine's *not* OK,' I had collapsed behind the TV monitor where the make-up girls used to work. The next thing I knew, there was this guy called Jez, the floor manager, going, 'Martine, Martine, can you hear me? Can you see me?' I remember lying there, looking at him and thinking, Cor, isn't your lisp bad! Apparently I was still laughing as I came round because I could see three Jezes, just like they do in cartoons.

There's always a doctor on duty at Elstree and they got him down to give me the once-over. I was fine and felt well enough to carry on working. Fine? OK, I lied. My head was in agony but the show must go on, you know.

That wasn't the only time I hurt myself on the *EastEnders* set. I sprained my ankle in the middle of the New Year's Eve scene when Tiff had a big argument with Grant. We had to have a big fight, which the stuntmen demonstrated to us both. The trouble is, when you go to do the take you get so into it, screaming, crying, shouting, literally hating this person in front of you, it's easy to lose track of what you're supposed to be doing. I am actually very flexible and bendy, and even though I am not built like a whippet, I get knocked about quite easily. If the wind is heavy and blowing behind me, I reckon I could fly down the street. It is just the way I am. If someone nudges me I will go right to the other end of the room. It doesn't take much.

Before the take the stuntmen were being more cautious than usual. 'Be careful,' they said as they watched us practise. 'Stop it now, you're getting carried away, Martine, and you are going to hurt yourself.'

Tiff always had bloody high heels and my little ankles were struggling to balance the violence I was enacting above. 'I hate you, Grant!' I was screaming while simultaneously trying to punch and slap him. I went to punch him in the mouth, missed – Ross just jumped aside – and fell off my heels. Bang! Splat! Everyone was laughing their heads off until they saw my ankle, which was already swelling up like an overripe watermelon. I'd sprained it falling off my heels and ended up being loaded into an ambulance. Oh, the indignity of it all! I was taken to hospital and had to wear a support on my ankle for about two weeks.

I've still got the scar from another 'heels' accident on set. Patsy always used to keep an eye out for me for any new talent that joined the show. One day she came into my dressing room full of the joys of spring: 'Have you seen the new director?' she gushed. 'Oooh, you're going to love him. He's a right sort! This director is right up your street.'

'Oh, Patsy, don't do this to me,' I said, feigning lack of interest, but Patsy was having none of it.

'No, no, have a little look.'

I had a little peek out of the window to where she was pointing but Patsy wanted us to physically go outside and witness this alleged vision of loveliness at close quarters.

'What we'll do is walk up to the Square, look lovely, strut

our stuff and then walk through the market so he's bound to notice you.' I was in such a fluster I agreed to her crazy plan.

'You've got to be sexy, you've got to strut,' she kept telling me – so strut I did. Indeed I was strutting so much I didn't look where I was going, missed my footing and promptly fell arse over tit. I skidded and scraped the top of my leg on the gravel – and still have the scars. The director laughed his head off. I imagine Patsy was disappointed by my performance. If she was she never said so.

One of Patsy's best friends, Sid Owen, was a good laugh to work with, too, but he has got the crudest mouth in the world – even if he is hilarious with it. I'd be standing behind the bar out of sight of the camera and he'd be pulling all these faces or thrusting his hips, anything to make me laugh, which I invariably did. As soon as Sid succeeded and I started giggling all the producers and directors would be screaming at me to shut up. Once people start shouting at me for doing something like that, I laugh even more. In the end I had to grass him up. Everyone was getting in a right mood with me so I pointed at Sid and giggled: 'It's him. It's him. He's standing over there grinding his hips thinking he's John Travolta or something while I'm trying to have a heart-to-heart with my husband here!'

When I first started on *EastEnders* Sid and I didn't get on. In fact we hated each other. I was nervous, while he was really loud and boisterous. He was also fiercely protective of Patsy, whom he'd known for years and years. Someone told him that I'd said something derogatory about Patsy. These rumours were flying around within weeks of my starting – the usual bitchy stuff, like, 'Oh, Martine, she thinks she's this, she thinks she's that. She said this about Patsy.' The truth was I'd never said a bad word about Patsy to anyone, but that didn't stop Sid being very offish with me for a long time. I *had* said that I thought Patsy was a brilliant actress and perfect for *EastEnders*. I remember telling one actor (again I'm not going to give them the pleasure of naming them here), 'If Patsy was the new girl and I'd been here a while I'd be really threatened by her.' I'd be intimidated by Patsy because she's just got such a presence about her. She's got the same thing on screen. You see her and she's so funny, comical and convincing.

But of course it all got turned round in the mix and by the time it reached Patsy it had changed to, 'Oh, Martine says that you should feel threatened and intimidated by her!' We didn't know each other well enough for Patsy to confront me over it so there was this horrible atmosphere in the air for a good few months. Her loyal friend Sid made me feel really uncomfortable and eventually spoke to me about the gossip. I explained what I'd really said and was quite blunt about it, saying finally, 'If you don't want to talk to me, you don't have to, but I think it's silly.' We ended up sorting it out but, as I said, a good few months had already slipped by then. Patsy, Sid and I became much closer after that – in fact I miss them both very much.

As Tiff's relationship with Grant developed, so did mine with Ross. We became quite good friends after a while, went for lunch, that kind of thing. Ross was, is, the consummate professional. I think he's got acting completely sussed, really. He never got too involved with anybody, loved his job and rightly deserved to get a lot of credit for that. Ross has got a very dry sense of humour. You think at first that he's a bit strait-laced. He's got a booming voice, too, and, if I'm honest, he frightened me a little until I got to know him better.

I'll never forget the time we went to film in Paris in September for an epic *EastEnders* special. That was where I really got to know him.

There were seven of us: Ross, Sid, Steve, Gillian Taylforth, Patsy, Sophie Laurence – who played Diane Butcher – and me. We thought we'd have a great time but we had a manic schedule because it was Grant and Tiff's honeymoon. The two characters were really happy at this time and Ross and I got to 'dry snog' a lot on a bed in a posh hotel and go shopping. Bliss!

The marriage was to take place in Gibraltar but all the action happened in Paris. The shopping scenes mirrored real life because I was having the time of my life dragging Ross round these fancy boutiques. His lines were like, 'Oh, not another shop!' while Tiff was going, 'Yes, come on, Grant, it'll be great!' The weather was fine and we all had a brilliant time. One night, Ross told us all that he knew this beautiful restaurant. That didn't really surprise me because, unlike his *EastEnders* character, Ross is a very cultured man. There's a lot more to him than people would ever guess – he can even speak fairly good French. He knows something about everything and is highly intelligent. Anyway, he said, 'Come on, we'll all go there for dinner.' For some reason a lot of the others had gone home, and Steve was working, and so Ross, Gilly, a runner called Will and I all went for a meal at this nice hotel.

Dinner was perfect – it was the wine that was the problem as Ross was a little too enthusiastic about getting a bottle or two uncorked. 'Oh, do we have to drink wine?' I complained. 'I can't handle wine.'

Ross grinned. 'You can't handle drink, full stop!'

'I can,' I insisted, 'I just have to pace myself.'

'I'll tell you what,' he said – because he and Gilly could drink like fish – 'for every bottle we have, you have one glass.'

That sounded like a fair deal. I mean, how many bottles

can those two go through? I thought. We're only having dinner. And so I foolishly agreed.

Anyway, about five bottles of different wines later, things were getting a little, er, rowdy in this very grand restaurant. We had all spotted this woman at another table getting a terrible dressing down from the guy she was with. She looked very unhappy and had sat there on her own for ages before the bloke had even bothered turning up. Ross decided to make her night.

There was a woman inside the hotel selling those pretty orchids women can wear on special occasions. Ross suggested we buy an orchid and get the flower lady to take it over to this poor neglected French woman. 'We'll get the flower girl to give it to her with an anonymous message saying that we've been watching, we think she's beautiful, and get her to ditch him!'

Will wrote it all out in French and got the flower lady to take it over. I tell you, when this guy read it he looked like he was ready to rip someone's head off! That seemed like a good time for us to get *l'addition*.

As we walked outside to find a cab I realised I was really quite drunk by now. Gilly and Ross were drunk, too, in a happy-tipsy sort of way, but I was feeling ill-drunk. Will, who hadn't touched a drop all night, had quite a job getting us all in the car. Somewhere along the line a bottle of champagne had come into my possession and I can remember (just) sitting in the back of this car, swigging champers out of the bottle and being very loud, saying, 'I love this stuff, I love France, I could live this life, it's bloody great, I love it.'

We hadn't been motoring that long when I realised all the booze had gone straight through me. 'Oh no!' I cried, a little melodramatically. 'I've got to go and wee.' Now you've got to remember as I tell this story that I'd had only a working relationship with Ross and Gilly until that night. Ross looked a little panicky and told me that we were in some dodgy district in gay Paris and that we couldn't possibly stop just yet. 'But I've got to go, Ross,' I slurred. 'I've really got to go otherwise there's going to be a very nasty accident in this car. Stop the car, stop the car, I'm going here.' Gilly was having kittens while Ross looked at me as if I was completely deranged.

He got the driver to pull over. 'Well, Martine, why don't you go here?' he said pointing to some dingy-looking alley. 'I'll make sure no one comes in.'

'I'm sorry, Ross, but I'm not walking in there by myself, you've got to be joking. I'm not going round there by myself – any old Tom, Dick or Jean-Pierre could be lurking in that alley!'

Gilly drunkenly suggested she keep watch and saluted Ross as if he was some sort of army general. Will looked profoundly worried – as we were his responsibility. He was supposed to get us back to our hotel by a certain time as we had a very early start the next day. Heaven knows what time it was by now.

I staggered into the alley and remember seeing all these stinking dustbin bags lying around. I can remember (vaguely) turning on Gilly: 'What have you bought me here for?'

I told Ross to turn his back.

'Don't flatter yourself, Martine, I ain't going to watch you having a wee. There are much better things I can look at, thank you very much.'

It was pitch black in that alley, so dark I didn't notice that I was weeing all over my brand-new Prada brogues. Ross didn't help by asking me to hurry up as I gave him a stage-by-stage account of my actions: 'I'm pulling my knickers up . . . I'm sorting my skirt out . . . I'm pulling my tights up . . . Right I'm ready.'

We arrived back at the hotel about fifteen minutes later and I was feeling dreadful. I felt drunk and queasy at the same time. Yuk! As I walked into our hotel, carrying bags from all these designer stores and doing my best to look like a glamorous TV star, I slipped on the marble floor and slid on my front from the doorway to the bar, where everybody, including all the senior *EastEnders* people, were standing. I ended up sliding right under a glass table. I seemed to slide for miles.

'Whoops!' I said when I finally slowed to halt. I was still on the floor. I could see everyone laughing as I looked up and gazed at my new surroundings. I remember seeing our producer, a rather well-built woman, staring down at me open-mouthed. I also remember (very clearly as it happens) looking up at her and shouting, 'Everyone's been saying you're a lesbian. Is it true? I just want to know, because I don't think that it should be a problem with you, you know, saying if you are or not, unless you want to keep it private.'

The woman was horrified. 'No, no, no, I'm not a lesbian!' she snapped, but I wasn't giving up.

'Well, then, if you're not a lesbian, prove it. Who do you fancy? I'm a girl and I definitely am not a lesbian. I know the blokes that I like so you tell me who you like.'

'Jeff Bridges,' she answered sharply.

'Call yourself a woman who likes men?' I said, making no attempt to hide my disapproval. 'Jeff Bridges? You've got to be kidding!'

I was slurring like you wouldn't believe while all the crew were at the bar looking on and thinking, Oh my God! What has she done? This producer, you understand, was quite a powerful woman and she was not laughing.

'Who else then?' I persisted.

She said, 'Brad Pitt is lovely.' A good answer.

'That's it, you see,' I said, eyes rolling in my head and still sprawled on the floor. 'We're sorted now!'

Embarrassed – dare I say humiliated? – by my antics, I was helped to my room by a few people Ross had gathered together for the purpose. Once alone, I must have felt some remorse for my behaviour as I made a drunken call to my Mum. 'Mum, I'm with all these French frogs and I think I've just insulted the producer cos I wanted to know if she was a lesbian,' I said. 'It's not a big deal. Have I showed myself up?'

Mum was aghast.

'Mum, right now I'm lying on this bed and the walls and everything are spinning round, it's really going round and round. I feel like I'm on water.'

'Oh, Mart!' was all I can remember her saying because I had to get up then and rush to the bathroom to be sick. Unfortunately I didn't quite make it.

I woke up the next morning to the sound of someone knocking on my door. Then I heard the key going into the door lock. I couldn't move. I lay there motionless listening to Will shouting through the door, 'Come on, Martine, it's your call. If you don't come out we're going to have to come in.'

I remembered not making it to the bathroom. 'Don't come in, don't come in!' I croaked back, trying to get myself up against the pressure of an almighty hangover. I looked around the room. It resembled a scene from a horror movie. Oh, my God! I thought. What have I done?

That day was not a good one. Ross and I had to do this scene where we had to keep going up and down these escalators. We were both exhausted and poisoned from all the booze. Ross even let his professional attitude slip once or twice because we both started snapping at the director, 'Can you hurry up and get this shot, please!' It wasn't his fault. It was a hell of a rough day – but my drunken escapades sometimes make great tales.

CHAPTER 12

Split

THE BETTER THINGS were going at work, the worse things began to go between me and Gareth, which may come as a bit of surprise considering how loved up we were. I increasingly felt Gareth wasn't fulfilling his end of the bargain, relationship-wise, while he was finding my growing celebrity status more and more difficult to deal with. Looking back, I don't blame him for feeling like that. It can't have been easy escorting me to all those showbiz parties, events you need to attend to maintain your profile, only to be ignored by everyone there.

I remember that one night at the Emporium nightclub a footballer came over to me with a beautiful watch on his wrist, immaculate clothes, and a great car waiting outside. 'Hey, babe, do you fancy coming out with me for the night?' he asked. Gareth was standing right next to me at the time.

'Thank you,' I replied, placing my arm around Gareth. 'But this is my fiancé and we're together and so no, thank you, I'll stay here.'

Gareth was treated terribly by some other famous people but there was nothing I could do to change that. If we went out for dinner people would always come over and chat to me but ignore him. It started to get underneath Gareth's skin. The situation wasn't helped by our different working hours. We had very little time together as he worked at least a couple of nights a week and most weekends while I worked days. I'd still go out with him on Friday or Saturday nights but would be totally shattered by the end of the evening and would spend the rest of the weekend in bed. It's a cliché, but we were becoming more and more like ships that passed in the night.

Both our lives were changing rapidly but, whereas once upon a time, before *EastEnders*, it was always down to me to fit in around his work, I now needed him to fit around *my* career. I suppose the first cracks in our relationship broke through not long after our semi-engagement – though neither of us would have admitted that at the time. We were both so in love that neither of us wanted to acknowledge that things had changed, but they obviously had. People started to book Gareth to work for them, people who would never have considered booking him before. There was a catch, though, because they also used to ask if I would be joining him. Gareth told me much later after we had gone our separate ways that his workload plummeted when we split. Club owners realised that without me in tow there would be no hordes of paparazzi waiting outside their doors.

In effect Gareth Cooke was fast becoming Mr Martine McCutcheon, as often happens when one half of a couple becomes famous. I'm not saying it's impossible for a celebrity to have a non-famous partner, but they have to be very centred emotionally and spiritually to put up with all that goes with it.

Instead of getting to grips with our romance, Gareth went the other way. Instead of rushing home as soon as he had finished his set, he'd stay on at the club, partying until nine in the morning. It's quite clear to me now that we'd stopped talking, stopped addressing the problems that were surfacing between us, and were avoiding the ugly issues that had begun to raise their heads.

The problems we were having didn't have anything to do with whether or not we loved each other. That was never in doubt. No, it was everything else around us that was going wrong. The one thing that I'd always wanted since I'd been a little girl, the one thing I knew I needed to make me happy – stardom – was the very thing that was destroying our relationship.

'Oh, well, that's the price you pay for stardom,' people say, but I don't feel it should be that way. It's a big price to pay but it wasn't as if I could chuck in my job overnight and stop being famous. They say once you become a regular in a soap you get recognised forever. The damage had already been done. The irony was that we'd talked about all this in the early days of our romance and so it wasn't as if we hadn't seen it coming. I can remember sitting in bed with Gareth at his flat in Dartford before I'd even been asked to audition for *EastEnders*. It was about five in the morning and we had just come back from a great night out.

'You know what, Gareth?' I whispered in his ear as we cuddled under the duvet. 'I'm going to be a star. Sometimes you talk about me outgrowing you but I don't want that to happen. I want to make sure you stay with me because I need you to make me strong. With you beside me I can be strong enough to make it, to become what I want to be. Please, please be strong for me.'

But that was Martine, the girl in Milan, talking, the

Martine that worked for £1.50 an hour in Knickerbox, the Martine that nobody knew. Ordinary Martine.

But Martine, alias Tiffany Raymond, the girl from *EastEnders*, was a different proposition, a bittersweet proposition as far as Gareth was concerned. As I became more famous, he became more attractive to the opposite sex. Girls would be all over him like a rash when I went with him to his gigs. They would be out of their minds on drugs or drink and I'd have to stand there and watch while they pawed him and took the mick out of his 'Tiff'. If I was acting like a jealous bitch, he was just as bad.

Things pretty much hit rock bottom at the end of May 1996 when I and a lot of the younger characters from *EastEnders* were sent on location to film in Blackpool. The plot line at that time was typically involved. Tiff was three months pregnant but didn't know who the father was. Was it Tony Hills (who it turned out was gay and got off with my screen brother Simon), or was it Grant Mitchell, who'd had a one-night stand with her three months earlier?

It was a rare treat to get away from Elstree and everyone was in fine spirits even if the Blackpool workload looked enormous. We set off at the beginning of June when the weather, surprise, surprise, was dire. At that time the vibe at *EastEnders* was just great. Everybody was trying their damnedest and the results were there to be seen on screen. The atmosphere at Elstree had been fantastic around this time. Everyone was helping each other and there wasn't much bitchiness going on. The show was on an all-time high. I remember every couple of weeks leading up to the Blackpool trip we were having meetings with the producers who would just sit there and verbally pat us on the back. But, as far as Gareth was concerned, the trip couldn't have come at a worse time.

He was in Italy working hard and we hadn't seen each other for long enough to iron out our problems. Instead everything had to be said over the phone, which was far from ideal. One evening after filming in the freezing cold on Blackpool Pleasure Beach, the cast and crew decided to have a few drinks back at the hotel. We all sat around this huge fire, bunging £1 coins in the jukebox, and taking turns on the pool table. There was a whole gang of us there: Mark Homer, who played Tony Hills; Andrew Lynford, my screen brother Simon; Bianca, alias Patsy Palmer; Paul Nicholls, who was a relative newcomer and played Bianca's weird but cute half-brother Joe Wicks; and Daniella Denby Ash, a.k.a. the religious fanatic Sarah Hills.

Despite the good-time atmosphere, Gareth was weighing on my mind and I broke away from the bar at around 10 p.m. to ring him from the hotel payphone. It was a bit of mistake. We ended up having an argument, a typical lover's tiff about absolutely nothing as I recall, just an outpouring of frustration, and I burst into tears. I tried to pull myself together discreetly in the phone booth, but didn't do a great job because as I walked back to the bar Paul saw me. He gave me a strange look which said: 'Oh, God, it's a girl and she's crying and I just don't know what to do.'

I decided to speak first. 'It's OK, Paul, you don't have to say anything. I'm fine,' I said, my voice quavering with emotion. 'Men? They're just a bunch of arseholes. My Gareth's a nice arsehole, I'm not knocking him, but sometimes he can be a complete and utter effing wanker. I know he loves me and I love him and it's all going to be all right. So don't worry about anything, I'm fine.'

Paul was for a moment lost for words. Then he mumbled, 'You're not fine. You're completely not fine.' Even though I was having none of it, he insisted I down a stiff drink.

He brought me back to the bar and ordered the drink. I'll tell you more about Paul in a minute, but right there and then he offered me a shoulder to cry on and I happily accepted it. I found myself opening up to him, telling him all about the problems I was having with Gareth. I think he already had a fair idea from my behaviour at Elstree over the previous few weeks. There had already been a few tearful conversations with Gareth and Paul would see me leaving my dressing room – his was two doors down – wiping a tear or two away.

That night in the hotel I remember REM coming on to the jukebox with their hit 'Everybody Hurts'. 'See!' Paul exclaimed in his thick Bolton accent. 'See!' he said again, only this time with a chuckle in his voice. 'Everybody hurts sometimes. *Sometimes*, mind, not all the time. Everything's going to be great, Martine. Everything will be fine, you'll see.'

Then Patsy came over and she, too, asked if I was feeling OK. 'Look, I'm fine,' I assured them both, doing my best not to make a spectacle of myself. It goes without saying that you need to be careful about who sees you when you're feeling all emotional, as you don't want to be the cause of gossip. I decided the best thing to do was go to bed and get my head down.

I took a while to get to sleep – I don't think I went under until 2 a.m. – as I had a lot on my mind. Evidently Gareth had a lot on his mind, too, because he rang me just before four o'clock. I woke up with a start and grabbed the phone. I was feeling woozy, not really with it at all. His first words to me were, 'Oh, it's you that's answered the phone, then.'

I was furious. 'Well, who do you think it's going to be? Of course it's me. Look, I am really tired. I don't want to have an argument. Can you call me in the morning? Can you call me tomorrow?'

I didn't think I was being unreasonable but Gareth was having none of it. Jealousy had got the better of him. 'Oh, right, so you don't want to speak to me today. It's only three in the morning, or whatever . . .'

'Look,' I said, 'it's nearly four. It's pitch black here and I'm really tired.'

Things started to get nasty. 'Oh, thanks very much, *EastEnders*,' Gareth said bitchily. 'I feel they've taken you away from me. I really feel like they've taken you away from me.'

That hurt me a lot because I thought everything I'd done, I'd done for us, everything I'd got, I'd got for us, I'd got for our future, for our little fairy tale. I went mad at Gareth's whinging. 'How dare you?' I seethed. '*EastEnders* pays for this, it pays for that and you happily reap all the good things it brings us, yet you're always the first to slag it off or anything else that doesn't come easy. Well, that's not how life is. There was a long time when I was just known as DJ Gareth Cooke's girlfriend and I'd be treated like shit. I used to have to stand there while girls would come over and flirt with you. There's a price to pay for everything. You can't take all the good and then blame me for all the bad stuff that happens in your life. You just can't keep doing that.'

Amidst my sleepy fug I found a second wind, drew a deep breath and continued. 'Gareth, you know *EastEnders* has brought us a lot of good things. If you're now realising you can't handle it then I need to know because I can't keep this relationship together by myself. I love you and I know you love me, but if you want this to work then you've got to stop putting obstacles in the way. If you're not going to fight for our relationship then we might as well just give up now.'

I could hear Gareth crying at the other end of the phone from a hotel room in Italy. I started crying, too, and somehow, between the sobs, we decided it might be best if we both hung up and waited till the morning to speak again. That plan lasted all of twenty minutes, since I couldn't wait any longer to straighten out the mess. I phoned him on his mobile, thinking he might be trying to kill himself or something awful. I burst out crying as soon as he answered. 'I love you,' I stammered between sobs. 'We can't give up this easily. I'll see you when I'm back in London.'

Something else had come into my life that was adding to my confusion. That something was Paul Nicholls, who had arrived at *EastEnders* just as Gareth and I were first experiencing our problems. You see, I thought Paul was the most amazingly handsome actor I'd ever set eyes on.

I wasn't the only one to take that view. I remember Dean Gaffney coming up to me in the Square a couple of months earlier looking most put out. 'I don't believe it!' he moaned. 'Paul bloody Nicholls is going to be working here. I can't believe my bad luck.'

'What do you mean? What are you talking about?' I said.

'Martine, he is so handsome. I mean the bit of fan mail I get at the moment is very nice, but now he's here I'm not going to get any, am I?'

I couldn't stop myself laughing, and even Dean was laughing with me. 'I bet you end up fancying him, Martine. Every girl here is going to fancy him.'

'No, no, I won't fancy him. How old is he?'

'He's about sixteen, I think.'

'Sixteen!' I shrieked. 'I'm not going to fancy him. I'm nineteen. I'm not going to fancy a sixteen-year-old boy!'

Dean walked away shaking his head. 'You will!' he muttered prophetically. 'You will!'

A day or two later I ran into the runners' room to collect my scripts. There, standing in front of me, was this handsome vision of a man. 'Oh, hello,' the Adonis said. 'I'm Paul Nicholls. I'm going to be playing Joe, Joe Wicks, Michael French's screen son.'

'Oh, hello, nice to meet you, I'm Martine.'

'Yes,' he said quietly. 'I know who you are.'

I felt butterflies in my stomach for the first time since I'd met Gareth at Hollywoods three years earlier. It wasn't like an 'Oh my God, I love you' feeling or anything like that, but I'd be lying if I said I didn't fancy him immediately. My heart and mind were completely flummoxed by the sensation as I'd never fancied anybody other than Gareth before. I'd never even looked at anyone else because I was so in love with him. But Paul was tall, slim, with long legs, beautiful green eyes that seemed to change colour depending on the light, a mop of dirty blond hair, big, full lips and fresh olive skin. To be honest he was far prettier than most girls I knew.

How confused was I by meeting Paul? Well, I actually thought there was something wrong with me because I knew I shouldn't be fancying anyone else. Of course, you're only human but this was the first time it had ever happened to me. And with someone so beautiful!

'OK, I'm off now,' I said, trying desperately to regain my composure. 'It's nice to meet you, Paul.'

'Nice to meet you, too,' his Bolton voice called after me.

As I walked back to my dressing room I could still hear his voice calling after me, asking, 'Do you know where the canteen is?' It was Paul's first day and he didn't know where he was, of course. I turned in the corridor to see Paul walking quickly towards me. 'I'm going for lunch, Martine, would you mind showing me where it is?'

'No, not at all. Just give me a chance to get my make-up off.'

He followed me into my dressing room. This'll get rid of him, I thought, scrubbing my face. Once I've got no make-up on he definitely won't look at me like that again! My nerves always show through my mouth and this time was no different. I found myself rabbiting away to the point where I was embarrassed by my own gob. I just couldn't stop talking.

'Yeah, it's great here,' I babbled. 'You'll make loads of friends. It's really, really great. Do I look awful without make-up on? Do I look dreadful?' Oh, Martine!

'I think you look really pretty, actually,' Paul replied, nonplussed.

Aw, that's sweet, I thought, all but ramming my fingers in my bloody big gob to stop it uttering any more dreadful inanities.

That night I went home to Mum and John. My house in Brentwood was still being done up and I'd been staying with my family whenever Gareth was away. I remember running into the house telling Mum about this gorgeous new guy on *EastEnders*. I told her how I felt when I met him, how my stomach had filled with butterflies.

'Oh, that's quite normal, Angel,' she answered matter-of-factly. 'You can look so long as you don't touch.'

I was very honest to Gareth, as well, and remember telling him, too, how gorgeous this lad Paul was. I didn't have a problem telling Gareth that – as I didn't consider Paul a threat to our relationship and I'm sure Gareth felt likewise.

But destiny, or more specifically the *EastEnders* scriptwriters, decided Paul and I were to spend a lot of time together filming. We both had intense storylines. Tiff was pregnant and getting engaged to Grant. Joe was turning completely mad, covering himself in petrol and playing with

Split

matches. Like mine, his postbag at Elstree was filling up fast. We grew closer and closer, with Paul asking for my advice on how to deal with the whole fame thing, the money, the friends you're never sure are real friends. I tried to help the best way I could, and amidst this the whole fancying thing switched off for a while. I'm a very loyal person and was determined to sort out my life with Gareth. Paul, however, had a knack of catching me off guard. He's very observant and would say stuff like, 'Martine, you seem really down today. Are you all right?' He was always spot on, too.

He was aware of my troubles with Gareth and could see them from another perspective. Paul was different from me, you see. He never wanted to be famous, whereas I've always loved the fame thing. I love my picture being taken. I love all of that. But he loathed it and that was the one thing we always disagreed on. All I wanted to do was shine, to go out and shine in my dress, while Paul would turn up to film premières only if I badgered him, and then he'd come dressed in a suit and white socks just to embarrass me!

He wanted to act. He didn't want to be a star. He wanted to be an actor because he was very good at being someone else, actually doing the job; all the stuff that came with it he regarded as excess baggage. He wasn't interested in money: he just wanted to get on with the job. And that focus paid off. I mean, how he played Joe so brilliantly aged just seventeen is beyond me. I'd have looked a loony if I'd tried. Everyone would have laughed their heads off, but Paul was the genuine article and genuinely intense with it. I think he sometimes took things too much to heart and beat himself up over them. A lot of actors are like that – very, very intense, piling unbearable pressure on themselves.

My relationship with Gareth took another knock when he refused an invitation to come with me to a wedding. It was one of the make-up girls who was getting hitched. It was never going to be a 'showbiz' do so I couldn't understand Gareth's objection. Maybe by then he was just sick of the whole Mr McCutcheon thing, I don't know. It was a great wedding and there were loads of people there, including Paul, of course. It was a lovely summer's day and the pair of us ended up talking for hours as the sun slowly set in front of us. The day turned into a truly gorgeous evening. 'Martine,' Paul began quietly when we were alone. 'If things aren't going right, I just want to let you know that I'm there for you. I know you're trying to be strong at work and everything else but I just wanted to let you know, if you do need to talk to anyone in any shape or form, I'm here for you. You put on a brave face, Martine. I don't think anyone has a clue about what you're going through but you seem very unhappy to me.'

I could feel myself gulp for air. 'Oh, thank you, that's really lovely, Paul, but I'm engaged and Gareth is lovely. We're fine.'

'I know,' Paul began again. 'I'm not trying anything on, Martine: I'm just letting you know . . .'

I thought, This is getting worse by the minute. My heart was all of a dither as my mind kept throwing up objections to my growing affection for this beautiful man in front of me. 'Paul, you're young, you don't know anything,' I said. I was only twenty myself.

To be honest, I think that, if I had been completely OK with Gareth, I'd never have felt so strongly about Paul in the first place. I just wasn't me at that time. I was going through such a bad time emotionally and everything I knew was changing. For as long as I'd been famous I'd had Gareth wrapped around me like a security blanket. I constantly battled with wanting my security, wanting someone to love me, and doing what I felt I should be doing for my career — to maintain my growing status. There were places I wanted to go, events I felt I should attend, people I felt I should meet. What I didn't need was my other half going, 'That's just a load of crap.' It was becoming clearer every day that Gareth and I as an item were not working out.

When our romance finally collapsed, it was not as I might have imagined. I was sitting in my dressing room on another fine July evening. I'd actually finished all my scenes but couldn't bring myself to drive home and face more aggravation. Things were pretty cramped at Mum's, too. Our house in Brentwood was still uninhabitable because of the builders so we'd been staying most nights with my parents and little LJ. I know that placed even more strain on Gareth and me because we weren't having any intimacy. If we had a row we couldn't even make up with a kiss and cuddle. I wanted some peace and quiet to myself, and so my dressing room at work was doubling up as my sanctuary. The peace was broken when the phone rang. It was Gareth asking when I'd be home.

I answered vaguely and Gareth snapped. 'Why are you hanging around at work? What are you doing? Why don't you come home?'

The truth was I wasn't doing anything but gathering my thoughts. I wasn't seeing anybody. I wasn't socialising with anyone at work. I was just sitting in my dressing room thinking, How can I solve this? How can I make Gareth and me all right again? Yet deep in my heart I knew there was no way I was ever going to make it work. We had both changed too much as people to go back to the way we were.

I went home. Mum and Gareth were both inside and the

atmosphere was tense. I'd been inside only a matter of seconds before the tears came streaming down my cheeks. 'I really need some help here, Gareth, because I don't know what's going on. What's going on? Why is everything feeling wrong?' My words came out as sobs.

It was Mum, not Gareth, who spoke first: 'I think I should leave you two alone.' And she made to go. But it was her house and I didn't want our problems to drive her out.

'No, Mum, it's your place. You should be able to sit where you want.' And then the floodgates opened. 'Look, Gareth, I'm starting to fancy other people and I've never ever fancied anyone since I've been with you because I've been so in love. I'm really sorry you're having a hard time dealing with what's happened to me, but you're a grown-up and shit happens. Can't you just deal with it? You're supposed to love me. Can't we just deal with it together? But you're not talking to me. I don't know what you want. Everything's getting on top of me. I'm trying to sort out the house and you're hardly ever there. We're working different times. You're working nights, I'm working days. I just can't deal with it all by myself . . .' I couldn't get anything else out. My larynx was overcome with sobs.

Gareth waited until I got my sobbing under control before speaking. I don't know whether he was shocked by my outburst or just numb from it all, but one thing's for sure: I'll never forget his response.

'I'm going to go and get some biscuits,' he said, and disappeared into the kitchen.

I followed him. His silence only added to my rage. 'Don't you care?' I screamed. 'Don't you care what happens to us? Don't you even want to try? Don't you even want to help the situation?'

Looking back now, I suppose he was keeping quiet because

he didn't want to say anything that might hurt me any more – or maybe he just thought, She's on one now and I'm not getting in the way.

Either way, we slept in the same room that night or at least tried to. We were in LJ's little room while he slept with my parents. We were both squashed on to this little single bed. I woke early and remember looking at Gareth, looking at the back of his shoulders, thinking, This is the day it's going to end. It's going to end. I can't do it any more, I just can't do it any more.

I frighten myself when I get like that because, once I've made a decision like that in my head, that's it.

I phoned Gareth from Elstree later that day. He was being a bit funny with me and I had no inclination to play along with his mood. 'This isn't happening, is it?' I asked him bluntly. 'I can't hold on to something by myself and you obviously don't want to hold on to it yourself. I tried to talk to you about it yesterday and you didn't have any answers. That's either because you're finding it too painful to talk about or because you don't care any more. Whatever the reason, I simply can't keep sitting in my dressing room because I don't want to face what's at home. I used to love coming home but I don't any more. I know things are changing but I thought you'd be able to change with me. If you don't want to, well, that's fine.'

And then the tears started again. Ironically, we talked more easily about our situation for a while. Gareth finally admitted that he was finding the whole fame thing hard to handle. 'I'm finding it really difficult sharing you with so many other people,' he said. 'I don't know why it's not working, but it's not.'

I drew a deep breath. 'I don't really want it to end, Gareth. I've just got to do this to help my own situation. It's not like

I can turn back the clock and go, "OK I am not going to be famous any more." It's been done. I can't say I'm not going to do this job any more. I could dye my hair blonde but people are still going to know it's me. Even if I wanted to, I can't change what's happened. That means it's over for us, doesn't it?'

Sad, painful and upsetting as that call had been – and it was all three of those things – I put the phone down, got into my car and then drove round the corner a couple of hundred yards or so to the BBC bar. I didn't tell anyone what had happened. I didn't say anything to anyone. I didn't take my ring off. But I did feel as if a huge weight had been lifted from my shoulders.

For the next few weeks I was utterly numb. I didn't speak to anyone at work about what had happened because I didn't want anyone gossiping about me. The only person I confided in apart from my Mum was Abby, one of the runners at Elstree, and a woman I felt completely at ease with. I trusted her enormously and used to confide in her quite a lot. Nothing I ever mentioned to Abby ever found its way back to me.

It took me a while before I opened up to Paul, it has to be said, despite his looking at me on an almost daily basis, giving me the kind of look that said, 'I know you're having a difficult time – come and talk to me.' By then Paul was living in a huge house in Buckhurst Hill. One of the wardrobe girls at *EastEnders* had fixed him up with it and Paul was in the enviable position for a lad his age of sharing the place with three girls I happened to know quite well. They were all older than Paul and reasonably responsible. They made sure he was OK, that there was dinner when he came home, that kind of thing. There was Jo, who worked in a bar, Vicky, who was great at doing girls' nails, and Charmaine, who loved keeping the place tidy, which was quite a job with Paul there. I used to go round to Buckhurst Hill quite a lot during the first couple of weeks after I split from Gareth, not because I fancied Paul – though we were getting closer – but because I couldn't face going home. I'd sit in the kitchen, Vicky would do my nails, and we'd all chat about, well, about nothing, really.

The real blow, the kind of smack that sends you reeling sideways, was still to come. It happened on 24 August 1996, a date it's hard to forget. Mum told me she'd had a call from one of the Sunday newspapers. 'Someone's doing a story on you,' she said, doing her best not to make that sound as alarming as it did. Then she added, 'All I can think is that it's Gareth.' Mum and Auntie Kim went to collect a first edition of the papers. Auntie Kim is very like me – very sensitive – and I thought how lovely it was that, before she even knew anything for definite, she was there with support for me and my Mum.

I was sitting in a chair by the fireplace when the front door opened. I will never forget Mum's face as she walked towards me, clutching the Sunday rag. Both Mum and Kim had obviously been crying. Mum's eyes literally welled up in front of me. 'I'm sorry, darling. It's him, it's Gareth that's done it. You need to read it, really, it's not for me to say.'

Mum was so upset because not only had she read what he'd said but she also loved Gareth – everyone in my family loved him. I opened the paper. The enormous headline told me all I needed to know about the article's content. 'MY MARATHON SEX SESSIONS WITH MARTINE McCUTCHEON', it screamed in huge letters – or something tacky like that. There were pictures of our engagement from *OK!* magazine.

For the past five weeks I'd been thinking Gareth and I

might sort our problems out. I often used to think about him when I went to bed, dreamily praying that we could mend our romance: Maybe he'll sort himself out and come back to me and say, 'I'm strong enough to deal with this,' I used to think. True, Gareth had tried to call me a few times and had sent me letters. Half of me would think, I'm never going to move forward if I keep reading this stuff; the other part of me thought, I really miss him.

But the article completely killed me. I knew then what kind of vengeful person Gareth was. There was no way I was going back to him. Absolutely no way was I going back. By talking to the press in such a tacky way, Gareth had totally betrayed both me and the good relationship we had had. I felt as if I had been cut in half. I felt terrible, physical, tangible pain as I read what he'd said. For five weeks I'd gone to bed each night in LJ's room wearing one of Gareth's unwashed T-shirts, taking comfort somehow from his smell. Never again. I got up, walked into the bedroom, shut the door and cried my heart out. Mum kept coming up, popping her head round the door to see if I was OK, but I was inconsolable. I cried until I fell asleep. I took my engagement ring off and threw it into a Roman pot on my dressing table which used to have all my lotions and potions in it. One day, months later, I went to retrieve it, but it wasn't there and to this day I've no idea how it vanished.

Paul and the girls rang on Sunday morning. They each took turns to try to tempt me outside. They'd read what Gareth had done, too, and were convinced that I needed to be out and about, preferably in their company, but I was having none of it.

What Gareth had done had floored me completely. The pain was far worse than actually splitting up and I didn't have the strength to brave it out. Instead I gave in to my grief and

Me and Denise Van Outen. We always knew we'd make it.

Me and Joan Collins at a star-studded night after the première of *Stop the World*.

Me and the late Anthony Newley. Tony gave me my first big break. He is sorely missed.

Me and Claudia Hill, originally a duo, but fated to become Milan in the future.

Me and LJ. He has a fascination for cars, nudity and hot weather!

Me, aged fourteen. Here I am with my dancer's figure – all my hard work at Italia Conti paid off.

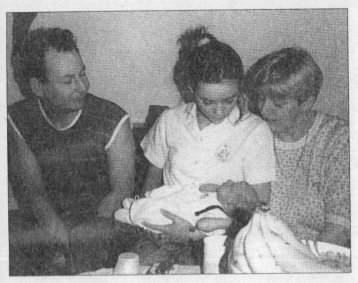

John McCutcheon, Mum, me and baby LJ, who was three weeks old. It was love at first sight for me.

Me, aged fourteen, posing on the settee in my new pink velour swimsuit!

Claudia Hill, Dionne Compton, Lyanne Compton and me on a night out at
Epping Forest Country Club.

Me, Howard Batty (my cousin
Carrine's husband) and Paul Nicholls
on a rare night out in Chester.

Me and Dionne Compton on our
first holiday in Tenerife. We were
young and free and on our first
grown-up holiday, and I'd had
my belly button pierced before
anyone else!

Me and Gareth Cook. The beginning of my first real relationship.

Me and Gareth in Paris, on the eve of our engagement.

Me in rehearsals for the Royal Albert Hall show, with David Arnold, the conductor of the Royal Philharmonic Orchestra.

Despite serious illness in the spring of 1998, nothing could keep me from the doors of the Royal Albert Hall where I would perform a selection of Oscar-winning songs including 'Don't Rain on my Parade'.

Me and Oliver. An unofficial visit to see a very sick little boy. Oliver didn't make it, but I will always remember him.

Me, Edie Cohn, Jonathan Barnham, Alan Tomlin (Mum's hubby), Kim Challinor, Mum and Natalie Cooke at my 23rd birthday party at the Belvedery.

Me and Mum at my 21st.

suffered what to all intents and purposes was a mental breakdown. The following two weeks passed in a delirious haze. I didn't get out of bed for that period. I lost loads of weight. My Mum tried to rouse me and would run baths for me but I refused to get up despite her pleading, 'Martine, please, you normally take such care of yourself and you haven't even changed out of your pyjamas. Please make an effort.'

I wouldn't budge. 'Mum, I can't describe it,' I'd say. 'If you stabbed me through the heart I swear I wouldn't feel it. I feel that sick and numb I would not feel it.'

I couldn't eat because my throat had swollen up, caused by the nonstop sobbing. I wish I could say I was exaggerating here, that I was being melodramatic, but I can't. I simply lost the plot.

The people at *EastEnders* were brilliant. I wasn't needed very much anyway and they shifted scenes about so I could try to get myself together without coming in and running the risk of meeting any more journalists. Paul popped round a couple of times just to ask if I was OK. Mum told him I was fine but wouldn't let him see me: 'She's just not herself, Paul.' Mum knew that he cared for me, and vice versa, and knew that it would upset him if he saw me like this – it was just not the time or the place.

It was Mum who eventually got me up to face the world. She came upstairs after I'd been out of it for more than two weeks and said, 'Martine, if you don't pick yourself up and get yourself together I'm going to have to take you to hospital or something because I can't watch you do this to yourself. I just can't.'

She'd spent the past fortnight trying to rouse me by tempting me with bits of chocolate, but for once in my life I wasn't interested in sweeties. I just wanted to die under the duvet. I used to think the notion of someone dying of a broken heart was a load of nonsense. But I've changed my mind now. I believe that people *can* die like that. In the end Mum grabbed me, literally picked me up out of the bed and stuck me in the bath. 'Right, my girl, you are getting yourself together. You're too beautiful and too lovely to let one man waste you like this. I'm sorry, but I will not allow it to happen. You can't just write yourself off just because somebody isn't strong enough to handle you. It's their problem, Doughnut, not yours. A lot of bad stuff will come to you in this life but a lot of fucking good stuff comes along as well. You've got to take care of yourself, put a bit of make-up on and get back to work. We've all had a broken heart, we've all split up with people we love. It's painful, but life goes on.'

She got herself quite worked up about it and really drummed her message home.

It took me months to get a handle on what had happened between me and Gareth, but as each day passed I certainly felt a little happier in myself. My friends were brilliant. All the girls round at Buckhurst Hill kept an eye on me. And Paul? Paul and I tried to date each other a couple of times. We had a few kisses but that was as far as it went. To be honest every time we tried I would break down in tears. It was just not going to happen between us and we both knew it. The timing was all wrong. There is, though, still something special there with me and him. Whenever I see him I think, Oh, look at what could have been. Paul and me could have had such a brilliant time together if the time had been right.

Chapter 13

Men

With tiffany going from strength to strength and in slow recovery from a personal life in tatters I began to revel in my new life as a single-girl celebrity, going to nice restaurants, parties and so on, and meeting some truly amazing people. One of the most important relationships I've struck in my life began, inauspiciously, about a year before I split from Gareth. It was with Matt Goss whom I mentioned before. I bumped into Matt, who sang with his twin brother Luke in Bros. We had met at Browns nightclub in London's Covent Garden. I was just having fun, dancing away with a couple of mates, when I spotted him at the crowded bar. I said a brief hello and wanted to tell him about the day I met Luke when he and Milan were on the same bill, but it was impossible to strike up a conversation as it was an insanely busy night. Everyone was squashed together and the club was heaving. Matt made to get past me, which led to a slightly embarrassing moment for the both of us as his baseball cap kept whacking me on the forehead each time he tried to shimmy past. He managed to get by in the end and said hello back before moving on. Little did either of us know after such an awkward first meeting that we would one day become firm friends.

Over a year elapsed before Matt and I were destined to meet again and a lot of water had passed under the bridge for both us. My split with Gareth was a couple of months behind me and I had thrown myself into the social scene. As a result I collided with Matt, by chance, at Sticky Fingers, a restaurant owned by the Rolling Stone Bill Wyman. Bill had invited me to a party he was holding that evening, which included some live music from Matt Goss. It was a great night and, as the party wound down, Matt and I found ourselves locked in conversation. We moved on to the Met Bar in Park Lane as the night wore on and we spent the entire night chatting intensely. As the hours flew past, I believe we could both feel a special bond developing. It wasn't a sex thing or even a male–female thing. No, it was more like a realisation that we were going to be very good mates. I felt he understood me, my crises of confidence and my bust-up with Gareth. Without being too deep and meaningful about it, Matt just knew exactly what type of a person I was.

About six months later we met again at the Atlantic Bar in Soho. Matt, by now, was living in New York and had returned to the UK only to sort out some legal matters. We yakked away like anything again and when the evening came to an end I remember feeling quite disappointed because Matt told me he was returning to New York.

'That's a shame,' I said. 'It would be lovely if we could stay in touch. Let me know when you're coming back and we'll all go out again – good luck with everything.' And that was about it. I never thought I'd see him again – but the fates had other ideas.

Some time later I was told that Tiffany was to be given a two-week break as a result of a bodge by the *EastEnders'* scriptwriters. If Tiffany wasn't required for two weeks, then neither was I. There was a new *EastEnders* executive producer, Matthew Robinson, and a new drama boss, Mal Young, at the BBC by now, and the atmosphere at Elstree was definitely suffering. I was chuffed to bits to be free of the place for two weeks – and even happier when I got a phone call from Matt.

It turned out he had been forced to postpone his return to New York and had at least another two weeks here in Blighty. Perfect! Especially as just about everyone we knew had to work. That meant we had only each other to keep ourselves entertained. By this time my relationship with Gareth had been over for almost a year and I was enjoying my freedom again – but that's not to say I had Matt in my sights, or that he was chasing me. We'd already got that male–female thing out of the way. I'd told him how I fancied a couple of people and he had done likewise. I explained how I immediately appreciated him as a handsome man – I even fancied him at first. I think that most women who meet him do – he is very charming. But once I truly got to know him, we developed an amazing friendship and bond that is much deeper than any of the more shallow, fancying-someone stuff. I truly love him as my friend. Matt, who is very in touch with himself, said he felt that same way and I believed him. We're just good mates, that's all. Plenty has been written already on whether heterosexual men and women can actually be friends. Well, I believe they can. Indeed Matt was the first person to suggest I date a friend called Jonathan Barnham, a recommendation I didn't take up until a long time later.

Those two weeks away from *EastEnders* were fantastic. Matt and I were inseparable, and ran around London like two little scallywags. We got to know each other well and Matt gave me so much good advice regarding the music business and my incipient dreams of leaving *EastEnders*, if only for a while, to release a single. Matt, who lost millions of pounds in the aftermath of the Bros split, had somehow managed to avoid turning into a bitter and twisted cynic. He was so well grounded and matter-of-fact about it all that I found I trusted him. It was a refreshing change to have someone helping me out as a friend rather than doling out advice and then sticking a big bill in the post.

One night we went to Langan's Brasserie in Mayfair and ate fish and chips washed down with vintage champagne. That says it all about me, doesn't it? Fish, chips and champers! Food played a big part in our relationship, as Matt, when he was in London, used to live a matter of yards from me. Whenever I felt like a midnight snack, as I often do, I'd ring him and we'd meet up at this bagel place in Fulham. They used to do this special curried-noodle thing.

Matt, I think, was impressed by my appetite. 'I've never met a girl who will eat as much as you at eleven o'clock at night and not even worry about it, not one bit of guilt,' he'd say. Matt was very aware of the emotional and physical collapse that followed my split with Gareth and used to enjoy watching me eat.

He was also encouraging to me, stressing that I should take things easy and that in time I would be back to normal. 'It will happen. In time it will happen,' he'd say soothingly. 'You're a very beautiful person, Martine. I'm not going to lie to you about that because you are.' He had a knack of making me feel everything was going to be all right. I believed him because I knew he was a survivor himself. From what he told me about Bros, how he came through that experience even half-way normal, I'll never know. Bros went from nowhere to being the biggest thing in pop almost overnight. Their build-up wasn't as gradual as mine has been, which was part of their problem.

People always think the Goss twins were just puppets but that's to deny them the credit they deserve. They are clever, talented guys. Matt's now in New York, where he's a respected songwriter, while Luke pursues acting in Los Angeles. I'm in touch with both the twins to this day and believe great things are just around the corner for them.

Surviving life in a boy band is something another acquaintance of mine knows a thing or two about – Robbie Williams. Again, I'd met him first while I was touring with Milan when Take That were on the brink of superstardom. Milan were playing the kinds of clubs Take That did at the start of the nineties. That was a good lesson because it made me realise how hard those five lads worked in the early days. Every single club that Milan visited, Take That had been to before us. Whether they were gay clubs, straight clubs, under-eighteen clubs, over-eighteen discos, ladies' nights, whatever, they had played every one. The more clubs we played, the more we realised how hard Take That had worked to make it

I first met Robbie properly in October 1995 at the first National TV Awards, which were staged that year at the conference centre at Wembley, not far from the famous stadium. A big group of us – I was in *EastEnders* then, of course – including quite a few from the cast and the Australian singer Natalie Imbruglia, went to Browns nightclub for a celebration drink afterwards. Mr Williams was already propping up the bar.

'Hello, Robbie,' I said before telling him how, like Take That, I'd played every toilet in Britain with Milan. Robbie had left Take That three months earlier and wasn't in a good way, but there was no stopping me. In fact I must have been quite gushy, because I know I said things like, 'You know what, Robbie? It's so mad to be here. I can't believe I'm talking to you. Me and the girls used to sit there and say what a sort you were compared to everyone else in the group . . .'

'Oh, really,' he smiled. My conversation embarrassed Gareth, who was with me at that time. 'Don't, Mart, you're embarrassing him,' he said, nudging me in the ribs. You could tell Robbie was still quite upset about leaving Take That but he was also very charming. We chatted for about twenty minutes, but I think we were imposing.

Seeing Gareth leading me away and giving me a talking to, Robbie piped up, 'You're a very sweet girl and your boyfriend is lovely. It would be lovely if we stayed in touch.' Then a guy who was with him gave us Robbie's numbers. I never called, though. Robbie, back then, wasn't in a place he wanted to be career-wise or emotionally. I felt it wouldn't be right to call and say, 'Hello, remember me? Fancy us all going out to dinner?' It was the wrong time for everybody, I suppose.

I saw Robbie next about six months later when I was at work one day on *EastEnders*. He must have been at Elstree to film *Top of the Pops* and I spotted him hanging about in the canteen. He looked awful, absolutely awful. We exchanged a few words before I plucked up the courage to tell him to take care of himself. 'You've got so much to give, Robbie,' I said. 'I know it's hard but you've been given something so special and you've got to look after yourself, you have to.'

Our paths were destined to cross again when I was invited to a party thrown by Robbie's mate and co-writer, the musician Guy Chambers, with my mate Sheree Murphy from *Emmerdale*. It was a brilliant night, which seemed to last forever. We eventually all bundled back to my place, where I put on some Frank Sinatra CDs and started singing.

Now Frank Sinatra may be my hero but I don't expect him to be everyone else's, so when Robbie went, 'Oh, I love Frank Sinatra,' and started singing along, I was in heaven. Sheree, Robbie and I ended up having a bit of competition to see who could sing the loudest. I wonder what the neighbours must have thought! The floor at my flat was marble and we both kept dancing and sliding around on it. Robbie was hilarious. One minute he was doing Frank Sinatra, the next he was doing the famous Michael Jackson moonwalk. It was also the first time I'd heard Robbie's voice properly and the first he had heard mine. As dawn broke I can remember telling him how much I wanted to sing. He listened carefully, despite it being the early hours of the morning, and said, 'Just do it. If you think you can do it, then go for it.' We must have sung the whole *My Way* album together before it was time to call it a night. We bundled Robbie into a taxi and sent him home, still singing.

I'm not a close friend of Robbie at all. I couldn't even say that he was a proper friend – we're more like acquaintances who are fond of each other – but I think he knows where I'm coming from. We both know we're essentially good people. We may have our problems or whatever but we've still got big hearts.

We ran into each other again early in 1999 in New York, where I was finishing my album, *You, Me and Us*. I'd been staying at the Soho Grande hotel and he was there, too, with his Mum, Jan. She had this remarkable presence about her – no wonder Robbie says she helped him sort out his demons. Jan is a very special woman. Anyway, we were chatting away and they invited me to go and see Robbie play some club in town. I didn't hesitate and am glad to this day I went along to see him in action. It was boiling hot inside this venue, absolutely steaming. I was virtually fainting from it just standing in the crowd watching. Robbie must have lost pounds through dehydration because he didn't stop running about for even one moment. I suspect the club owners had turned off the air-conditioning to persuade fans to go to the bar, but the intense heat did nothing to diminish Robbie's show. He was superb – one of the best live performers Britain has ever produced.

And so, too, is Mick Hucknall, a man I can claim to call a friend, although I was a fan long before we ever met, as you now know. My prophecy back at Italia Conti that I would one day get to count the Simply Red star as a pal came true in the summer of 1996, just after I had split from Gareth but a few weeks before he broke my heart by running to the papers. I had gone to a cinema complex in North London where Arnold Schwarzenegger had chosen to premiere his latest film, *Eraser*. I was in *EastEnders*, of course, and the whole Tiffany phenomenon had exploded. As my relationship with Gareth had not long broken up I was quite keen for a night out. I'd been offered a couple of tickets to the premiere but didn't fancy going on my own so I asked Howard Antony to escort me. 'No problem, Martine, let me just call the girlfriend,' he said, whipping out his mobile phone. A few minutes later he got off the phone and said, 'I've called her and she's OK about it. She just said, "As long as there's no stories about you in the paper, it's fine with me."'

I was wearing a black dress from Next that had cost only a tenner, knocked down in the sale. It was a completely strapless Calvin Klein-style number. It was floor-length, black, split up the back and off the shoulder. It looked lovely.

Almost as soon as we walked into the party, which was done up like a giant fairground, I spotted this nutty-looking girl in a leopard-skin outfit with short cropped peroxide hair. Her name was Deirdra Murren, though she's known to most as club hostess Miss Dee. I never thought in a million years I'd be friends with someone like that because she was simply barking mad – although I was pretty loony at the time. But Dee was something else, a complete nutter. She was the epitome of the club world and stood out a mile at the party. I had no idea who she was when I said hello, but she seemed fun. Everyone thought she was having this raging affair with Mick Hucknall – she said the rumours used to drive her mad. Nevertheless, as we were chatting he came over and said hello. All three of us nattered for a bit and Mick was absolutely charming. I could have stayed all night talking to my hero but I had to go because Howard was leaving the party and we were sharing a car. Mick and Dee walked me out and as I turned to go, he said, 'I'll see you later – it was lovely to meet you.'

I'd exchanged numbers with Dee that evening and saw her a couple of times socially after that. I loved hanging out with her and still do. She has a brilliant and infectious laugh and a deep throaty voice. She's been a truly wonderful friend to me over the years.

Anyway, one August afternoon, a few weeks before Gareth's kiss-and-tell came out, she called me and said, 'Mick's invited all of us to go to Knebworth to see Oasis. Do you want to go?'

'I'd love to go – that would be brilliant,' I said.

'Great,' came the reply. 'I'll put him on the phone.'

There I was at Mum's place in Romford, Essex, speaking on the phone to my teenage idol. Mum soon cottoned on something was up when I put the phone down and started dancing about the living room.

'Mick's invited me to go to the Oasis concert,' I explained without bothering to say who Mick was.

'Mick who?' she asked. When I told her it was Mick Hucknall she nearly collapsed. 'Mick Hucknall? Mick Hucknall? And he's asking you to go and see Oasis? That's fucking brilliant, that is. He's got the voice of an angel. I can't believe it: my little girlie has been invited out with Mick Hucknall.'

With that she ran over to the old stereo and put on Simply Red's *New Flame* album and started dancing around the room like a loon because she was so excited for me. I was excited, too, but was doing my best to keep cool, thinking, I've got to take this in my stride now because I'm one of them now, I'm famous too.

One of them? Part of me felt quite frightened at the prospect of hanging around with the likes of Mick Hucknall because I hadn't been part of that clique of rich and famous stars until now. I was an *EastEnders* soap star, that was all. It was only because the whole Bianca-and-Tiffany thing had become so trendy that things had changed. Patsy and I had become very fashionable for a while. We'd had features about us in *The Face* magazine, the bible of style, and other mags, and we'd always camp it up with plenty of black eyeliner and fake fur coats, leopard skin, that kind of garb. I never thought I'd see the day that Tiffany and Bianca would become the fun, camp thing to be into, but we were and that fun time lasted for about a year. At this stage, though, the idea of people like Mick Hucknall wanting to hang out with me was a daunting prospect.

On the day of the concert I went over to Fulham to hook up with everyone. Loads of people were round at Dee's getting ready for the day. She lent me this little top, like a vest, which had pretty tortoiseshell link things on it. It went well with a stripy long coat I had, with my hair up and fake-snakeskin trousers. I felt like I was getting funky in my old age.

As we got ready I remember Mick put on a Terence Trent D'Arby LP. 'I love this,' I squealed.

'You're into your music, aren't you, Martine?' Mick replied.

'Oh yeah,' I said before taking a deep breath and launching into one. I felt I needed to clear the air. 'Mick,' I began. 'I've got to tell you this just to get it out of the way. You're a phenomenal artist. I say that hand on heart. I think you are brilliant. I saw you in concert when I was young and it was the best concert to this day I've ever been to. There was a bit with just you and a guitar and it was absolutely amazing. So you understand I'm a bit of a fan but I can handle it if you can.'

Mick smiled at me, flashing the ruby that's set in one of his teeth. 'I think the car's ready, Martine. Come on.'

The day itself was quite extraordinary. There must have been at least a hundred thousand people at the concert, as Oasis were huge at the time. There were some heavy-duty people there and loads of nutty partygoers. I felt quite out of my depth but Mick was lovely and a total gentleman all day, always asking if I was OK, if I needed anything. I was so nervous I couldn't even think about eating, but I did have a drink or two of champagne. By the time it got dark I'd had quite a few, but had still had nothing to eat and was starting to feel under the weather. No joke, I could actually feel all the drink inside me fizzing away in my tummy.

I must have started to look a little pale because Mick asked me if I was OK again, this time with a genuine air of concern. 'Yeah, yeah, I'm fine, but I think I need to go home,' I explained. 'I've seen the show and it's been a great night but I think I need to get home now. I don't feel very well.'

'No problem' was Mick's reply. 'We'll get everybody together and if anybody wants to go out to a club or whatever they can but we'll drop you home first. It's not a problem.'

'But I live miles away, Mick. Don't worry about me. Just drop me off in London. I've got to get to Essex!'

'No, Martine, we'll take you home, and please, don't worry,' Mick said calmly. By now I was very drunk and struggling to keep myself together. What followed was one of the most embarrassing experiences of my entire life. He put me in the back of his car while Dee sat in the front, talking at a hundred miles an hour, rabbiting on about where we could party next. 'Where shall we go now, Martine? Shall we go to Browns? Shall we? Come on! You'll feel better in a minute.'

But I knew I wouldn't. All I could manage was, 'I'm sorry I can't concentrate, Dee. I can't concentrate at all.'

Mick slipped into the seat next to me and we were off. I don't know if it was the motion of the car or what but, when he asked once again if I was feeling OK, I replied with a terrifying noise. I don't know whether it was trapped wind or not but I made a noise that sounded like something from *The Exorcist*.

'I'm sorry, Martine, what did you say?' Mick asked again, this time with a strange look on his face. I replied by being violently sick all over him. I was sick everywhere, over and over again, in the back seat, down the side of the car, but mainly over Mick and his famous red dreadlocks.

All I remember Mick saying was 'Oh my God' as he scrambled to get out of the car, the floor of which was swilling with my foul-smelling vomit. I was sitting right in the middle of it, apologising out loud while in my head all I was thinking was, You silly cow, what have you done? You get an opportunity to meet lovely people that you admire as artists and then you throw up all over them.

I'm a one-glass wonder, me. I'm not a drinker and never

have been, as my body can't tolerate too much alcohol, especially if I haven't eaten much. It just sits in my stomach and my body doesn't absorb it. If I've eaten, I'm OK, but even then I can have only two or three glasses before I run the risk of disgracing myself like that. But, if I haven't eaten and I'm drinking on an empty stomach, then forget it: it's over. I've learned that the hard way, as you can tell.

I was in bits about my behaviour. Mick had finished doing his best to clean himself up and was back in the car, mopping down the leather upholstery. I apologised over and over again, my drunken state not exactly helping me keep control of my mouth. Worse, I noticed Mick still had bits of my sick in his dreadlocks. I was later told that he had to cut his dreads off because he couldn't get the smell out. I don't know if that was just a myth but one thing's for sure. The next time I saw him the dreads had gone. How he ever forgave me for that night I'll never know.

But the night was only just beginning. Mick had a spare jacket in the boot and changed into that. The last thing I remember for some time after that was asking him if he was OK. Apparently I then giggled to myself and passed out! My next memory was of rain hitting me in the face. When I opened my eyes I realised that my head was out of the window and my chin was leaning on the car door.

I don't know how long I had been out cold, but we were back in London. 'Right, Martine,' Dee said. 'I'm getting out here. We've tried to find out where you live but you've got nothing on you. We couldn't wake you up. I'm going to Browns but don't worry. Mick's safe as houses and you'll be fine. He's got loads of bedrooms in his house. He's going to look after you and we'll probably be coming along later, so don't worry. You'll get some sleep, he'll make you something to eat and everything will be fine. Don't worry.'

I wasn't worried because I passed out again.

I came round just in time to catch a glimpse of the enormous gates to Mick's house in Surrey. 'Oh,' I giggled stupidly to myself. 'It's not like my Mum's semi-detached in Romford, is it?' Despite having to leave the concert early and putting up with my throwing up all over him, Mick burst out laughing at my observation. 'Come on, girl, let's get you cleaned up,' he said, leading me inside his mansion.

He took me indoors and told me to phone my Mum. 'Let her know that you're not coming home,' he said. 'Do you know the number?' I nodded. 'Phone her now. I know it's late but leave a message for her. Tell her you're not going to be coming home and you're not going to be at your other house that you mentioned earlier. Just tell her you'll be home safe and sound tomorrow, OK?' I nodded again. 'Do you want anything to eat?' I didn't make a sound. 'Martine,' he said, his voice genuinely concerned. 'I'm trying to look after you here so I've got to ask: have you done something I should know about? Have you taken anything?'

To the best of my knowledge I hadn't, though Mum reckons I had my drink spiked. 'No, I haven't,' I answered hoarsely. 'I promise you. I know you might not believe me, but I don't do drugs. I do *not* do drugs. I can't even have a drink. Look at me on drink. I'm so sorry, I'm such a lightweight. I know I should be ultra-hip and cool and be able to hold my liquor and everything else but I just can't. I'm sorry. I am an angel, Mick, I really am.'

'You're an angel, are you?' Mick sounded understandably sceptical.

'Yeah, I am. I've even got it tattooed on my ankle, look.'

Mick wandered off to make me a sarnie while I got on the blower to Mum. I got the answer machine and must have sounded hilarious as I was slurring all my words. 'Mum, it's me. I'm with Mick, he's cooking me a bacon sandwich to make me feel better. I've had a bit too much to drink. I'm safe as houses and I'll see you in the morning.'

If Mick hoped the food would quieten me down, he was wrong. I took one look at the bacon sandwich in front of me and then started laying into him because he'd made it with brown bread. 'You can't make a bacon sandwich with brown bread,' I ranted. 'What's the matter with you, man? You're a Northerner and working class. You should like white bread like me.' Oh, the shame of it!

Mick never lost his cool. 'If I'd known you were coming I'd have got the right bread in,' he laughed.

'I'm not being ungrateful,' I said ungratefully. 'I'm just saying I can't believe you've put a bacon buttie in brown bread – it's a sin. You just don't get it, do you?'

Mick howled with laughter at my cheek – or at least I thought it was my cheek. When I told him to stop laughing at me, he urged me to go upstairs to the bathroom and I'd see why. 'I'll get you a top and tracksuit bottoms while you're up there because I think you need to get some sleep,' he called after me sweetly as I disappeared.

I soon found out why Mick found me so funny and it had nothing to do with my cheek. It had more to do with my eyes. I looked like Alice Cooper. I had mascara all the way down my face. I'd been chatting away to Mick, saying what an angel I was, having a go at him about bacon sandwiches, while all the time I had these massive, satanic, black mascara smears down my face. As I was washing it off, I shouted down to Mick in a silly voice, 'You might hang out with all them supermodels, Mick, but I reckon I just take the biscuit. I am Miss World by comparison – I look absolutely gorgeous. I am the beauty. I am the most beautiful thing you've ever met in your life!' I think I must have still been drunk.

'Don't forget to brush your teeth,' he yelled back. 'And then we'll get you to bed.' He showed me to a bedroom, handed me a Milan T-shirt – Milan the place, not the group – and then sat around while I grilled him about life as a pop star, asking questions about his songs.

'I want to start writing and doing songs,' I explained as he made up my bed. 'I know you're going to think, She's a soap star, she can't sing and she's going to be a load of old rubbish; but I promise you I can. I know everyone's going to slag me off for it, but fuck 'em. Do you think I'm bad for wanting to sing? What do you think will happen?'

To his credit Mick said the same thing as Robbie had said: 'If you can sing and you believe you've got a voice and feel you've got something to offer with your writing and stuff, then go for it. But keep your options open. Make sure you've got your options open.'

So what does Muggins end up doing when I finally get a record deal? Only get myself killed off in the soap, that's what – no options left open whatsoever!

But that was still some way off. Right there and then, though, lying exhausted in one of Mick's bedrooms with the taste of stale champagne, toothpaste and bacon in my mouth, all I wanted to do was sleep. I think my last words that night were, 'Thanks for looking after me, Mick' – and with that I slipped into the land of nod . . .

The next morning I opened my eyes, head throbbing like a bass drum, and looked around me. 'Where am I?' I asked myself as I took in my totally unfamiliar environment. It was a few moments before I remembered. As my mind raced over the hazy details it threw up – excuse the pun – of the previous night, my hangover seemed to get ten times worse. I crawled out of bed, tiptoed out of the room and headed downstairs.

'Good morning, Martine,' said a grinning Mick Hucknall

as he busied himself in the kitchen, indulging his passion for cooking. 'What would you like for breakfast?' Ever the gentleman, he didn't even mention my behaviour the previous day.

'Oh, I'd love boiled eggs with Marmite soldiers, please.'

They went down a treat. I rang Mum, assured her I was fine and then started raving about Mick's boiled eggs down the phone. Mick had the Grand Prix going in the background on the biggest TV I've seen in my life.

'Could you order me a minicab?' I eventually piped up. 'I need to get home. I've got to go back to Romford and leave this paradise behind me. Oh, and Mick. Thank you so much for looking after me.'

He never once tried it on with me. He was nothing but a perfect gent. No wonder women love him. He has charm, talent and charisma in abundance – and yet somehow is so down-to-earth he comes across as being completely, well, normal. He just took everything I did in his stride. Each time I tried to bring up the sick thing he would say, 'It's OK, if I can deal with it, you can deal with it.

'I know you might not remember this,' he went on. 'But you were talking about your music and stuff last night. If you ever need any help, just let me know.'

'Thank you, Mick,' I said. 'Maybe one day I will.'

When you spend the night at Mick's, you don't get sent home in a common-or-garden minicab, a beaten-up old Datsun with a clueless driver. Nope. I got into a beautiful Mercedes, which took me all the way home, no charge, as Mick had already paid for it. He even rang the next day to check that I'd arrived home safely. It seemed that, despite my antics at Knebworth, Mick and I were to be mates.

The next few times we ran into each other I would automatically apologise for what I'd done. Eventually Mick, now with much shorter hair, put an end to my embarrassment.

'The being-sick thing,' he said. 'You've got to stop talking about it.' He also stuck to his word as far as my music dreams were concerned. When the time came he turned up at my showcase concert at London's Café de Paris. He also helped with my music, giving me advice about songwriting and chatting about contracts, suggesting what sort of clauses I should put in that would guarantee I retain creative control.

Matt, Robbie and Mick weren't the only three men in my life after Gareth. That winter, six months after finding myself a single girl again, Reece was back with a vengeance. His letters, it transpired, had been pouring through the letterbox, but most had been kept from me. Now he was getting crazy. One day Reece rang the switchboard at *EastEnders* – he'd made something like three hundred calls a fortnight earlier – and told them he had a machine gun and would kill anyone who prevented him from seeing me.

The BBC told the police who, thank heavens, went round to his flat in Brixton, south London, and arrested him. Reece is now off my case, as far as I know, but there have been others . . .

CHAPTER 14

Sick

I MAY HAVE been living like a star, hanging out with famous people and going to all the smartest parties, but I certainly didn't feel like one as far as my bank balance was concerned.

Now I'm not going to deny that I'd win a gold medal if shopping was an Olympic sport, but after two years in *EastEnders* I still found it strange that I didn't seem to have two pennies to rub together. I was certainly doing all right for a twenty-year-old but I couldn't help noticing that many of my fellow *EastEnders* actors appeared to be substantially better off than I was. Howard Antony had a BMW convertible and Dean Gaffney drove a brand-new Vauxhall Tigra, so why was I having problems paying for a Fiat Punto?

I first got thinking about my lack of cash way back in the early days at *EastEnders*. Maybe I wasn't doing enough personal appearances to make ends meet. But, although I was mystified by my lack of money, I didn't do much about it. However, as each month went by, I'd look in my Woolwich account and see little more than a dribble of cash going in.

I'd chat to people at *EastEnders*, as you do, and get a rough idea of what they were spending their earnings on. Some were into nice clothes, others were buying properties. The more I listened, the more I wondered why I wasn't in the same league. You get paid different rates at *EastEnders* and when I started I was on one of the lower rates. But after two years I was earning more than double – not that you would have known if you opened my purse. I decided to look a little deeper.

My agent at this time was Mark Devene. I had been to his house in Notting Hill some time beforehand. I was with Gareth at the time, and I remembered thinking then what an incredibly smart pad it was for a man who didn't seem to have too many working clients. Mark always used to bang on about how he came from a very wealthy family. He used to wear a ring with a crest on it on his little finger and told me that he had royal connections. I can remember thinking he must be some sort of trust-fund baby as we left that night, though Gareth suggested that it was time I got an accountant.

I spoke to Tony Margaritelli, who was my Uncle Lawrence's accountant. He was a bit worried that the *EastEnders* cheques were a bit slow in coming. He asked to look at the paperwork I'd collected and said he would write to Mark and see if he could clear the matter up. He wrote quite a few letters but never got any replies, so he suggested we contact the BBC and get them to pay my *EastEnders* money directly to him, and pass on Mark's ten per cent after that.

I wasn't sure at first. Mark had got me the job in *EastEnders* and I felt very grateful to him. I didn't want to create waves but went ahead anyway. A lot of letters were mailed to various departments at the Beeb explaining what they had to do. Eventually Mark caught wind of this and went ballistic. He was annoyed, perhaps feeling that I'd gone behind his back, and offered to take me out for dinner to explain himself.

Now, I'm no accountant, and so, by the time Mark had finished going through all the facts and figures, I thought, This man has got nothing to hide. He got me the job in the first place. I'll let things carry on as normal. When I told it all to Tony he was unimpressed, and decided to check the whole thing out.

The BBC operates a very sensible system as far as payments go, attaching a brief statement to each cheque detailing its amount, what it was for and what date the episode was broadcast. It even carried details of the relevant cheque number. Tony looked it all over and decided it was time to pay Mark Devene a visit, so he went along to his office in Kensington unannounced. Tony explained who he was and then asked to cast his eye over Mark's books. Freaked out by the surprise visit, Mark nevertheless agreed. It turned out that Mark's bookkeeping was hopeless, and Tony thought the time had come to part company.

We spoke to the actors' union Equity about what we had found – who were helpful – and eventually to the Government's Department of Trade and Industry. A guy there called Hugh Fraser agreed to take on the case on our behalf, and they brought a prosecution for which a trial was held in March 1997. It turned out that Mark had contravened the laws governing the conduct of employment agencies, and pleaded guilty to all eleven charges brought against him.

The magistrate said he was mindful of Mark's ability to repay a fine, costs, or make any compensation payment, and gave him a conditional discharge for two years on all eleven counts.

I later discovered that Mark, at the time that my problems with him occurred, had run into financial troubles trying to keep the agency going after Joelle left. I heard that he had borrowed some money from some people who had started getting quite nasty with him. I wish he had just come to me to ask for my help – which I would have given him. The legal proceedings taken by the Department of Trade and Industry required a lot of effort, as all legal proceedings do. But I'm glad I've had the opportunity to set the record straight and put an end to all those rumours about Martine 'dropping' the agent who had brought her into *EastEnders*. The truth was very different.

There's also a lesson here for any other youngsters with dreams of going into show business: get yourself a damn good lawyer and a damn good accountant. You might not think it's worth it at first when you're earning only a little, but finding the right people to look after your legal and financial affairs can save you a fortune in the long run. I'm not the only actress to have got stuck with a dodgy agent. It's happened to quite a number of household names.

With no agent and no money, I needed to get my act together and turned to my friend Barbara Windsor for advice. She's been in this game longer than anyone, I thought to myself. At least she must know an agent who will send me my money when it's due and find me some decent work. That was in the winter of 1996, about four months before we finally got Mark Devene in court. I told Barbara what had happened and she was really great about it, putting me on to her own agent, Barry Burnett. I went to meet him and thought he was a lovely man. I sensed he was more a theatrical agent than a telly or music-business expert, which ultimately meant we were to work together for only a relatively short time, as I made no secret of my ambition to get into music and movies. But Barry was well respected in theatre and got me a great panto that Christmas, which I'll get on to in a mo.

So I had to sort out my finances, which were in a complete mess. One of the chief problems was the house I'd bought in Brentwood the previous year, thinking it would be home for both me and Gareth, on which I'd spent a fortune doing it up. It was beautiful by the time the builders had finished. The only problem was that the house wasn't the only thing that was finished by this time. So was Gareth's and my relationship. I'd bought the place thinking we would have two incomes, but by then there was only me to pay for any of it and I was struggling to meet all the bills – the house had to go. I didn't want to stay there, anyway, because the place held so many memories of Gareth and happier times long past. The solution, I reasoned, was to buy a little pied-à-terre in London just as my screen heroine Holly Golightly did in *Breakfast At Tiffany's*. I found just what I was looking for in Westbourne Terrace.

In the months between selling Brentwood and moving to Westbourne Terrace I became a nomad again, at one point living in the back of my car. I didn't want to go running back to Mum's house in Essex all the time. She was having problems of her own with John and the vibe there was all wrong. Instead I used to crash over at friends' houses and became a regular fixture at Louise Nurding's place in Chelsea. I needed to be in London to keep up with all the extra work I could get doing photoshoots for magazines, personal appearances and so forth. I was determined to make some money, and got Barry to fix me up with as much work as I could take on.

PAs were a great way of meeting the public as well as making extra cash. From meeting people in this way I got to realise just how big Tiff was becoming. Men fancied me and the wives were OK with it – they'd even ask for my autograph for them. Thanks to Tiff I had become an allowable fantasy for thousands of men. I wasn't used to this, as a lot of women in my life had always been jealous because I was getting on with things. Strange how life turns out.

A typical PA would involve turning up at a nightclub alone or possibly with someone else from the cast. You would get looked after and driven around in a stretch limo, which was very nice. Then you would meet the public, chat about the show, answer questions and sign autographs. I couldn't believe how many people would queue up to meet me. We *'Enders* folk seemed to be guiding people through rough patches in their own lives and we didn't even know it. I used to get loads of fan mail – a big brown supermarket box full of mail – and I suppose from reading those letters I began to realise how much you were admired and what a difference you made to people's lives. But meeting people in the flesh made everything said in those letters seem so real.

I remember guys at the clubs who used to get really drunk and would chase me around, telling me they were in love with me. The DJ would often give a running commentary and laugh while these guys were pestering. I remember one was desperate to give me a red rose he had brought. 'He's after her,' the DJ giggled into his mike. 'Come on, mate, run faster, faster.' Eventually this lad threw his rose at me. I caught it and everyone went wild.

It wasn't just PAs that Barry fixed up for me. He had also been approached by a guy called Kevin Wood, a very straightforward businessman, who was interested in casting me for a panto he was staging at the Marlow Theatre in Canterbury, Kent. He'd settled on *Cinderella* and wanted me to play the part of Cinders, the girl who shoots from rags to riches thanks to a fairy godmother. Perfect.

First I had to get clearance from the BBC, who were pretty good about it. Everyone on 'Enders used to take it in turns to do a panto or some other project once in a while. By and large it's a good idea as it keeps you fresh, getting away from Walford from time to time. I asked for permission and was chuffed to bits to get it, as panto can be a really good earner – and I needed the money badly. As it turned out I was well paid for six weeks' work from mid-December to the end of January. But after commission to your agent and forty per cent to the Inland Revenue, a lot of it disappears. But I was happy – happier still when I learned that my friend John Pickard, who starred in the BBC sitcom *2 point 4 Children* (his brother Nick is in Channel 4's *Hollyoaks*), was also going to be in the show playing Buttons.

The scriptwriters at *EastEnders* were sending Tiff off for a holiday in Marbella, Spain. It was a good idea, because she needed the break. She was heavily pregnant and had only recently got married to Grant. In real life I got stuck into the panto rehearsals and started searching for somewhere to stay near the theatre. I ended up settling on this cottage in the middle of nowhere which John and I were to share. We had a fantastic time there – well, for a while, anyway, as it snowed that Christmas. The pair of us used to go bob-sleighing using dustbin liners for sleighs. It felt like a proper fairy-tale Christmas.

Cinderella was hard work, no two ways about that, as we were doing as many as three shows a day. Kevin wanted to get his money's worth. I loved it all the same. I had a gorgeous Zhandra Rhodes ball gown, a pink one, dotted with what looked like loads of pink Kleenex tissues and sprinkled with diamanté baubles, the most over-the-top fairy-tale dress ever. The kids loved it almost as much as I did. Sometimes on that stage I felt as if I was a five-year-old again, dressing up in Mum's clothes.

But after the first week disaster struck. My voice started going funny. I sounded more like E.T. than Cinders, and the kids would look at me with horror on their faces. I felt as if I was coming down with flu. I went to my dressing room at the end of the matinée performance and tried to pull myself together. Scott St Martin, who played one of the Ugly Sisters, came in to check up on me, armed with a smoked-salmon bagel from Marks & Spencer. My Mum came in a few moments later. I told them I felt bloody lousy, feverish. My make-up was running all over my face because I'd started sweating, too. I honestly didn't feel like I could do the evening show, but they both assured me I could, that I would be fine.

So I went on stage that evening. My voice was still awful and I felt worse as the show went on. Just as the curtain came down at the end of the first half, I felt very faint. I had this burning feeling in my head and couldn't breathe. The next thing anyone knew, I'd hit the deck and collapsed. The rest of the cast realised I'd definitely picked up some sort of bug and helped me to my dressing room, where people took turns assessing me. Kevin, of course, was convinced I was OK. After all, thousands of people had bought tickets for the show to see Tiff as Cinders and he didn't want to disappoint them. Everyone else thought I needed to go straight home to bed – and they were right.

I didn't make the second half of the show and spent the next seven days at the cottage feeling lousy. John Pickard came home each evening but was so busy with the show he would often forget to pick up provisions. We were living out in the sticks and there were no corner shops nearby, so if John forgot to get food we had to go hungry. I spent the first two days living off two Pot Noodles and some tangerines while gazing deliriously at the flowers and get-well cards that John *did* remember to bring home. For the next four days I literally lived on tangerines. He didn't *mean* to let me starve: he just kept forgetting. Even worse, all my friends and family who rang to see if I was OK were driving me nuts. We didn't have a land-line phone in the cottage, only my mobile. We were so off the beaten track I couldn't get a signal to talk, so each time they called I'd have to throw a coat on and trudge out into the snow to ring them back. Mum must have called me about twenty times a day and just didn't seem to get it.

I was in quite a bad way that week. I'd get out of bed and the sheets top and bottom would be drenched in sweat. The doctor came out to do some tests because I felt as if I'd had the stuffing knocked out of me. I can remember telling Mum that I wanted to see Gareth, as he was still very much on my mind, and my bitterness towards him over his kiss-and-tell to the press had worn off a little by then. I felt that a hug from him would make me feel so much better. Mum called him but he couldn't make it for various reasons. That hit me badly, too. To this day I think that was why it took me so long to recover properly, because I was still an emotional mess. Mum did her best to cheer me up, saying things like, 'If he doesn't want to come and see you then he's not the one for you. It's horrible but there's no point crying and you'll only make yourself feel worse.' It was a horribly lonely time.

After a week off I decided to go back to *Cinderella*, because Kevin was desperate for me to take the stage again, even if I couldn't sing solos and could only croak my lines. I still hadn't had the results of my blood test from the doctor – it was only later I would find out that I'd had pneumonia – though I did start to feel a bit better as we hit New Year, and I started singing again.

In fact I felt well enough to go to a New Year's Eve party.

The venue? The Chilled Eskimo bar, run by the Pickard brothers. The attitude? Do the best you can, girl. It was a wild night, all right, but I couldn't quite get into the swing of it, no doubt because of the pneumonia. This bloke kept looking at me, which ironically only made me feel a little down. The split from Gareth was still weighing heavily on my mind and I also had to contend with everyone else at the party snogging their partners. I wanted someone to snog, too! I left the bar and walked round to the Pickards' living room, where the brothers' closest friends were having a quiet glass or two. I'd been in there only a minute when the bloke who had been looking at me came in, too, and joined us.

'Hello, I'm Jonathan,' he told me. 'I just wanted to say hello. I'm not clear on your name as everyone keeps calling you different things so I thought I'd introduce myself and find out, first-hand, what you call yourself.'

'Oh, I'm Martine.'

'Not Tiffany, then?'

'Oh, no, don't say that,' I protested, thinking he was mocking me, but Jonathan Barnham, to give him his full name, looked genuinely confused.

'What have I said? What have I said?' he asked.

'Well I'm an actress and I'm on a TV show,' I explained, still not sure if he was taking the mick. 'In the TV show I'm called Tiffany but in real life I'm Martine – the real me is Martine.'

'I bet that's irritating, isn't it?' Jonathan asked. I nodded and we continued to chat.

We became good friends dizzyingly quickly and I suppose the reason was that he really didn't have a clue who I was. It can be a pain when people want to talk to you only because you're on the telly. Sitting there chatting in the Pickards' living room, I learned a little more about him. Jonathan, it turned out, had been in the UK for only six months, as he'd lived in Spain from the age of nine. He went to a normal Spanish school and was fluent in the language.

Like me, he'd been to a stage school when he was much younger, in his case the Corona Stage School, and had now returned to the UK to get some acting work and kick-start a career in the business. He was best friends with Nick Pickard, who was a little bit older than I was and hung around in slightly different circles. I was much closer to his brother John, as we were doing panto together. I admit even then I thought Jonathan was nice and told his cousin Sarah, whom I was introduced to at the same party, just that. Indeed Sarah and I got on so well we ended up swapping numbers with the intention of going out for a girls' natter sometime. I felt quite perky by the time New Year dawned, yet couldn't quite put my finger on the reason why.

The panto wound up in the middle of January. I cleared out the cottage over the weekend and drove back to London ready to start work on *EastEnders* the following Monday. Despite the fact I was still feeling a bit groggy and increasingly depressed, the irony was that everyone said how well I looked. I'd lost loads of weight and none of Tiff's clothes fitted me properly any more, especially as the character was about eight months pregnant by the time I returned.

I may have been thin but I felt terrible. Work on 'Enders was hard. I felt as if I was just going through the motions and felt increasingly numb and isolated from what was going on. Looking back now, I believe that all the events of the previous seven months had started to take their toll on me mentally and I began to slip into a depressive state. Those close to me at Elstree noticed something was up. I'd finish a scene, go back to my dressing room, have a little cry and then go back and film another scene. I was finding it difficult to cope with life on my own. I didn't know what was going on, who I was, what I was doing and why Gareth wasn't with me. All around me people seemed to be taking money from me, selling horrible stories to newspapers, betraying me. I realised I had all these people clinging on to me, who were out for what they could get while I seemed to be riding this crest of a wave. You know the sort, the ones who will always order champagne and simply assume I'd pay for it. It wasn't house champagne, either, but bottles of Cristal, one of the world's best champagnes, which is all very well for special occasions, but not every weekend. I didn't even feel properly in contact with my friends because I'd been so busy. Louise had met footballer Jamie Redknapp and had moved out of London, and I didn't want to put the three girls who lived with Paul Nicholls in a difficult position what with their connections with the show, so I didn't even see them. I would like to thank them here and now, though, for the tremendous support and loyalty they showed me. Not one of them was ever tempted to dish the dirt on me when I was at such a low ebb. Thanks, girls!

Instead, my whole life seemed to centre on Elstree and Tiffany Mitchell. Both Barbara and Patsy realised I was losing the plot. Patsy even suggested we take some time off together. Her own love life was having a few ups and downs, too, as things weren't going well with her boyfriend and future husband Nick Love. She had already booked a couple of weeks off and asked me to do the same. We could both run away together to Spain and have a girlie holiday together. I agreed and we set our sights on two weeks in Marbella at the end of July.

The next six months passed in a blur. Nothing went on in my private life, and work was just, well, work. Tiff was still the public's East End darlin', her baby Courtney was born in March, followed by a DNA test which established Grant, not Tony Hills, as the father (which was just as well because Grant and Tiff had married the previous November). The scriptwriters were planning my holiday excuse and settled on Tiff's simply not being around much.

Did I say nothing much happened in my private life? Er, that wasn't quite true. The lad that I had met at the Pickards' New Year do? Well, we met again. Back then I was still heartbroken from splitting with Gareth. I preferred girlie nights out. But I admit now that I was still chuffed to bits when, a couple of days after New Year, I got a phone call from Sarah, Jonathan's cousin, inviting me out for a drink. I was keen and arranged to meet at the Bluebird restaurant, where I'd once been for dinner with Michael Douglas.

Maybe I was a little slow off the mark but I didn't think anything of it when midway through dinner Sarah's phone rang. It was Jonathan allegedly at a loose end. He invited himself round to join us. Odder and odder, I thought. He popped by about twenty minutes later and ended up staying until we left sometime after midnight. He was very polite, not at all pushy, and offered me a lift home to Westbourne Terrace. We swapped numbers just before I got out.

From then on we became firm friends but there wasn't a hint of romance, certainly not on my part. It was another five months before Jonathan came clean about his own feelings. We went to the Hanover Grand club off Regent Street for my 21st birthday. I was dolled up to the nines if not tens, wearing a little black sequin boob tube and satin trousers, and felt the bee's knees. It was a great night and all my friends from *EastEnders* were there, including Dean Gaffney and Michael

Greco, who had just started on the show, playing Beppe di Marco.

At one point I was sitting down when Jonathan ambled over. 'Do you know what, Martine?'

'What?' I replied.

'I could fall in love with you,' he said. 'But I'm not going to because you're not good for me at the moment – you're a bit mixed up, you're a bit here, there and everywhere; but when the time's right I'm going to give it a go.'

I sat there in shock for a couple of seconds. 'Oh, will you now? Will you really?' I said all flustered.

He smiled. 'Yeah I will, honestly, I will. You just watch.'

'You can have a go, Jonathan. I'm not saying you'll get anywhere but you can have a go. I don't want to be with anyone at the moment so don't say such things to me because you're supposed to be my friend.'

'I am your friend,' he insisted. 'I'm just saying . . .'

I didn't give him a chance to finish. 'Men!' I said theatrically. 'You're all the same.'

Fortunately that moment didn't affect our friendship adversely – and it continued to blossom. We'd go out and have a great time, particularly on Sundays, when we would meet for a simple lunch at Pizza Express in Notting Hill, and then see a movie.

I've got this thing about Sundays which Jonathan seemed to understand. Ever since I was a little girl I've always felt sad on Sundays. I call them Sad Sundays. I use to hate them because Mum would work so hard during the week that on Sunday she'd be no good to man or beast – especially her little girl. Saturday nights were her only night out and by the time Sunday came she really had nothing left to give me. The kids over the road didn't want to play with me because they obviously thought I came from a rough family as Mum would always have a black eye or some other unpleasant reminder of Keith's late-night visits. The Indian kids I used to hang out with – and nick their saris during weekdays – always had a family get-together on Sunday.

There was never anyone around and, truth be told, I used to get really bored. That was when death first raised its ugly head in my consciousness, way before Uncle Chrissy died. I used to watch all the black-and-white films while Mum caught a few Zs on the settee and I remember one day asking her what happened to all the actors in these films. 'A lot of them have passed on and died,' Mum answered – that got me thinking.

Then *The Antiques Roadshow* came on the TV. 'Mum,' I'd ask annoyingly, 'Where do antiques come from?'

She explained how they were items passed down from generation to generation.

'So the people that bought these things in the first place, are they alive?'

'No, Mart,' she'd say, 'they're not alive any more. They're dead now, they're in heaven.'

Top that lot off with a load of programmes in the evening about Jesus dying and I think you can understand why a young child might go off Sundays. I used to cry my eyes out every Sunday night as a kid because I didn't want to go to sleep in case I died, too, while I was snoozing.

My Sunday afternoons with Jonathan were much more fun and became a regular fixture of my life, yet not once did I ever see what was staring back at me. Not once did I consider Jonathan as a potential boyfriend. Instead I had these brief flings which never led anywhere. I was very much disillusioned with dating and was genuinely looking forward to spending a girlie fortnight with Patsy. With hindsight, of course, I reckon I just couldn't see a good thing when faced with it.

By this time, Patsy and I were very close. But we had our own agendas, our own families and our own lives. We trusted each other though, as we were the same – normal every day girls with special jobs – and it was a good time to be in each other's lives.

We decided to go to this very upmarket resort called Las Dunas, a few miles outside Marbella. The record producer Nellee Hooper, who knows just about everyone in the music business thanks to strong connections with the likes of Madonna, had recommended it to me. Nellee, the epitome of trendiness and cool and the most sociable, party-loving man on the planet, was going to Spain at the same time and had borrowed a friend's enormous boat and was planning to stay on that.

For the first few days it was great fun. We went out together and with a few of Patsy's friends who were in Spain, too, and it was hilarious watching the British tourists who spotted us. They just couldn't believe they'd seen Tiff and Bianca sipping cocktails in a Spanish bar. Then one afternoon I got a call from Nellee, who had just arrived in town, and we arranged to meet that evening by the harbour.

I spotted Nellee's party first – and it wasn't hard. The Oasis star Noel Gallagher was there with his wife Meg Matthews, and Nellee was bounding along arm in arm with the supermodel Kate Moss. There was a huge crowd of them and they were all being incredibly rowdy. Nellee got us all on to his boat and the party began. I can remember having quite a heated discussion with Nellee, who kept banging on about what was cool and what wasn't. I kept arguing that there was nothing wrong with being pop or mainstream, though he was having none of it. The astonishing thing was that Noel backed me up – much to Nellee's chagrin. I realised that night just how clever Noel was. He sat there, quietly listening to what everyone was saying, taking everything in, and then he'd come out with a classic comment. Far from putting me down, when I said I wanted to do some singing and put a record out, Noel was bang up for it. Louise Nurding's manager, Dennis Ingleby, had once suggested to me that I do a collaboration with Burt Bacharach. When Patsy told that to Noel he was impressed. Thank God – I'm cool, I thought to myself, looking at the people around me. Meg was a right sweetie, just completely normal, and ended up getting all the girls dancing on the boat. 'Come on, Kate, let's have a boogie,' she shouted, and the pair of them were up on their feet in no time, just like any girls on holiday.

Nellee's boat party rounded off the end of our first week. Patsy and I decided to spend the second half of the break just chilling out at Las Dunas, sunbathing and taking life easy. I can remember waking up one evening to find Patsy leaning right over me. 'Martine,' she asked anxiously. 'Are you OK? I'm worried about you. You've been asleep for the last twenty-four hours. I've been trying to wake you up.'

I felt utterly exhausted and told her so.

'Well if you feel knackered just carry on sleeping, Mart. I just wanted to make sure you were all right.'

I assured her I felt fine and made an effort to be a bit more fun in case her mates thought I was completely boring. I agreed to go out with her to a club with the hair colourist James Galvin, Daniel's son. The three of us decided to check out the fabulous Olivier Valere Club. I still felt exhausted but I knew it was a great club and couldn't resist. We had a strange evening right from the start. I can remember Princess Diana's former lover James Hewitt, who was subsequently branded the world's biggest love rat, coming over to say hello.

I didn't know what to do. Part of me thought I didn't want to talk to him as he seemed to have been behaving despicably after their affair had become public knowledge. The other part of me thought, given my own experiences, that I should make my own mind up, rather than believe everything the media had said about him. So I said hello back.

We ran into each other again at the nightclub and chatted for a little longer. It was all quite strange but I have to say in James's defence that he was nothing but a gentleman in terms of the way he behaved to me and Pats. The night was full of promise – the trouble was I just couldn't pull myself together. Eventually I could push myself no further and told Patsy I was heading back to the hotel. 'I'm just so tired, I can't seem to get over it,' I explained as I turned to go.

I went straight to sleep almost as soon as I hit the mattress and was miles away when the phone rang. It was possibly 7 a.m. or even a little later. It was Patsy and she sounded in a right old state. She was sobbing and having difficulty getting her words out. 'Oh my God!' I said, panicking madly. 'What's happened?'

'Oh, Martine, you haven't heard? I can't believe it but Princess Diana's had the most dreadful accident . . .'

'Are you winding me up? Stop winding me up. Don't pull my leg just because we saw James Hewitt tonight.'

'I am not joking,' she said. 'Put the telly on now. Put on Sky News.'

So I did.

'Tell me what's happening,' Patsy said when I got back to the phone. 'What's going on?' she asked.

'I don't know,' I told her. 'Give me a chance.' There were constant updates but the outlook was grim. 'Patsy, I've got a horrible feeling she's going to die,' I told her.

'That's it. I'm coming straight back. I'll see you in a few minutes.'

I was glued to the screen. Patsy arrived about ten minutes later. We were together when they broke the news that Princess Diana had died.

We threw our arms around each other and burst into tears. We cried for ages. The news was totally incomprehensible, let alone weird. Only hours earlier I'd been chatting with her one-time lover.

The next day Las Dunas was a place of silence. The whole resort seemed to be in shock. Nobody was talking; it was quite bizarre – more like a ghost town than a holiday resort. Everybody was just so unbearably sad. Patsy couldn't get her mind off Diana's sons William and Harry because she's got her own little boy.

'What are those boys going to do without her?' she kept murmuring, half to herself.

Even now I struggle to put the weirdness of it all into perspective. A couple of weeks before that holiday the *Mirror* newspaper had asked me to model one of Diana's old dresses, which the paper had bought in a charity auction. I was immensely flattered to be asked. The picture ended up on the front page and is one of my treasured mementos, a memento permanently tinged with sadness. I regret to this day that I never had the chance to meet Diana. She and Frank Sinatra were the two people I would most love to have met. It was a horrible end to an otherwise fabulous holiday.

When I got back to Britain I headed straight to Bethnal Green. My Mum had left John a few months earlier, and with some financial help from me had gone back to the pub trade, but this time as a landlady in her own right. She was running the Railway Tavern, a rickety, horrible old pub. She had started full of hope. She even roped me into pulling pints on the opening night. I remember her talking out of the side of her mouth as I was pulling away saying, 'I bet you're hating this, aren't you?' She wasn't wrong.

Anyway, Mum was pleased to see me back, especially as it seemed her pub dream was already turning sour. There was one bright spot on the horizon in her life, though. She had met a nice new man called Alan Tomlin, who used to drink in the Railway. Mum pointed him out to me one day when I dropped by. It's funny, people have subsequently pointed out that Alan's ten years Mum's junior, but that never struck me at all, perhaps because Mum's so young at heart. Anyway I thought Alan looked a bit like Sylvester-Stallone-meets-Al-Pacino. He was dark and rugged, with heavy-lidded eyes, a strong nose and a good body. I knew Mum fancied him immediately – he was right down her street.

Mum thought I'd got a nice tan but I still felt dreadful, lethargic and utterly devoid of energy. I couldn't really keep awake. My belly had started to swell a little and my chin puffed up too. I thought I might have reacted badly to the flight, even though we were up in the air for only a couple of hours. Anyway, the following day I was shooting for *EastEnders* and I was determined to be there bright as a button.

Barbara Windsor clocked that there was something wrong with me as soon as we did our first scenes together.

'Martine, darling, something's happening to you. Your face is swelling up right here in front of me, love. Are you feeling OK?'

I didn't see any point in lying. 'Actually, Barbara, I feel a bit sick, weird more than anything,' I said. 'I just . . .'

'Everyone stop filming,' Barbara ordered sternly.

'Something's wrong with this girl. Look at her!' I did look bad – yellow-tinged and horribly swollen. 'You better get to the doctor, darling.'

I was taken to see the local GP in Elstree, who thought I'd gone down with tonsillitis. He gave me antibiotics, and I was put in a car and sent home to Westbourne Terrace.

Once inside I collapsed and fell into another deep sleep. I couldn't get up the next day and went back to sleep in my clothes. I woke up not knowing what day it was when my doorbell rang. There was a car outside waiting to take me to Elstree – I'd been too ill to drive myself home the day before. So I grabbed my antibiotics and jumped in feeling as queasy as anything. I don't think the pills were helping because not long after swallowing one I felt like I was going to throw up.

'Stop the car,' I told the driver. 'Pull over – I need to be sick.' We were on the Edgware Road heading north. The driver pulled in at a petrol station.

'Christ, you don't look at all well, love.' I didn't hear what else he had to say as my head was outside the car window and I was being violently ill. My body was reacting to the antibiotics. As soon as I pulled my head back inside the car I passed out cold. The driver turned out to be a bit of a lifesaver. He grabbed my mobile phone and started going through the numbers stored in its memory. He found Mum's, rang her and told her what had happened.

'I've got your daughter in the back of my car,' he explained. 'She's really not well. I don't know what to do with her and she's, er, just passed out in the car. I've radioed through and told the BBC and they've said bring her into work!'

My Mum told him to take me straight back to my flat. She was going to make an appointment for me with another doctor, and would pick me up later.

An hour or so later I was sitting opposite Dr Peter Ryan at his practice in Wimpole Street. He took one look at me and said gravely, 'You're a very poorly girl, young lady. You have to get some rest. I've looked at your records. You've got to take some proper time off work.'

'I can't,' I wailed. 'You don't understand: I'll be letting everyone down. Scripts are written in advance . . .'

'I don't care,' he replied. 'If you carry on working you won't have a career to worry about. If you don't rest you can forget about even *having* a career.'

He then patiently explained how my immune system had collapsed over a period of time, dating back some seven months to when I contracted pneumonia. I'd never given my body a chance to regain its strength. Instead I'd kept pushing it and pushing it until something had to give. I was devastated and more than mildly alarmed. I began to tell Dr Ryan about my life. One thing led on to another and I was soon weeping to him about Gareth, the house in Brentwood, pneumonia, work, everything.

'You're just not doing yourself any good at all by punishing yourself all the time with so much work,' he said. 'We'll stick you in bed for about a month and then, day by day, you're going to have a set programme of things to do. Try to eat what you can but drink plenty of fluids.'

'I can't,' I said. 'I look all swollen as it is. I look fat, I look horrible . . .' But when he put me on the scales I didn't weigh any more than normal.

'See, you don't weigh any more,' he continued. 'But I'm telling you now: get this whole weight thing out of your head. Forget what the press says, forget it all. It's just vanity, girlie stuff, put it all to one side. You've just got to let all that take a back seat because without your health you won't have a career.' He was worryingly serious and very firm with me. It was quite frightening, too, because he was having none of my nonsense. 'You know you could be feeling like this for about eighteen months,' he went on. 'You've just got to get used to it.' He said my internal organs were all inflamed, and some were seven times their normal size.

That was August. The *EastEnders* people may not have liked the doctor's diagnosis but they were in no position to argue. Scripts were hastily rewritten. Tiffany was suddenly diagnosed with chickenpox. If anyone in the Vic asked where Tiff was, Grant or Peggy would say she's upstairs feeling poorly. Hardly original but it worked.

Another shock was in store when I got a call from the BBC saying that I was up for Best Actress at the National TV Awards in October. I mentioned this to Dr Ryan next time he visited me at home, where I'd already been confined to bed for the best part of a month. 'I've got to be better by October,' I explained irritably. 'I'm up for Best Actress. I've got to go.'

'Well, if we can get you better in time, you can go and have one glass of champagne there, but then you'll have to come home – and that's only if I think you're well enough by then.'

Jane Harris, the executive producer, had already been on the phone making sure I was OK and sounding me out about the awards. I was still pretty poorly with a month to go to the bash. I didn't even have the energy to go downstairs and get some fresh air. Even lifting the TV remote control left me knackered. Mum would have to come round and literally lift me to the toilet. I just slept all the time, catching up, I suppose, on all the late nights, all the work, all the illnesses, all the pain, all the upset of the past eighteen months. I had to sleep and recharge all my batteries because not once, during all that time, had I stopped for even one minute.

Towards the end of September I began to feel more like

my old self and Dr Ryan confirmed that I could go to the awards – but not stay long. I let the BBC know but was totally unprepared for the reaction from many of my colleagues.

There was lots of hurtful bitterness from the cast, a lot of resentment. Some even told me to my face. They had all been forced to cover for me but, then again, I'd done the same for some of them when they had been forced to take a couple of weeks off at short notice for personal problems. If someone goes off sick for just a week it can throw the entire schedule into chaos, so I wrote an open letter to the *EastEnders* lot thanking them for all their hard work, apologising for my absence and so forth. I ended by saying how I hoped to make it to the TV awards and that I would see them the following Monday at work. For some reason my letter was never pinned to the staff board as I'd requested. I think Jane Harris had a change of heart and felt that by pinning the letter up I would only irritate the rest of the cast more – and Jane was into the whole 'happy ship' concept.

I was lying in bed, contemplating missing out on what I hoped could be my finest hour, when the postman arrived. There was a letter from the BBC, from Alan Yentob indeed, then controller of BBC1 and one of the most powerful men in British television. 'Under no circumstances do you *not* go to the National TV Awards,' he wrote. 'You make sure you turn up at those awards and do us all proud.' Nice one, Alan. I think he simply felt sorry for me because he saw me losing out on a major opportunity that was there for the taking. I still feel people should have been more supportive of me. It wasn't the cast's fault. They didn't know that I'd written the letter. If they had seen it on the staff notice board I think they would have understood.

October arrived and I felt well enough to venture out and

join my Mum for a trip to Harrods to find a couple of frocks for the big night. I'd decided she should come to the awards as my special guest. I settled on a gorgeous black dress with a black velvet basque and a big net skirt.

On the evening as Mum and I got dolled up I felt something of what it must feel to be going to the Oscars. I was chuffed to bits that I fitted into my frock because I'd got a size twelve and I didn't *look* a twelve: I *looked* about a fourteen. But getting into that dress made my evening. Mum looked fab, too, even though she's never been into clothes; she made me feel so proud. I'd been to get my hair done at Nicky Clarke's salon in Mayfair and Nicky did me himself. What's more, he sorted me out for nothing, just to say good luck, he said. We were to be joined for the night by Paul Fitzgerald, an old friend of mine from Milan days. He looked very impressed by the two lovely ladies who greeted him at the door when he arrived at the flat.

As the limo pulled away from Westbourne Terrace carrying the three of us to the Royal Albert Hall, Mum leaned over and told me, 'Whatever happens tonight, Martine, you know you're the winner in my eyes. I love you. Enjoy every moment and don't worry about any bad feeling from whoever. Just go and do what you're supposed to do, do what you do best.'

I had been given no advance warning as to whether I was going to win or not – sometimes that happens at awards – and consequently I was a bundle of nerves. I knew there was a big fuss being made about it all by everybody at the BBC and, of course, Alan Yentob had really wanted me to go. I had my suspicions. I'm not just here for the pictures, I thought, or to get *EastEnders* in the papers or to get press for the event. I must have a chance of winning.

As the awards – hosted by ITN's Trevor McDonald –

went on, all I could think was, Come on, hurry up, hurry up! I tried to relax but couldn't. When it finally came to my nomination I started praying that the organisers had chosen a good clip of Tiff in action, because if they choose a bad one it makes you think, No wonder nobody had voted for me! Paul Fitzgerald tried to keep me calm by holding my hand. Sweet! The clip, as it turned out, wasn't too bad: a scene of me and Ross Kemp fighting. Now *there's* a surprise.

My head started going at a hundred miles an hour as I argued with myself: You've got it, girl, you've got it, I thought, followed by, No, you haven't, you haven't got it.

As all this was going on I heard Leslie Grantham, the celeb booked to hand over the award, and himself a former *EastEnders* star, prepare to read the winner's name: 'And the winner is . . . Yeah! Martine McCutcheon.' My mind was still arguing with itself when Paul gave me a little hug and said, 'Well done, off you go!' I got up and felt as if I was floating on to the stage. The best actress on British television! Who would have thought it? I'd already won a few awards but this was the big one. It *was* Britain's own Oscars. At the very least, I thought, winning an award like that keeps you in work for the next twelve months!

I walked up, kissed Leslie and turned to face the glittering audience. Almost everyone who was anyone was sitting there gawping at me. I didn't have a clue what I was going to say. I very rarely prepare a speech (I think it's tempting fate to do so), so I improvised. I thanked the cast for covering for me during my illness; Carolyn Weinstein, the 'lovely Jewish girl', as she calls herself – a wonderful friend with her curly hair and endless supply of yummy digestive biscuits – for her support and friendship; Jane Harris, even though things were a bit funny between us by then, for giving me the opportunity to say more than 'Here's your pint'; and then I thanked my Mum: 'As far as I'm concerned this is for Mum because without her I wouldn't be standing here,' I said. 'She made all my dreams come true.'

From the moment I stepped down from the stage, the evening was like a dream. I had endless people coming up to me, wanting questions answered, asking to book photo shoots. I was Miss Popularity that night and I was absolutely knackered by the time we left the Albert Hall for the party at a posh Royal-connected place nearby. The party was crammed with famous people and journalists but there was no aggro. Everyone was swilling champagne and having a natter. There was a tremendous atmosphere inside the bash. I knew I could stay for only one drink but I didn't mind. I was following doctor's orders and I wanted to make sure I was ready and raring for work the following Monday. I stayed for my one glass of champagne, said hellos and thank-yous to a few people, and headed home.

I had other things on my mind, too, and knew I had to make a call I really didn't feel like making. That night I made up my mind to end my professional relationship with Barry Burnett. It was always supposed to be only a temporary arrangement anyway, but he was such a lovely man I dreaded breaking the news to him. I didn't want him to hear that I was unhappy, that I was looking at other options. No, the last thing I wanted was for Barry to hear my news through the grapevine. That's not the way to do business. I didn't make the call that evening but the next day Mum was on my case first thing. I made the call but felt so bad about it I wasn't even relieved when it was over.

And then it was back to work. My body was still messed up. I was swollen and felt very tender for a long time afterwards, maybe six months or more. Ross and Barbara were always very conscious of me whenever a scene called for them to brush past me. I still find it quite amazing how many glands the human body conceals. Glandular fever brings them all out in places you would never imagine. I was swollen almost everywhere. I didn't feel very good about myself physically but that was counterbalanced by the gratitude I felt at having a bit of get-up-and-go again. I sincerely believe my illness gave me a different view on life. Ever since, I've believed that if the worst really does come to the worst, as long as I've got my health, I can deal with it.

Another change that followed my illness was my growing interest in spiritual books and healing. Patsy was always very into it, as was Lindsey Coulson, aka the Square's Carol Jackson. Patsy had also been to therapy. I often used to wonder what that involved and she was very open about it to me. I understood why someone would want to talk about private things, to get their feelings out in the open, but in a way that stopped those secrets becoming public knowledge. I also felt I could do with putting things in order inside my head. Patsy recommended a couple of books, which I happily devoured. I even started buying my own and still do.

Patsy also asked me if I had ever felt the need for therapy. 'You know, have you ever thought about talking to somebody, Martine?' she enquired, adding, 'It's literally therapy for your mind. You go to a doctor when you hurt your leg – it's the same if your heart's hurting or your head's hurting.' I agreed and looked into it.

I'd heard of the Charter Nightingale clinic in London and arranged to see a guy there. I went just five times but found those visits had enormous long-term benefits. He told me to write things down, identify the problems in my life – and I did just that. I realised that I was finding it hard coming to terms with the realisation that life isn't a fairy tale, that there's a lot of pain to go through and a lot of guilt to carry with you. I suppose I hadn't realised until then how pressures can test your heart and soul.

My therapist and I discussed everything I noted down and I started to see things more clearly after a while, and decided to narrow things a bit by rewriting my little book. Again. And again. In the end I condensed it all down to two pages. I realised that I felt life's knocks more clearly because I was now standing on my own two feet, without the security of man, a comfort blanket, to cushion life's blows – and that I found quite tough. But then I think most actors and actresses are like that, a little insecure, a little vulnerable, however bold they may seem outwardly.

I think this period of reflection in my life could not have come at a more appropriate time. It changed my outlook. Inner peace is very hard to achieve but it's so important and beneficial. As a performer living my life in the public eye, I have to rely on my emotions and state of mind. I've learned that to preserve both I must stop myself giving 110 per cent to every job. We're like batteries, you know, and will soon run out of energy – or emotions – if we're run at full steam all the time. Instead of doing every single interview offered to me when I was promoting something, I learned to pick and choose and commit only to the most beneficial jobs. Life doesn't revolve around you: there are a lot more important things out there, but paradoxically there's nothing wrong with putting yourself first, provided you don't go out of your way to hurt anyone. It's all karma. What you give out you get back.

That said, I found living in Tiffany's shadow was playing havoc with my mind, too. When I went out at the weekend as just plain, ordinary Martine McCutcheon shopping for knickers, I felt people viewed me as an impostor. They didn't want to meet Martine. They wanted to chat to Tiff with her sharp one-liners and gutsy determination to survive whatever was thrown at her. I was playing Tiffany from 7.30 a.m. until 7 p.m., five, sometimes six days a week. I'd go out at weekends and people would shout 'Oi, Tiff!' at me over and over again. Perfect strangers as far as Martine McCutcheon was concerned, but they all knew Tiff, didn't they?

You learn, of course, that it's just a job, a very well-paid job for some, but that doesn't stop a character from becoming intrusive, eating into your private life. My problem, I suppose, was that I always wanted to please everyone. I wanted to succeed but I didn't think I could succeed in my own right. The public, I started to believe, wanted Tiffany, not Martine.

CHAPTER 15

Don't Rain On My Parade

I WAS STILL totally committed to *EastEnders* but was beginning to dream of a life away from Walford and Tiffany Mitchell – but how would I get there? Who would advise me? I had to find a new agent, someone more in touch with my views on where I wanted to go.

It took a lot of asking about before I was pointed in the right direction, but as soon as I met her I knew. There was something about Ginette Chalmers – a tall, attractive blonde woman with a wonderful warm smile and twinkly eyes, from the West End agency Peters Fraser and Dunlop – that I connected with on sight. I sensed immediately that here was someone who would have a major impact on my career. I owe this happy meeting to Dan Hubbard, a casting agent, who runs a family business called Hubbard Casting. I was put in touch with Dan by an old friend called Tammy, who had worked for him and knew he would be able to help me. Dan did help me, and put a lot of time and effort into looking for the right agents for me to meet. He's a life saver – thanks Dan!

I walked into the bar, spotted Ginette and introduced myself with a cheerful, 'Hiya, how are ya?' She almost snapped at me and said I should 'stop all that' right away. 'Stop what?' I asked, slightly fazed. 'All that cockney Tiffany business,' Ginette said. 'This is Martine McCutcheon I'm talking to.' I thought that she'd read my mind, that she knew me already.

We began to talk. Ironically until meeting Ginette I had grown increasingly fed up with telling people what I wanted. I wanted someone to *tell me* where they saw my career going, and she did. 'Listen,' she said, 'this is how I see things, you tell me if you agree or not. I see you as multi-talented, I think you've got star quality. There are a lot of people on *EastEnders* and I'm sorry if they're your friends but I'm afraid half of them I wouldn't give a two pence for . . .' I sort of nodded, taken aback by her frankness. She continued. 'I think you're very versatile and I think you're showing only one tiny dimension of yourself. I think there's a lot more to you that's currently being wasted. I think the time is coming soon when we'll have to take you out of *EastEnders* because otherwise you'll be there too long and be stuck with Tiffany for ever.

'I heard you like to sing and that you're very good. We want to get you a nice musical, get you to Broadway, get the Americans to see you, they love anything typically British. We need to get you doing things as far away from Tiffany as possible. You need to do something different.'

I managed to catch my breath. 'Well, that's great because I want to do some recording, some different things. I definitely want to release a record.'

Ginette was refreshing in that she wasn't daunted by the prospect of saying 'enough' to the people at *EastEnders*.

I knew then that I wanted her to become my agent and told her so.

'We're going to do great things, Martine, we really, really are,' Ginette told me conspiratorially.

'Well,' I replied, 'I love everything you've said. There's nothing you've said that I don't agree with. 'That's how I like to work – no beating about the bush.' I gave her a big hug and I felt instantly close to her – and since then she's been a complete diamond.

In November of 1996, just before my ill-fated panto in Canterbury, I'd been part of an *EastEnders* line-up singing a musical medley on the BBC's Children In Need Appeal. I sang 'Wouldn't It Be Lovely?' from the musical *My Fair Lady*. Afterwards David Arnold, who was the conductor of the Royal Philharmonic Orchestra, asked me if I'd come back the following year and sing again. I agreed, of course.

At the time of the National TV Awards in October 1997 I'd forgotten all about David's offer. I'd had glandular fever, sweated and fretted my way through it as best I could, and had gone back to work. Before I knew it, however, it was Children In Need time again and a call came through from the telethon office asking if I'd still sing. This time they wanted me on my own, and they suggested I sang Barbra Streisand's 'Don't Rain On My Parade'. I thought there could scarcely be a harder song to sing, especially after my illness and with only six weeks to prepare, but sod it. I'd have a crack at it – they could always arrange it in a lower key if I couldn't make the high notes.

Singing alone on television for the first time was quite a big step for me, but I'd done it quite a lot on stage at Mum's pub in Bethnal Green. Mum used to throw music and jazz nights, jamming sessions and all that, down there at the Railway Tavern, and I used to love popping into the bar every once in a while unannounced and surprising the regulars by singing a few numbers. Mum was always getting different sorts of punter dropping by, and people would come from miles around to take part in the jamming sessions. Word of mouth brought some talented musicians in. People would say to friends: 'Have you heard about this little pub in Bethnal Green? It's really great and they're getting really good musicians down there. Did you know Martine McCutcheon's Mum runs it? The girl from *EastEnders*, that's right. Well, she gets up and sings with you sometimes.' Or something like that, I guess.

Anyway, singing solo on Children In Need was a challenge, but one I couldn't resist – and besides, I'd always loved the song (which I'd learned off by heart as a little girl long before Italia Conti). Right, I thought after accepting, I'm going to practise this over and over again, although I truly didn't think there was any way I would be able to hit the high notes.

It's a hard song to sing. You've got to be really controlled because they're difficult lyrics to get out and there's a lot of them. Simply saying the words can get your tongue twisted, let alone singing them, but I was determined to give it a shot. Luckily all my classical training came in handy. I'd had private classes outside school while I was at Italia Conti because there were at least a dozen other pupils learning there at any one time and I felt I needed more tuition in vocal techniques, needed to learn all about the diaphragm and how to use it to increase the power of your voice. I started lessons with a lady who lived near Wanstead in east London. She was a classical singer, and taught me about opera as well as giving me a real insight into singing properly – all those technical details like how to breathe correctly, something I'd first heard about from my schoolteacher Miss Smith.

It was just as well that I'd had a good grounding because

the demands of televising something as long, complicated and live as Children In Need meant that I had just one rehearsal with a piano to check the key before committing myself. That was a scary occasion, I can tell you, and took place two weeks before Children In Need hit the airwaves. I had an attack of nerves and lost my bottle just before I stepped up to the piano.

'I can't sing it in that key, I need to sing it a bit lower,' I told the accompanist.

'Well, we think you *can* sing it. Can we give it a try anyway?' replied David. I nervously agreed.

Prior to that I'd only practised singing along with Barbra on a CD, which always makes you sound better than you really are. So I sang it with the piano and was surprised to find I really got into it. All the notes came out and I gave it some welly, too.

Afterwards David and the pianist sat there like they'd witnessed a miracle. You could see it written all over their faces. 'I think we've got a little star on our hands – I'm dumbstruck,' David said. 'You've blown me away. Martine, that's fantastic and by the way, you're *not* changing the key. You will sing it in Streisand's key ... This is going to be fantastic.'

I walked away feeling excited and rather proud of myself. David was chuffed too because he'd found this talent in me that until then, no one outside of the Railway Tavern knew existed.

The afternoon of Children In Need came round very quickly – and I felt rather jittery as I travelled to the BBC Television Centre. I went to my dressing room and tried on my outfit. I'd already met a costume designer called Linda Martin a couple of times at the BBC. She'd asked me what I wanted to wear and I'd said that I wanted something flattering, comfortable, something I could breathe in as I stretched for the high notes – but something that sparkled too. Laughing, Linda reassured me. 'It's Children in Need. We'll camp it up as much as we can.' She really made me feel confident about myself. 'You've got a great figure. You're still in proportion and you're really curvy. You've got a great cleavage, Martine, and a nice little waist. I'm positive I can make you look great.'

She came up with this long, black tailored coat, with satin lapels, covered with black rhinestones, matched with black satin trousers and black high-heels. I was to have my hair up in a bun with feathers in it, very *Hello Dolly* style. I felt fantastic just thinking about it.

About an hour before I was due to go on, Ulrika Jonsson was holding the stage singing 'Making Whoopee'. I remember watching her, feeling quite relaxed, especially as I knew I wasn't on for a while. When Ulrika finished, I nipped off into make-up. I had barely sat down when one of the production team ran in. 'Martine, Martine, we've had to bring your spot forward, we're going to need you, not for the next act but the act after, so you've got about fifteen minutes. All right?'

The make-up lady looked like she was going to have a seizure because she had this fiddly hairpiece to fix on my head and hadn't even started. I don't know how the poor woman did it. She'd already put my hair up in the start of a bun and I'd done a little bit of my make-up but not much. Then Linda, who was waiting to dress me, remembered that she'd still got to stitch the hem of my jacket. She ripped it off me saying, 'I'll bring it back in two minutes,' before running off down the corridor to her room.

Suddenly I had four women frantically working on my hair, clipping this hairpiece on. The make-up lady was all of a fluster: 'I'm so sorry if it looks like a doughnut, Martine, but I've just got to try and put this on for you otherwise I've got nothing to pin the feathers to.' She put the hairpiece on while the other ladies stabbed it with feathers here, there and everywhere.

Minutes later I was standing in the wings ready to go on, minus my jacket, when I spotted Linda running towards me saying, 'Martine, Martine, you've got no heels on! I can't find the high-heels so here are your black boots . . .' They were the ones I'd worn to the BBC studio and didn't match the outfit at all, but I slipped them on anyway and didn't even have time to do them up.

I ran on to the stage to my spot and tried to calm myself down, just as a couple of feathers fell out of my hair. Was that, I wondered, a bad omen? I was panting because of all the panic backstage and had no time to prepare myself. Oh my God, I thought, clenching my hands, I'm not going to be able to sing – I'm not going to have enough breath left! I could feel my heart pounding away. I'm not going to be able to do this, my brain screamed at me. I can't remember the words. What am I going to do?

I was still standing there panicking when I heard Terry Wogan launch into my introduction: 'Doesn't she look fabulous, ladies and gentlemen? This is Martine McCutcheon, she's come a long way since Albert Square.' Then the music started up, I calmed down enough to remember my cue . . . and, well, the song just happened. It was just magical.

I came off set feeling exhilarated. I knew I'd done my best – although I can't remember much about the actual performance. Everyone in the studio seemed pleased and said I'd done well as I made my way back to wardrobe, but I wasn't prepared for the reaction that confronted me when

I stepped into the corridor outside. Linda came over to congratulate me and Ginette dropped her tough-girl façade to say my performance was 'wonderful'.

Then the producer came up to me while I was having a drink to calm myself down. He said that loads of people had phoned in to say they wouldn't pledge their money unless they showed a clip of me singing again. I was gobsmacked. 'You're joking,' I said. But he insisted that he was serious and that the switchboards had been jammed with people asking to see me sing again. I was over the moon. Shortly afterwards Terry Wogan went on television to say those magic words: 'By public demand we're going to show you Martine McCutcheon singing "Don't Rain On My Parade" again. She's signed the sheet music of this classic, beautiful song for us, which we'll auction off to the highest bidder.'

I watched myself on the repeat and thought, Good on yer girl. All right, your laces were undone and you felt like your hairpiece was going to fall off at any moment – so much so that you were frightened to move your head – but you did it!

Later, a guy called Alex who worked with David, the conductor, came over to me and said, 'We need to talk to you. We're doing a celebration of all the Oscar-winning tunes from various movies at the Royal Albert Hall next spring, and were wondering if you would come along and sing for us, do a few of those songs, you know, things like "Don't Rain On My Parade", "Cabaret" and "Secret Love".'

I didn't have to think for long. 'I'd love to. I'd absolutely love to. I'm not going to say no to an offer to sing at the Royal Albert Hall. It's my dream place to perform in, along with Madison Square Garden in New York.' And all that from singing just one song. Obviously I still had no idea how that performance was going to affect the rest of my life.

Over the next few days there were stories in the press about my performance, all saying flattering things. The phone didn't stop ringing either. Production companies rang and messages were sent from all these bigwigs to say how great I was. Not to mention the flowers – I got loads of them. I was thrilled to the core – but it made me think even more deeply about my future with *EastEnders*, and I suppose it was then that I started considering coming out of the soap for a while.

I was unbelievably nervous about performing at the Royal Albert Hall. Children in Need is Children in Need – it's OK for a soap star to sing for charity and afterwards, that's it, thank you very much, you can go back to doing your soap now. Performing at the Royal Albert Hall was something else.

I worked very hard on my voice and the songs over the next four months. I tried to build up as much strength as I could – because I wasn't just singing the one tune, I was to sing for almost an hour. To make matters worse I was still suffering from the lingering effects of glandular fever, which meant that one minute I'd be feeling fine and the next I'd wonder how I'd ever get through the next two hours. It was unpredictable, which makes the illness even more debilitating.

My heartache over splitting from Gareth had eased considerably, however, now that the split was more than a year ago and I could feel my strength building up again. Midway through my rehearsals for the Albert Hall concert I decided to hook up with Dee at a private bar just off Shaftesbury Avenue in Soho. It was early February 1998, just a week or so before the Brit Awards, Britain's 'pop Oscars'. We were having a drink at this club called Teatro, which is owned by former footballer Lee Chapman and his wife, the actress Leslie Ash. Robbie Williams' hit 'Angels', which had been number one at the beginning of the year, was playing in the background when we were joined by the photographer Terry O'Neil who had done a session or two with me in the past, and his friend the nightclub owner Johnny Gould.

I'd spoken to Johnny over the phone a few weeks earlier. I'd been working with Terry at the Café Royal in Regent Street at the time, doing some pictures for one of the glossy magazines to promote the Albert Hall concert. Terry kept gushing on about how cool this Johnny Gould was and how he was a big fan of mine, so much so that he ended up calling him on his mobile and putting me on the line. I remember Johnny had this huge, booming voice that sounded wonderfully friendly. When he invited me to drop by his club one night, I said I would but was so madly busy with *EastEnders* and the concert that I never set a date.

When we met face-to-face at Teatro, Johnny bounded over with Terry and asked me again to visit his club. His voice made him sound like a big, friendly bear. 'I would love to have you and some of your friends as my guests for dinner one night at Tramp, my treat,' he said. I had always known that many great movie stars and recording artists had been there. The place had so much history, so I was honoured and accepted.

The filming at *EastEnders* eventually quietened down and my preparations for the concert were going well enough for me to fix a night out with a couple of friends, Sheree Murphy and a friend of ours, Anthony. I can't remember where we originally planned to go, but something came up and we were told that our party had been cancelled. I had a thought: Why don't we go to Tramp? I phoned Johnny, asked him if it would be OK, and was sitting in a cab, heading to the West End, a few minutes later.

When we arrived at the club Johnny welcomed me like a long-lost daughter. 'Listen, Martine, there's somebody coming tonight who you might know, but then again you might not – you might be too young to remember him . . .' I looked at him blankly. 'His name is Jack Nicholson. He's supposed to be coming down tonight. Jack's a lovely guy . . .'

'You know Jack Nicholson?' I said incredulously. 'I can't believe it!'

'Oh, yeah. He's a great friend and a lovely, lovely fella.'

My jaw was still hanging in mid-air when Johnny nudged me discreetly and asked: 'Do you know him? Michael Douglas?'

Did I know Michael Douglas? Johnny, are you mad? Michael Douglas as in *Basic Instinct, Fatal Attraction* . . . ? I looked over and there he was, walking towards us. I thought I might need a few moments to prepare myself but, rather surprisingly, I found myself instantly put at ease by the movie star's manner. He sat down with us. 'Michael, good to see you,' said Johnny, making the necessary introductions. 'This is Martine, she's my guest for the evening. These are her friends Sheree and Anthony.' Of course Michael didn't have a clue who we were but that didn't stop him chatting to all of us. 'Martine is going to be a great actress,' Johnny continued much to my embarrassment. I made a face, reckoning that Mr Douglas must be wearied of such remarks, but Johnny was having none of it. 'No, Martine, you are a great little actress and I will tell him so.' Turning back to Michael, he went on, 'She's actually in something here at the moment, it's the biggest TV show in England.' I was mortified with embarrassment, but Michael seemed genuinely interested.

Everyone was ordering food and the club was beginning to feel quite buzzy. Michael was rabbiting away but I couldn't make out what he was saying most of the time because of the music. I heard him mention a Barbara. I seized on the moment and gushed something about how much I admired

Barbra Streisand. Michael then said they had actually been talking about that Barbra. I was truly starstruck: 'Oh my God, what's she like? She's my idol! I'm sorry, Michael, but she truly is. She's fantastic. I've based my entire career on that woman. She's funny, she can sing, she's beautiful in her own unique way, she's got staying power, she's good behind the camera as a director. She can do it all. She's fantastic . . .'

As the night wore on I became less and less shy with Michael. Indeed, I found myself talking to him as I would to any other new friend. He was a fascinating raconteur and held the entire table spellbound. That said, he still had a remarkable aura about him, a real air of intensity. I'd say even if you don't find him attractive sexually, Michael would still draw you in like a magnet. You can't stop looking at what he's doing. People were constantly coming over to our table, perhaps as many as eighty in all that evening, just to say hello to him. And Michael, dressed all in black, was charm and patience personified with each of them. It was impressive: this then is how a *real* star behaves. Wow, I thought to myself. Some of these big stars, superstars, come across as more humble than a lot of people who aren't half as big.

Lost momentarily in my own thoughts, my ears took a second to catch up with Michael and Johnny's conversation again. When I did tune in, I realised the two men were chatting about Jewish people. 'Oh well,' I piped up. 'You know what the Jewish are like? They can be quite tight, can't they?'

Both men turned to look at me and then burst out laughing. Of course I'd never realised – I can't believe I'm such an idiot – that Michael Douglas is Jewish, as is Johnny Gould. Anthony, who's very dramatic and expressive (another performer – how did you guess?), looked like he was going to explode with laughter.

I still hadn't twigged as to what I'd said, but I knew I'd done something majorly stupid. Then the penny dropped. I could feel my cheeks flush as I realised. 'Do you like musicals?' I asked Michael in a flustered bid to divert attention from my gaffe. He said he loved them and began citing his favourites such as *Seven Brides for Seven Brothers* and *Calamity Jane*. Well, the next thing, we're all up on our chairs singing 'Whip crack away, whip crack away, whip crack away'. Everybody was drinking and getting tipsy apart from me – I was determined to remain sober – not that I needed anything to enhance that evening. Who would?

We were all up, either on chairs or in Michael's case simply standing, singing away and laughing at the lunacy of it all. Johnny, beaming with pride – I said he treated me like a daughter – turned to Michael and said, 'You see, she *sings*.'

Michael fixed me with a stare and replied that this was obvious. 'Martine, you must keep singing as you've got a beautiful voice, it's really lovely . . .'

Johnny interrupted: 'She's going to be doing a concert at the Royal Albert Hall . . .'

Now it was Michael's turn to cut in. 'Really? You know what, I'll try and get back for it. If you're going to be singing these kind of numbers I'd love to come. I'm not lying to you. If I'm free, I'd love to come and see you . . .'

Suddenly all conversation was cut off as the DJ took off whatever clubby drum and bass tune he was playing and swapped it for some Frank Sinatra. 'Come on,' Johnny shouted. 'Let's all go and dance!'

We didn't need asking twice and all but ran to the dance floor. Michael even picked me up and swung me round to 'For Once In My Life I Have Someone Who Needs Me'. He was swirling me out and swirling me in, passing me to Johnny who would then pass me back after a couple of twirls.

I felt like the Belle of the Ball. What's more I could sense everyone else in the club looking at Michael and me, saying: 'Oh my God, Tiffany's dancing with Michael Douglas!'

At one point Michael spun me around so hard my hair burst out of its bun – I only had one pin holding it in place – sending my dark hair tumbling down my shoulders. Michael loved that.

I knew he was enjoying himself but he struck me as a very intelligent and serious man beneath the swinger. He's known for his interest in politics and even met British Government ministers in the spring of 2000 – but with me he was relaxed charm personified.

Then my friends got a bit too tipsy for everyone's good. They weren't badly behaved, just a little messy and loud. I realised it was time to go and thanked Johnny and Michael for a lovely evening.

'It's been great meeting you, Martine,' said Michael. 'I'm in London for a while, and if you're doing anything, let me know.' I nodded. 'If you need to get in touch with me,' he continued, 'call Johnny – and if I need to get in touch with you, I'll do the same.'

The phone rang late the next day – it was Johnny. 'Listen, Martine, my wife and I are going out to dinner with Michael. He said you were such fun yesterday, he would love you to come out again tonight. Can you?'

I mumbled something about not being sure if I could be as amusing again but Johnny was adamant. Immensely flattered but trying to keep my cool, I said I'd love to join them.

My next thought was a typically girlie one: I've got nothing to wear! I hadn't had time to get any dry cleaning done and nothing in my wardrobe seemed right. Even though there was no frisson of potential romance between us – and that's the truth – you still want someone like Michael

Douglas to think you're beautiful. I had a little short French fringe at the time with the rest of my hair hanging straight down. I eventually found a little Ben de Lisi black dress with a sash at the back of the wardrobe. I decided to go for a French look. I put on black sheer tights and black high heels. I threw a purple coat over the top of that and grabbed a tiny antique silk bag. I thought I'd sort of play it safe . . .

Johnny had booked a table at the Bluebird in the King's Road, Chelsea, a gorgeous modern restaurant owned by Sir Terence Conran. We all sat down and the evening began, quite soberly, with a discussion about politics, American politics, about which I knew very little. As far as politics in this country is concerned, I have quite simplistic views. I know what I think is right and I know what I think is wrong. Michael was mentioning all these American politicians who, with the exception of the President, I'd never heard of, but he was obviously into it in a big way. Then the conversation drifted on to his career. I never realised how many strings this man had to his bow. He'd produced *One Flew Over the Cuckoo's Nest* with Jack Nicholson, based on the bestseller by Ken Kesey, and told me about his early days as an actor in the American TV series *The Streets of San Francisco*. Perhaps sensing my awe, Michael turned to me at one point and said: 'Don't knock the TV stuff, I did loads of TV for a long, long time, and I still went into movies. You can do it if you don't doubt for a second you're capable.'

He struck me as being both a realist and an optimist, an unusual combination. Not once did he talk down to me, and I wanted the night to go on and on like that for ever. I asked him if he fancied going to the Met Bar. He agreed, though he had no idea what the Met Bar – *the* celebrity drinking haunt in London at the time – was. Johnny and his wife declined to join us but agreed to drop Michael and me off.

It was the start of February and London was freezing. The Brit Awards were being staged that evening and when we got to the bar it was crammed with pop stars and record company people. Once seated in a booth at the back Michael began chatting about his son, telling me we were about the same age – I was twenty-one at the time and Michael was fifty-three. 'You know what's more, you're a very beautiful and talented girl. I think you've got something special about you. If you ever come to New York and you ever need any help, please, just let me know.'

Of course I replied that I would, even though I'd never dream of doing such a thing. I mean I could never phone someone like him. I just couldn't! I'd feel like an idiot. Yes, we got on great but I'd never want anyone to feel like I was getting in touch simply because I wanted a leg up the next step on the ladder. We had a few drinks in the booth before deciding to call it a night, leaving Jay Kay from Jamiroquai – who was later to go out with my friend Denise Van Outen – to dance in the middle of the bar on his own. And who could blame him. I remember the music being wonderful that night, and feeling resentful that I had an early start.

As we rose, one of the bar's staff warned us that there were a lot of press photographers outside because of the Brits. That panicked me slightly as I didn't want to be photographed with Michael – as people, I thought, would then look on me as Michael Douglas's bit of fluff for the evening while he was in London. I'm a bit old-fashioned like that and don't want to be seen on loads of different arms. I felt embarrassed for Michael, too, as I'm sure he didn't want our night to be turned into a big 'affair' by the papers. 'Listen, why don't you walk ahead of me,' I whispered. 'I'll be fine . . .'

But Michael would not hear of it. 'No, no, no! You go first. We'll make sure that you get in the car first.' He was completely calm. 'They're going to take the pictures, it's no problem. We know what's happening so it doesn't matter what anyone else says.' As we walked out to the car Michael kept cracking silly little jokes about what the press would say about us, which made me laugh. In the end, I walked ahead of him. He was just taking it all in his stride.

A couple of weeks later, Johnny phoned me. He'd had a call from Michael who was stuck somewhere in Europe on a promotional tour. The sad but courteous news was that his schedule did not permit him to make the Albert Hall concert but that his warmest wishes were with me.

That wasn't the last I heard of Michael Douglas. Although we have never clapped eyes on each other again, our paths were destined to cross a few years later . . .

The challenge of singing at the Albert Hall gave me a massive buzz, something to shore me up as I became increasingly unfulfilled at *EastEnders*. Tiffany was a great character, for sure, but the scriptwriters knew that too, and I got the feeling they were bleeding Tiff dry as far as credible new stories went. I knew that there was going to come a point where I would have to stop, otherwise it would be unfair on myself and the public. It was bound to get boring eventually.

In the last few weeks before the concert I made sure I didn't take any time off from *EastEnders* after my lengthy absence the previous year. The executives on the soap responded reasonably, too. They finished filming early on the night of the concert, so that those who wanted could come and see the show. I'd been busy getting friends to ring round all the major record companies pretending to be my personal assistants, asking them to send their A&R people – that's artist and repertoire to the rest of us, the people who check out new talent – down to the concert. On top of that, I'd formed a temporary business relationship with a guy called

John Toon who was keen to get into music management. He had previously worked for the Spice Girls' legal team but had seen the get-rich-quick possibilities of music management and wanted a slice of the action. The trouble was he wanted too much from me in terms of his percentage. Even so, I send him a smile because he was instrumental in helping me secure a good record deal. Good being the operative word.

The night itself went very well. I performed 'Cabaret', 'Secret Love', the Little Mermaid song from the Disney film, and I finished off with 'Don't Rain On My Parade'. The TV presenter Darren Day did the other numbers. The concert, billed as a Tribute to the Oscars, went down a storm and I was chuffed to bits to see I had been singled out for rave reviews. Even more importantly, it transpired that all the major record companies had indeed sent people down to watch me. Simon Cowell, a consultant to the BMG record group, and the mastermind behind Five, was very enthusiastic. He had enjoyed huge success turning Robson Green and Jerome Flynn – two actors who stole the show in the ITV drama *Soldier Soldier* – into reluctant pop stars a few years earlier.

The other record company man to show a lot of interest was the fair-haired, public-school figure of Hugh Goldsmith, head of Innocent Records which was part of the Virgin group, and the man who turned a fourteen-year-old model by the name of Billie Piper into a major pop star. Both labels wanted to talk to me about my music and were keen to offer me a deal.

I think the gushing hyperbole of the newspaper reviews must have caused a bit of rumpus at *EastEnders*, because I got the feeling when I went back to work that the executives were beginning to realise that Martine McCutcheon wouldn't be around for ever. Ginette spoke to the BBC anyway and dropped a few hints that I might well be thinking about leaving. She wasn't stirring anything up, either, because the arrival of two new executives with responsibility for *EastEnders* the year before had pretty much convinced me it was time to go anyway.

When Mal Young and Matthew Robinson arrived at the BBC there was a lot of change. Some of it I agreed with, some of it I did not feel was necessary. Storylines did not seem to be high on the agenda. Drastic ones were to come later. The new producers seemed very interested in erecting a 24-hour web camera to give the public a better idea of what we were all up to at Elstree. I cannot speak for the rest of the cast, but I can say that towards the last few months of my time at *EastEnders*, I felt that there was a sense of despondency and low morale. We all felt trapped and under constant scrutiny by the producers and the web camera, which watched us during rehearsals on set, going through our lines, and even while we had on-set make-up. This was obviously great for the fans, but how would you feel if your every waking moment was beamed on to millions of computer monitors twenty-four hours a day, seven days a week? I think most of us felt our lives were virtually public property anyway. It's not just about the invasion of our privacy. It's also that we are actors doing a job, and we want the public to see us at our very best – not while we are rehearsing.

Once dramatic storylines were introduced, filming schedules became more intense. Punishments were drawn up to guard against any perceived lapse by the cast. People were being fined, for heaven's sake, if they arrived late. These were changes, I thought, that didn't need to be made. The two new execs came and wanted to make their mark, as anyone given the responsibility of that job would want to do. But I found it hard to adapt to the new regime, so God knows how people who'd been there for ten years must have felt.

Suddenly there was an end to money-spinning pantos and personal appearances. Not that they happened often, as the tight schedule was getting harder and harder as time went by. Pantos and PAs were regarded by some of the actors at *EastEnders* as a legitimate way of topping up modest wages. Robinson and Young banned us from doing that, a move which made some of us feel hard done by. You were expected to put up with people shouting at you in the street but banned from doing anything – from helping out a friend by opening a new shop, to earning a good fee just to do a PA at a club. It also felt like double standards on the part of the BBC as they were planning to exploit *EastEnders* through a new internet site without paying the very people who made the website a public draw – the actors – any extra money.

Even more irksome for me was that Ginette had discovered I wasn't even being paid what the other lead characters in the show were earning. Ginette told me: 'Martine, you're working all the hours that God sends. You, Ross, Patsy, Steve, Gilly and Sid are carrying the show at the moment but you, Martine, are earning a lot less than they are. You're big in this show and you should be earning the same money.' The BBC, of course, didn't want to know.

All of which meant Simon Cowell's and Hugh Goldsmith's overtures were that bit more appealing. Simon was a great guy and I felt I had a real rapport with him. It was obvious that he knew how to make money quickly for his artists but, as far as my music was concerned, a quick buck wasn't the issue. I wanted to have a long-term career in music and avoid anything that would be damaging for me in the long run.

Robson and Jerome never wanted to be serious singers, or

have a long-term career in music, but were more than happy about the millions their cover versions of classic pop tunes made for them. I wanted to be happy with both aspects of the job, the music and the money. Simon understood what I meant but it was Hugh who seemed to embrace my views whole-heartedly. He wanted me to write songs, he wanted me to develop my talent, he wanted me to go to America, he wanted me to do all of the big stuff and was happy for me to take my time. It was just a different approach. Either man would have been great, but Hugh was the one I felt more affinity with. The added attraction of his proposal came in the form of his A&R expert, a lady called Cheryl Robson.

I can remember her playing me 'Perfect Moment', the song that became my first number-one single, at one early meeting. Cheryl, who has a marvellously throaty voice, just said, 'This is your song!' She's a very talented woman with a knack for matching a great song with the right artist.

At that time 'Perfect Moment' was a very raw, Annie Lennox-type ballad and completely different to how it ended up but I liked it immediately, even though I knew it needed a few McCutcheon touches. I told her straight: 'It's great, but I want it to have a more magical feel to it, Cheryl, because it's the ultimate wedding song, isn't it? I want plenty of strings, I want it to have a big, classical feel but still remain contemporary.' She understood completely and later put me in touch with a producer called Tony Moran, who worked with superstars such as Celine Dion and Gloria Estefan, and who I still work with. He got 'Perfect Moment' spot on.

As talks went on, it became clear that the music business was prepared to throw a lot of money in my direction. I earned a fair whack from *EastEnders* but the amounts being talked by Hugh and Simon were big enough to finally convince me that I didn't have to stay there to pay my mortgage – or more accurately the rent on the little two-bedroom flat over looking the Thames in Chelsea that I'd taken on a few months earlier after selling Westbourne Terrace, a decision I regret to this day.

I thought it all over and decided that Virgin's Innocent label was the one for me. Hugh instructed his lawyers to start drawing up contracts which meant that it was time for Ginette and me to talk to the BBC. But first I decided to take a short holiday and booked a flight to Hawaii for a break in paradise.

But the fates, tragically, had other things planned for me. A few days after I arrived I got a call from Mum in the middle of the night. She was absolutely panic-stricken and kept telling me not to worry, without actually telling me what she didn't want me to worry about.

'It's your Dad, John, he's had a terrible, terrible accident and they don't know if he is going to live,' she said eventually, her voice full of tears. She went on to explain how he was working, as usual, cleaning windows when the harness supporting his platform, which was some thirty feet in the air, gave way. He fell straight to the ground breaking bones in his back, feet and ankles.

The call was a double blow because relations between me and John were very poor at the time. Mum and he had gone their separate ways, but he simply couldn't forget about her. Every time he spoke to me it was never, 'How are you doing, Mart?' but a rant about Mum. Heaven knows how he would have acted if he had known she was seeing Alan Tomlin regularly. Anyway it had got to the point where I said I simply wouldn't speak to John if he carried on like that and we had all but stopped speaking to each other by the time of his accident.

That made my grief at Mum's news even worse. I felt

incredibly guilty and decided to rush back to Britain on the first plane out of Hawaii to give him a cuddle. And that's just what I did. What a flight! I had eighteen hours by myself, worrying like mad about Dad and sobbing non-stop. I got back home where my friend Jonathan Barnham was waiting for me, had a quick change and dashed off to hospital.

Things weren't that much better when I got there. The doctors wouldn't allow me to see John until he was half-conscious. He was still in intensive care when I got to the hospital and I had to wait for hours until I was finally let into the ward. Dad could hardly move at all. He didn't know if he was ever going to be able to walk again and was very distressed. I looked at him, this simple man with his black and white views, with tears streaming down my face and thought, 'Christ, I love you so much! No one deserves this to happen to them.' I gave him a silly Elvis shirt I had bought on my holiday – he was a huge fan of the King – and listened as he told me what little he could remember of the accident.

Then he started up about Mum again – but instead of slagging her off to me he dropped the bombshell that he, too, had met someone else, a lady called Helen. 'Your little brother's obviously got no idea,' he said. 'And I've only been out on a couple of dates with her so I've not said anything to your Mum, but Helen's been really sweet to me . . .' His voice started to go all wobbly. 'But, Martine, I don't know if she's going to want me like this, you know . . .' His voice trailed off. I tried to fight back the tears by smiling and joking to him but it was incredibly hard.

I only saw him in hospital three or four times after that but stayed in constant touch by phone. There were lots of reasons for that. One of my best friends, Natalie Cooke, who had been in a very nasty accident when she was younger, was now having recurring problems in her legs and had to have a major operation. I was worried sick about her and went to visit her twice. But with the schedule at *EastEnders* and with Dad in hospital, too, I honestly did not feel I could bear any more hospital visits. Lots of people hate hospitals and I'm one of them. There was another reason, too. I was also worried that I might bump into other members of John's family at his bedside, and they had taken a dim view of Mum's decision to leave him. The last thing Dad needed was a row blowing up around him. However, the most overwhelming reason for me keeping my distance was that seeing John in plaster casts up to his eyeballs just broke my heart.

There was more heartbreak lying round the corner, too, at Albert Square.

CHAPTER 16

You're Dead!

I'D BEEN IN *EastEnders* for three-and-a-half years at the time of Dad's accident. Leaving the general unhappiness among the cast at Elstree to one side, I felt increasingly that Tiffany's storylines were starting to feel tired. I was no longer enjoying being strangled by Ross Kemp every other episode!

I didn't want to admit it to the other people there as the general view was that the plotlines had been working well. Everyone from make-up artists to the other members of the cast, who are normally very wrapped up in their own storylines, were regularly doling out praise to me and Ross. However, the variety needed to keep Tiff fresh wasn't there any more. A lot of different angles had been exploited over the years, so it wasn't that surprising towards the end to find we were running out of options. I mean, Tiff had had Grant's baby, married him, contended with his family – which was almost a full-time job in itself – and had more rows with Grant than she'd pulled pints. It made for good television, but what on earth could Tiff do next?

Initially, I reasoned to myself that I didn't want to leave the show for ever, I just wanted to go and do what all the other old timers had done when they needed to refresh themselves artistically, which was to have a break and try something different for a while. They say a change is as good as a rest, and that was all I wanted then. Loads of the cast had done it before, everyone from Michelle Collins to Mike Reid, and that's what Ginette told them at the BBC. The next thing I knew, I was being summoned to a meeting with Matthew Robinson.

Matthew had not been at *EastEnders* long, perhaps a year, but he had already made quite an impact with his new rules and punishments. His office was a tiny old-fashioned dressing room which had once served as a sort of chill-out area for the cast, or as a quiet room for informal meetings, actors discussing their storylines and so forth. Matthew commandeered it for himself almost as soon as he arrived because it meant he could remain close to where all the action was taking place. He was a very hands-on person who liked to know what everybody was up to. He used the dressing-room table complete with its mirror surrounded by lights as his desk.

I went in during a gap in filming and sat down. 'Ah, Martine,' he said. 'You know your agent has spoken to me about various things that have been happening to you? Well, she's raised the issues of how long you want to stay here at *EastEnders* and what you want to do, and I just wanted to find out from you first-hand how you felt about everything.'

'Well, Matthew,' I began, 'you know I've always sung and have always enjoyed music; my concert at the Royal Albert Hall went brilliantly and led to a few interesting offers. I'd like to have a go at my music, to develop it a little, and so the truth is I'd really love to leave for a few months, do something different, come back and hopefully we can all see things for Tiffany in a fresher way, as I'm beginning to feel everything's repeating itself a little bit. I think a break could do us all good.' I thought this was a perfectly fair response.

The meeting was businesslike and at the end Matthew said he would see what he could do. Excellent, I thought, and got up to go, pausing just before I reached the door to bring up the subject of money and the fact that I was earning a lot less than the other leads. I wasn't sure if Ginette had mentioned my salary to Matthew. But seeing as I was there with him, I didn't think it would hurt.

Again, he gave little away. 'We'll see' was the best I managed to get from him. I'm not being mean to Matthew because of what happened a short while later. He was just one of those people I couldn't warm to, no matter how much I tried. Perhaps he had a problem with women with strong personalities, I don't know, but I do know I wasn't the only one who wasn't his number one fan.

Matthew was the architect of many changes at *EastEnders*: the arrival of the di Marco family along with Melanie, alias Tamsin Outhwaite, led on to one of *EastEnders'* most powerful storylines – the murder of Saskia by Steve Owen, once better known as Spandau Ballet's Martin Kemp. Lots of the cast that I worked with have decided to leave, including Lindsey Coulson who played Carol Jackson. Her screen husband Alan, played by my friend Howard Antony, had long gone by then and so had Sid Owen. Luckily most of them, such as Patsy Palmer and Sid, can return as they are not dead – unlike me!

A week later I was still waiting to hear back from Matthew, hoping that everything would be sorted out and looking forward to a break and a change. Meanwhile I just decided to get on with *EastEnders* until I heard from him, and was quite enjoying the late summer sun. I was driving to work one morning listening to a tape and enjoying the fine weather when the cassette came to an end and the stereo switched automatically to the radio. I was quite near Elstree when the familiar voice of Heart Radio's breakfast-show host Jono Coleman came through the speakers.

'We cannot put up with it,' he roared in his familiar Aussie accent. 'We've got to have a march, a demonstration! We've got to all march up to Elstree – that'll sort it out . . .' My ears pricked up as I wondered what one of our lot had done now. I turned the radio up a bit to make sure I didn't miss any juicy gossip.

'I'm sorry,' Jono continued, sounding surprisingly serious. 'If you've just tuned in and are wondering what we're all talking about, take a look at the front page of the papers today. Tiffany Mitchell, the best barmaid the Queen Vic has ever had, is going to be killed off! We cannot stand for this. The BBC must not be allowed to do this . . .'

I was stunned. I quickly pulled over on to the hard shoulder and sat there listening incredulously to the rest of the broadcast. At the same time all these voices were racing around my head, screaming: No, no, no! This cannot be happening. This is wrong! Calm down! Something's gone horribly wrong, Martine . . .

I picked up my mobile and started dialling every Elstree extension I could think of, but everybody I tried was out. I couldn't get hold of anyone. I tried Mum. She hadn't seen the papers or heard the news on the radio either. I didn't have a clue what was going on – but I had a suspicion, just a suspicion at that stage, that a very big decision had been made for me. I restarted the car and carried on to the studios while my Mum got on the blower to Ginette, who was outraged and disgusted to the point of exploding.

She had spent the previous two days calling various BBC executives to find out what decision they had reached with regard to me having a break. Not one of her calls had been returned.

Once at the studios I was surprised to discover there wasn't a single *EastEnders* executive to be found. Matthew wasn't in his new office on the ground floor and his boss, Mal Young, couldn't be traced either. Nobody, but nobody, could tell me what was going on. The other actors certainly didn't know. Ross was totally bemused by the news, but was a support for the rest of the day. It also wasn't fair on him – we had become such a big part of each other's screen lives, that anything that affected me, affected him. Barbara, supportive as ever, gave me a cuddle, and asked me what I'd been told by the powers that be. 'Nothing,' I explained, 'only what I heard on the radio this morning.'

'It's disgusting,' Barbara rasped. 'This has to be put right. Nobody should be treated in this way. You've worked here all these years, you give them everything you've got because you want it to work, and then they turn round and do this to you. There are lots of ways of doing business but it should never be done like this.' Barbara was not messing, either, she meant what she said.

My eyes welled up as I listened to her, but I was determined not to cry especially as I had about twenty-two scenes to film that day. I couldn't understand why I'd been treated so harshly, why no one had bothered to even mention my character was to be killed off. I'd always been polite, gracious, worked hard, always been on time. I'd never had any drug or drink problems or brought scandal to the show. The worst thing I'd done was to work so hard my health had suffered. Other than physically being too ill to make it in, I'd been there all the time and had done one stretch of two years without a holiday, partly because I had covered for some of the cast's absences. What reason did the BBC have for telling the whole country before *me* that life as I knew it was going to end?

As I said earlier, Matthew and I had never got on famously, but I knew he had a challenge ahead of him and that he wanted to prove himself. Whatever it took, he felt he should do it, obviously with Mal's approval, as Mal was the boss of bosses.

It took another two days of uncertainty before I finally got to see him. 'I'm very sorry about what's happened in the last couple of days, Martine,' he began but I cut him off straight away: 'Where were you, Matthew? Where have you been?' I demanded. He made a couple of pathetic excuses which only confirmed my suspicion that he had been avoiding me and busying himself at BBC TV centre in West London instead. I felt I was being fobbed off and decided not to pull my punches. 'Wherever you were, Matthew, somebody should've been here to explain what was going on. I went home the day that story broke and there were twelve paparazzi and a group of journalists outside my front door asking me how I felt about Tiff being killed off. I couldn't say how I felt because I didn't know whether it was true or not. It's nothing short of disgusting to put me in that kind of a position. I'm not saying we've ever got on great, Matthew, but I've always done my job, I've always been polite to you and everyone else, so how come I'm the last person in the country to discover a character I've been so close to for so long was to die? Is this true, Matthew? Is what I'm hearing true?'

Matthew just smiled nervously at me. 'Well, I wouldn't say it was *definitely* true, Martine, I wouldn't say that we've got any *concrete* plans at the moment. It was just an idea that we had. Someone must have got hold of the idea and leaked it to the press.'

He must have thought I'd been born yesterday. 'Oh, really, Matthew, and just how did that idea get to the press? By itself? Matthew, I'm asking you how it got out. I've had to pay a price for that little leak, which makes me look totally stupid. I don't know what's going on and whatever happens, whatever you're plotting, you shouldn't make the people you're supposed to be looking after appear like that . . . .'.

Matthew looked quite freaked out as I tore into him. 'You seem a bit, er, upset,' he stammered.

'Of course I'm upset,' I said, my voice rising with my anger. 'I'm outraged! I'm disgusted! This has absolutely shattered my illusions of everything here at *EastEnders*. You've only been here a short while, Matthew, but all the good that the other people have done to me over the years has been just swept out of the window by your thoughtlessness.'

I was making my views pretty clear judging by how red Matthew's face had become, but he refused to acknowledge anything I was saying. Instead, he said things about there being several different storylines on the go at any one moment, and that this was only one of a number of options . . .

'Yes,' I said, 'but that should never have even been written or discussed without someone – you – letting me know. Only a couple of weeks ago I told you that I just wanted some time off – so what's this all about? Is anything different going to happen with the storyline if I stay? Would I get more money?'

Matthew shook his head. 'We don't know, Martine,' he replied. 'We've got lots of changes planned and we've got more new families coming in. The honest truth is that we're not quite sure what's going to happen to Tiff.' A penny dropped. I asked him if he was saying that unless I put up with the same money, with the same sort of storylines, then Tiff would be killed off.

'Yes,' he replied. 'Well, it's a possibility.'

'Fine,' I spat back. 'To be honest with you I don't want to be sitting around here letting you work me to the bone, making me too terrified to leave early in case I get killed off as some sort of punishment. I'm not going to have that hanging over my head, not for anyone, not for anything. I'm very grateful for what I've had so far at *EastEnders* but I'm not at all grateful for the way you've treated me.'

He carried on mumbling blandly about it only being one story option. 'Well you go and discuss your options with someone else because I've got my own options to think about now,' I said and stormed out.

Looking back now it shocks me how I behaved. I had never had a cross word with any of my bosses before, and did not realise just how much it would upset me until I sat there and actually heard him say those words. Matthew had got a bit of a raw deal from my behaviour and my outburst, but then so did I. Seeing Matthew had given me the opportunity to focus my anger. As I left work that day I was still upset, sure, but I was also feeling surprisingly resilient. Sod you all, I thought. I'm going to go on and conquer the universe, you just watch me! I felt almost sorry for the people I would be leaving behind, people who had been with *EastEnders* since day one and were now facing a hell of a lot of changes. I didn't envy them at all. But maybe they would have dealt with it better than I would.

Killing Tiffany was part of a new drive to increase the ratings for the soap. Matthew had started to dine out with the media. Obviously killing a character like Tiffany, who was just about a national institution by then, was guaranteed to grab the headlines and help push up the viewing figures.

Maybe Matthew thought that he would get the support of the press after having meetings and dining out with them, getting the cast to do extra photo shoots and interviews, and giving different tabloids exclusives on what future storylines would be. But there was a backlash – when most of the tabloids decided to do their own thing and were organising campaigns to save Tiffany.

Matthew maintained a public front that no decision had been made to kill Tiffany off – it was just one of a number of possibilities. That was something he had over my head for some time, but few believed him. I was lucky in that I had already made my decision to go, regardless of whether they killed Tiffany or not. I was not going to worry myself too much about the politics at *EastEnders*. I was going to sign my Virgin record deal and make it a wonderful success.

About two weeks after that meeting with Matthew I finally found out what was really going to happen to Tiff. I was invited to the BBC Drama offices in White City with Ginette for a meeting with Mal and Matthew. We were made to wait for fifteen minutes in reception before being shown into Mal's large office. A nice touch, that. Matthew arrived after us with this over-enthusiastic grin spread all over his face. I gave Ginette a look which said: just look at his face and you'll know *exactly* what Tiffany's fate is going to be. It wasn't that I identified so personally with Tiffany that her death would somehow also be mine, but I had got under the skin of her character, portrayed her thoughtfully, and in some sense she was as much my creation as that of the writers. I don't think it was strange that I felt protective about the character as well as my own, separate, professional position.

We sat down and were obliged first to watch some clips from a couple of new dramas Mal was shooting, including *The Scarlet Pimpernel* with Richard E Grant. Ginette and I kept exchanging glances, wondering why on earth we had to watch all this stuff. Didn't we have important business to discuss?

Eventually Mal got the ball rolling: 'We've decided what we're going to do and, Matthew, would you like to explain what we're planning as far as the character of Tiff is concerned?' It turned out to be a slow and laborious lecture with Matthew refusing to give away the bottom line – the bit where we would find out whether Tiff lived or died – until the last minute. It was like slow torture.

'Grant, as we know at the moment,' he said, 'is struggling not to flirt with Tiff's mother. He loves Tiff, he loves Courtney, but you know he's got this self-destructive personality that wants to go and muck everything up all the time. Tiffany meanwhile is feeling quite happy: she knows things aren't great but Beppe is still completely in love with her. That all comes to a head when she and Grant go through a particularly tough time. They end up separating and Tiff responds by going out on a date with Beppe. On the same night Grant ends up in a clinch with your mother and they have lustful, passionate, intimate time. The difference is that when Tiff goes home with Beppe you decide that you cannot go through with it, that you're still in love with Grant, despite all the battles, despite everything that's gone on. Tiff wants to keep him even if she has to fight for him for the rest of her life. She goes back to Grant feeling full of guilt, full of guilt . . .'

All this time Mal just sat there, listening and nodding occasionally with this smile on his face, making comments like 'Great mate . . . carry on' while Ginette, stony faced, kept flashing looks at me, her mouth becoming more pinched by the second as she resisted the urge to leap up and throttle the pair of them. Matthew just carried on regardless. 'Grant does end up going to bed with Louise, doesn't really know how he feels about it, but does appear to be regretting his actions a little later. It occurs to him that only by sleeping with your mother does he finally realise that he is truly in love with you.

'Outside it's raining very heavily. Tiff goes back to the pub, tells Grant that she loves him and hugs him warmly. For his part Grant is full of remorse. He finally accepts he's in love with Tiff but also recognises he's done a dreadful thing to her so he starts making it up to Tiff like you wouldn't believe. He buys her a beautiful black sequin dress and they go out for dinner. Tiff can't believe that Grant's looking at her with so much love in his eyes. He tells her that he loves the way she is with the baby, he tells her that he loves the way she is with just about everything. He even says he loves the way she sings . . .' I was going to say something at that point, but thought better of it.

Matthew continued. 'That night Peggy has been looking after the baby who is asleep upstairs. The baby monitor is downstairs in the pub. Tiff goes back to the Vic and finds everybody's having a New Year's Eve party, there are people doing the conga. Tiff feels so happy, thinking about Grant and Courtney and all the people enjoying themselves in the pub. Tiff is thrilled to her core and for the first time in her life she starts to feel complete.

'Tiff picks up the baby monitor and tells Peggy that she's popping upstairs to check on the baby. She doesn't know that Grant has nipped upstairs to do just that. Tiff is standing at the bottom of the stairs, taking her coat off, and she hears voices over the baby monitor. She stands listening to it and hears Louise talking to Grant about their night of passion. "You've never loved Tiffany," Tiff hears her Mum say. "You've never loved anyone but yourself otherwise you wouldn't have done it to her, Grant. You're the one that

wanted it, you're the one that kept persisting." Then Tiff
hears Grant's voice. "I don't want you around here any more,
Louise, I don't even want you to look after the baby tonight.
I love Tiffany, I want to make it work with Tiffany . . ." By
this point Tiffany's not listening any more, she's crying her
eyes out. She drops the monitor on the floor and rushes
upstairs – not for a confrontation but to make out that
everything's fine. She's heartbroken but this is war. She starts
to panic. She needs to get her clothes together and she needs
someone, Beppe, to help her. She has decided to get away
from Grant, to get away from everything. She knows Beppe
loves her and will help her pack and make her escape.

'Tiff decides to confront her mother with what she heard
over the baby monitor; she also tells Bianca that she's
planning to leave, taking the baby with her. The plot spirals
and spirals onwards until it all comes to massive head when
Grant catches Tiffany getting the last of her bits and pieces
together. I think we'll have her struggling to put the boots on
Courtney, I'm not sure, then she picks up Courtney, turns
and finds Grant waiting for her. "You're not going
anywhere," he argues but Tiff is having none of it. "I'm not
having you do this to me any more, Grant . . ."

'He snatches Courtney out of her arms, runs down the
stairs. She follows, chasing him through the crowded pub
where everyone's singing and the chimes are heralding in the
New Year. Above the racket you can just about hear Tiffany
scream: "Peggy, someone, someone help me! He's taking my
baby, someone stop him, please . . ." But all the locals are too
merry to hear her cries. Tiff runs outside where a film of light
snow has landed in the Square, still chasing Grant and her
baby but it's very icy on the street. Meanwhile Frank Butcher
(Mike Reid) is driving over to the Vic. He's only a matter of
yards from the pub when Tiff darts out in front of his car and

he knocks her to the ground. She lies motionless in the street with blood pouring from the back of her heard into the gutter . . .'

Matthew stopped talking, looked at Mal and then the pair of them looked at me, awaiting my response. 'Right, that's fine,' I said calmly. 'It sounds like a great storyline.' I was determined not to give the two producers what they wanted – shock and dismay. Ginette must have read my mind because she was also very calm. 'Yes, that's good, almost what we expected but we didn't realise quite what a wonderful build-up there would be. It'll be great for Martine's exit, absolutely fantastic, and it ties in with everything we wanted.'

Matthew looked more than a little disappointed. Mal sat there and simply stared at me for a while as if to ask 'What sort of creature are you?'

'It's going to be fantastic for me to play,' I piped up. 'I want people to miss me – and you guys are certainly doing your best to help me achieve that, so thanks very much. Is there anything else you need to discuss?' They shook their heads. Talk about wind being taken out of sails . . .

Mal asked me one more time, 'Are you *sure* you're happy with it?'

'Of course,' I lied. 'I'm over the moon. I think it's going to be a fantastic exit. What more could an actress possibly want?'

Of course in my heart it hurt dreadfully. The graphic detail, the blow-by-blow description of the storyline, the lack of warning – but I didn't let any of that show. I didn't even let them see me swallowing hard as I listened to Robinson rabbit away about Tiff's demise. Instead I smiled at them throughout. Ginette brought the meeting to an end by getting up and shaking hands with the pair of them. I did likewise even though I wanted to punch their heads in! I smiled and was very courteous as I said my goodbyes.

I think the men from the BBC found the whole experience a bit of an anticlimax. I think they were expecting me to be upset. That's the way it was and, as unbelievable as you may think, that's exactly how it happened. They say it takes all sorts to make the world go round, well, those two were definitely two 'all sorts'.

As we left the BBC Ginette said, rather proudly, 'I think you showed 'em girl. You came across as a lady with complete faith in yourself and if they're disappointed with that then that's their problem.' I agreed with her, weary but proud of myself and still attempting to maintain my dignity. I'd done all my crying weeks earlier when I'd first heard about Tiff's death on the radio. That evening after the meeting I didn't shed any more tears, but I did feel a bit subdued. I put on as brave a face as I could, and met up with Jonathan. In my mind *EastEnders* was already over. It was soon going to be time to establish Martine McCutcheon in her own right.

While all this was going on my contract with Virgin's Innocent label was being drafted. Taking the sound advice I had received from friends like Mick Hucknall and the Goss twins, a good team of lawyers got to work, ploughing through every detail. It was a slow process as I wanted everything to be perfect, but it was worth it as the last thing I needed was to be as quickly forgotten by my new paymasters as Milan had been. I was completely anal about the detail in the contract. I wanted to make sure I had artistic control. I didn't want my solo singing career to go the same way as the group experience.

By the time the deal was ready to sign I had all but finished shooting at Elstree. I signed my record contract at Virgin's head office in Kensal Rise, north-west London. Paul Conway, Virgin's head honcho was there, along with Hugh

Goldsmith and my Mum. Despite all the months it had taken to draw up the contract, the deal was signed in a second. Afterwards I threw a celebration party at the Atlantic, a spectacular-looking bar in the heart of Soho. I had a little side-room off the main bar and had loads of people drop by from the record company so we could get to know each other, as well as a few mates from *EastEnders.*

I didn't have time to dwell on the show any more. I still had a little less than two months filming to complete, but Innocent wanted me to get on with my songwriting straight away. So those last weeks were spent writing at the Metropolis studios in Chiswick, west London, shooting at Elstree, and dashing off to New York – for anything from a couple of days at a time to a few weeks – to record. I didn't have time to think about Tiffany as the record company, like me, wanted to make sure my album came out as soon as possible after my disappearance from *EastEnders.* Flying to New York on Friday to record with Tony Moran and then dashing back for filming on Monday morning almost killed me, but I was a driven woman once again now I had something new to get stuck in to.

Despite the frantic pace, I still found my last few months at *EastEnders* a bit of a drag. I never thought I'd be excited about leaving Elstree as it had been my first taste of job security, not to mention fame, which are rare feelings in the acting world. I used to be so wrapped up in the whole Albert Square thing, the history, the people . . . I had a real respect for it, but that respect wilted in the last weeks.

I was angry with Matthew and Mal, of course, but I wasn't angry with anyone else there. The thing I really wanted to do – and Ross, Barbara, Patsy and the rest of the cast helped make it happen – was to make my last few months as fantastic as possible. I didn't want to leave with people thinking: 'She didn't really want to be here at the end, did she?' I wanted people to say 'Martine's going . . . isn't it sad?' I really wanted them to miss me.

Paradoxically perhaps, the newspapers' continuing and initially flattering Save Tiff campaigns meant less and less to me. I didn't really want the press to keep banging on about Tiffany because I had got something completely different now. The public were great – and, even better, people seemed to understand what had gone on behind the scenes. More than one person stopped me in the street and said, 'Oh, those BBC bosses don't know what they're doing, girl!' Others would plead: 'Please, don't go!' When I said I was definitely off they'd say they had heard all about the reasons why and how unfairly the BBC had treated me. Indeed it was *the* topic of conversation between the public and me for a good six months after that.

My last scenes were filmed on 6 November. They threw a little party for me at Elstree but there weren't any tears on my part. Steve McFadden unscrewed the brass plaque on my door and gave it to me, which was a bit of choker, but then he said 'I think you're making a mistake. I don't think you should leave, Martine.' Maybe he had forgotten that I didn't really have any choice in the matter.

'Oh well,' I told him, 'we'll just have to see, won't we?' He was very sweet and honestly thought he was saying the right thing. But I was too busy with my music to care.

I had hit it off with Tony Moran from our very first meeting at The Ivy restaurant in London. He's a very handsome Puerto Rican man who has worked with many of the best, including Janet Jackson, Luther Vandross, and Celine Dion. He had enough money in the bank from his past hits not to need to work any more, but he still does because he loves it, especially with new talent. All he knew about me was that I was a well-known TV star in my home country, blessed with a good voice. Cheryl had told him I'd sung a lot of show songs from musicals, that I wanted to do some big ballads and that Streisand and Frank Sinatra were my ultimate icons. He's a very calming man to be around, is Tony, but quite firm about what he wants in a studio.

I had done a lot of my writing in the UK with Ben and Jason as they are known professionally. Ben Parker and Jason Hazley were a formidable partnership from my point of view and we wrote a lot together including a song called 'Tremble' which ended up on the album. I was on one of my red-eye visits to New York when I first started work on that song, one of my favourites, jotting down lyrics while eating in this fifties-style retro restaurant-cum-bar. I just got these lyrics in my head while I was there and had to write them down double-quick.

My few weeks at the Metropolis studio stand out for another, completely unwelcome, reason in the shape of my second stalker, Mark, an escapee from a psychiatric hospital. He too started by writing Reece-style letters. He was young – about thirty – and had apparently turned up at the set of *EastEnders* a couple of times before I left although I was never informed about it. Apparently he was quite good looking and appeared totally normal, but he was very twisted mentally and successfully put the frighteners on me not long after I started working with Ben and Jason.

Nick Pickard had rung and invited me to a *Hollyoaks* video launch which was to be held at the Aquarium club in London. I never mentioned it to anyone else which made it doubly strange when I got home that day to find the porter at my Chelsea flat had received a surprise visit.

'There was a lad here today,' he explained. 'He's left you a note. He wanted to go up to your flat but I wouldn't let him.'

I opened my letterbox and took out the note and read it with a mixture of terror and shock. 'I hope you look beautiful – I shall see you tonight at the Aquarium,' it read.

Somehow Mark had managed to find out about my meeting at the Aquarium. A couple of days later he turned up again. Luckily I had spent the day recording with Ben and Jason and instead of going home alone to Chelsea as I usually did, I agreed to join the boys for a drink in Islington. It was quite late by the time I got home – about eleven – I would have normally been back at 9 p.m. I was very surprised to see all these police cars with sirens blaring driving past my apartment block as I pulled up, and I asked the porter what had been going on. Mark, it transpired, had turned up at the flat at 9.30 p.m. and asked to see me. When the porters refused he became very angry. He then dodged the porters, ran into the lift, went up to my door and started kicking it in, screaming and shouting as he did so. He must have been watching me regularly to have found out which flat I lived in and what time I normally arrived home.

I gather that, when the police caught and questioned the nutter, he told them we were married! He said I was the mad one for not wanting to admit to it! He said that we'd married very young, before I'd got into *EastEnders,* explaining to the detectives that it was a big secret and that I'd never told anybody because he didn't fit in with my life any more. Later that night the police rang me at home to ask if any of what he'd said was true. Apparently he was incredibly convincing as he knew so much about me and the police felt they had to ask. 'You've got to be crazy!' I screamed. 'Of course I don't know him.' Mark was a total fantasist and was later restored to a psychiatric ward by the courts.

One final word about stalkers, about which I hope you will

take careful note – I've been followed several times by fans when I've been in my car. Even normal fans don't realise how much something like that can freak you out; they sometimes just find it tempting to chase you so they can get a better look at you. Please don't. You have no idea how terrifying it can be and after the murder of Jill Dando, who lived only a short distance from me, security has become my number-one priority. Fans don't always understand why their idols sometimes appear slightly aloof or distant. Sometimes we have to be like that, not because we want to, but because you're not safe if you act any other way. It's hard because we get knocked for it all the time.

I am still very hands-on with the public. I will give fans a cuddle or a kiss, that's just the way that I am, and I don't want to stop behaving like that because of a few crazed people. So don't wind people like me up by following us. It's dangerous. Right. Enough said. Back to the music.

People often ask how I write my songs. The answer is there are no set ways. Sometimes I have a tune and lyrics in my head at the same time, sometimes just the tune or a lyrical phrase. If I'm really lucky they both come together. I got most of the lyrics to 'Tremble' right there in the New York bar, but there were still some bits missing which I filled in back in London. Ben and Jason were always on hand to help especially when I first started writing the album. We also wrote 'If Only' and 'Falling Apart' together – two of my favourite songs on the album along with 'You, Me and Us', which became its title song.

'I Don't Want To Cry Again', another album track, I actually wrote with a guy called Nigel Lois before I got a record deal. We collaborated for a while as a sort of experiment. The other writer I should mention is Matt Rowe who co-wrote most of the Spice Girls' biggest hits. I think he is a wonderful writer, but unfortunately we didn't really get long enough to work together.

The whole of the album was recorded in New York where I was based full-time from December through to January 1999, and the longer I spent there, the more fun I had. Matt Goss was around most of the time and if I wasn't going out with him of a night, I would be hanging around with Tony. I love shopping and New York is one hell of a place to do it. I found a great shopping mall called Anthropology which was close to my hotel, the Soho Grande, and I became a regular there.

That was the easy side of life in New York, of course. Recording, on the other hand, was very tough because everything had to be absolutely perfect. I was used to singing live, and had recorded a few demo tapes, but this was something very different and testing because Tony wanted everything to be just so. There were times I'd be in the studio literally sweating from exertion. Nevertheless I wasn't particularly daunted by going into Tony's studio as I'd been in a few with Milan and later when I was doing demo tapes for my album. The studio itself was all light wood and glass, based on the sixth floor of an office-style building in New York's Chelsea district. The lift ride up to the sixth floor was unpleasant, as the elevator reeked of glue for some reason. Once out of the lift you would be confronted by a heavy door – with tens of thousands of pounds worth of expensive recording gear inside, security was paramount. Beyond the door everything was light wood, glass and blue as the light reflected off the carpet. Some of the rooms were literally wallpapered with platinum discs – Janet Jackson, Luther Vandross, Celine Dion . . . The recording studio itself was made with very dark wood and soundproof glass.

When it came to recording 'Perfect Moment', I was

determined to get the ambience just right. I had the studio filled with candles and the main lights off, which really helped get me in the mood. Tony loved it so much I later bought him a Donna Karan candle made with all these essential oils as a little thank you gift.

'Perfect Moment' was destined to become one of *the* wedding songs of 1999 so I knew I wanted to get the sound, well, perfect. Tony completely understood and got the production spot on. Because I didn't think I had anyone special in my life as I was singing, I concentrated instead on imagining life with an ideal man. I settled on the gorgeous movie star Ethan Hawke and as I sang each lyric I fantasised about Ethan coming towards me saying, 'Let's get married'. All that corny kind of stuff!

The music minus my vocals sounded quite mystical. Then Tony mixed in my voice and managed to create this amazing feeling of space in the final mix. It was the obvious first choice for my debut single.

With work progressing on the album at full tilt there was no point in returning to Britain for New Year's Eve. Instead I decided to meet up with my fellow ex-pats in the Big Apple. I called Matt, saying how weird it felt to be away from home as we welcomed in the last year of the millennium. Mum was busy with Alan and my little brother. Matt already had tickets to all these different parties and we agreed to hit a few of them together.

There was a large crowd over at Matt's including a few friends from England who were crashing out there too. I decided to join the happy campers as two friends of mine needed somewhere to stay for a bit of romance and I'd lent them my hotel room. Matt got a call from Matt Rowe, the songwriter, who had bunch of tickets to this really posh-sounding do at the Mercer Hotel and restaurant and wanted us to join him. So I put on this foxy-looking black frock covered with black rhinestones. I'd worn it to a Royal Variety show – where I sang Frank Sinatra's 'They Can't Take That Away From Me' to Prince Charles. Then we hit the town.

It was the most incredible and bizarre party I think I've ever been to. At one point Tom Cruise and his wife Nicole Kidman came running in, sat themselves at one of the tables, put paper hats on and start blowing those silly hooter things. I burst out laughing because it was such a madcap sight. They both wished me a Happy New Year as the chimes started, which made me feel really chuffed. I then thought to myself, look at your life, Martine. A couple of weeks ago you were slogging it out at Elstree and now you're in New York, at the Mercer, partying with movie stars. Then my brain started nagging at me. Next New Year, it ordered, you've got to be a big enough star in your own right for Tom and Nicole to know who you are . . .

Just then Mel C from the Spice Girls came over and asked in her Scouse way if I was feeling all right. 'You look deep in thought there,' she pointed out. I nodded as she wished me a Happy New Year and gave me a friendly kiss on the cheek. We ended up chatting for ages, having a right laugh together, but that didn't stop me from feeling a little homesick.

'I feel like I want to have a bit of England, something English, around me,' I told Matt Goss. 'It's great in New York and all that, but right now I need a bit of England to make me feel at home. Any ideas?' He knew exactly what I meant and had a great idea. He got a load of us to leave the Mercer and head off for this bar he knew. We had to walk miles in our glad rags in the freezing cold New York night because we couldn't get a taxi, until we reached an Irish bar which was the closest thing to England we could get. As it turned out there were quite a few limeys there. That bar was the crowning aspect of an excellent night. No one knew me in New York and after seeing Nicole and Tom whooping it up, it was quite a boost to the old ego to suddenly find myself surrounded by fans. 1999 certainly started with a bang.

With the festivities out of the way, it was time to put the finishing touches to the album and shoot my first proper pop video. We wanted a crisp, cold yet romantic feeling for the video and New York seemed like the perfect place to shoot it. I also had some new pictures taken, lovely black and white shots of me wandering around the city. Even though my health and figure were not yet how I wanted them to be, they were very stylish photographs, a million miles away from my old life in *EastEnders*. I was conscious of my need to move on, to leave Tiffany Mitchell behind.

CHAPTER 17

You, Me and Us

BACK IN ENGLAND, on a freezing January night, I hooked up with Matt Goss again as he, too, was in London. We met for one of our regular midnight feasts at our favourite bagel shop and I remember him looking at me quite seriously as we munched through our food. He started talking about my friend Jonathan Barnham. 'I think you quite fancy Jonathan, don't you?' he half-stated, half-asked. Rather defensively I asked him what he meant. 'I think you do, that's all.' I denied it and said we were friends and no more. 'Well, I think you're going to be with him in a boyfriend-girlfriend kind of way . . .'

I told him to lay off. What he was saying was making me feel weird. Matt, the wretch, would *not* lay off. 'Mark my words, Martine,' he continued, 'I think you're going to be with him.' And he was right.

Matt, as I said earlier, is very perceptive, spiritual and in tune with what's going on around him. Sometimes I feel we even share a telepathic bond, as I'll be thinking of him one minute and the phone will ring the next with him on the other end of the line. He recognised something in my relationship with Jonathan that I had refused to acknowledge. But even there and then in that bagel shop, dating Jonathan, as opposed to seeing him as a friend, simply wasn't on my agenda.

From the moment Jonathan and I had first met at the Pickard brothers' bar, I didn't think he had a chance of being with me, as I knew I was fed up with trying to find a decent man. I don't know if he was truly in love with me during those subsequent lunches or whether his interest was whetted just because I was the first girl who hadn't fallen under his spell. He's an incredibly good-looking boy, well-tanned from his frequent visits to Spain where his family lived, with blond hair and sharply chiselled features. Real male model material – and that was exactly the kind of work he was getting at the time. He had plenty of girls after him but like me, none of his relationships ever lasted more than five minutes. No, hand on heart, I can say I genuinely wasn't overwhelmed by the Barnham charm and he couldn't understand it, which I think did him good.

Instead we spent a lot of time together talking. He got to know me, he got to know what I wanted from a relationship, because we'd talk about it. He'd tell me about the various girls in his life. One Sunday over pizza it would be how in love he was with such and such, two weeks later he'd be crying into his tricolore salad! I admit during those two weeks I wouldn't see him as often and I'd miss him desperately. Hey, I'd even feel a little bit jealous and wouldn't know why.

We must have been seeing each other as mates for more than a year before I started hearing word about his true feelings towards me from third parties. I knew if he ever saw me with an old flame like Stuart Bilton, he would hate it, make his excuses and leave whichever club or bar we were in. Stuart was typically my type – tall, dirty blonde hair, lovely fat lips, very handsome. I'd always admired him because he was so wonderful to look at and such a lovely man to talk to. I first met him at Patsy's house and at the time he was going out with Victoria Beckham, or Posh Spice. I didn't know this at the time and remember telling Patsy how lovely he was.

A couple of weeks later Patsy and I were sitting in a bar when she started telling me that Stuart was single again. 'You little cow, I can't believe you haven't told me before,' I said. 'How long have they been split up?'

Patsy grinned. 'Long enough!'

I really quite fancied the idea of going out with Stuart but felt insecure. 'He won't be interested in me,' I said. 'Victoria's really glamorous.'

'And you're not?' asked Patsy, adding, 'He obviously likes dark girls, sexy girls. I'll phone him for you.'

We ended up going on a couple of dates. I remember one in a little tapas bar in the square where Patsy lived in Bethnal Green, but it just wasn't destined to be. We had a kiss and it was very nice and we dated for a couple of weeks but it never went beyond that.

I was just not ready to commit myself in any shape or form with anyone. I couldn't understand why Jonathan was so funny when I would talk about, or see, an ex-boyfriend or someone he knew I fancied. It wasn't as if it was a big romance or anything. I found out why when a couple of friends told me: 'You do know Jonathan's in love with you Martine . . .' I asked how they knew. 'Because he keeps telling us,' was their reply.

I didn't find out just how much he loved me until more than two years after we had first met, and then, only through somebody else's misfortune. Early in 1999 I was going to

Barbados for a magazine photoshoot in the run-up to the launch of 'Perfect Moment' – an all expenses trip I planned to share with Mum and Alan, her boyfriend as he was then, plus a few others including a friend of mine named Karl Gordon, better known as KG, a writer and producer for All Saints among others.

The night before we were due to fly to the Caribbean was a big night, too, the British Soap Awards. I knew loads of people who were going including Nick Pickard, many of the cast of Channel 4's *Hollyoaks*, and Jonathan. I remember telling him that evening that I wouldn't be seeing him for a while as I was going off on holiday for a couple of weeks and wondered if he wanted to join me for a late dinner after the awards ceremony. Maybe it was because I hadn't invited him on holiday but Jonathan seemed to have the hump. For the first and only time in our relationship he turned my dinner invite down. He planned to go out with the lads for a booze-up after the awards. 'Why don't you come with us?' he asked. I explained that I couldn't do that as I had to be up early in the morning to get packed. 'Well, we'll have to leave it, then,' he said and disappeared. I remember thinking he looked so handsome – and felt rather disappointed not to be seeing him for a fortnight – but I knew he had loads to do while I was away so I didn't feel that guilty about not taking him with me.

Earlier Mum had seemed about as miffed as Jonathan by my decision. In fact I think she reckoned I was stark raving mad. She'd met him a couple of weeks earlier and couldn't believe that I'd insisted on maintaining a platonic relationship for so long. 'This man is your best friend, Martine. Are you mad? Are you fucking mad?' she ranted. 'He is fucking gorgeous. He is an Adonis and you're going out to lunch with him at Pizza Express on a Sunday as your *friend.* You must be madder than I thought before. I've heard about this Jonathan for so long I thought he was going to be pig ugly. I thought that must be the only reason you're not going out with him, but I've seen him now and he's gorgeous. Are you blind? He loves you – he'll do anything for you. He puts you first AND he looks like *that.* You've got to have something missing upstairs, girl.'

Early the following morning I got a phone call from Karl. 'Martine, you're not going to believe this but I can't find my passport,' he said. 'I've got to be the biggest idiot on earth – I've got a free holiday to bloody Barbados and can't find it.' KG was coming out as my guest. I had agreed to do a picture spread for *Hello!* magazine because it meant my little brother, Mum, Alan and another friend Kim all got the chance to have a holiday they would never, ever normally have the chance to enjoy. I might have been doing well but I still couldn't have afforded first-class travel and accommodation for six people.

In the end we had no choice but to leave KG behind while he tried to find his birth certificate to get another passport. He couldn't find that either, as it turned out. Then, as we finished packing Mum suggested I call Jonathan and invite him along in KG's place. I thought about it for ten seconds, rang him and he excitedly agreed to follow us a few days later.

I was very pleased when he arrived as I'd really missed him for the first couple of days of the holiday. We were in a beautiful hotel called the Coral Reef, in a classically elegant resort. LJ had met him before and had taken to him instantly. He was over the moon when Jonathan arrived and has been ever thankful that Jonathan taught him how to swim properly. After years living in Spain, Jonathan was obviously au fait with water sports and spent days in trunks surfing, swimming and jet skiing. He did all three brilliantly. It was only then that I started to appreciate what I'd been looking at for the past two years. Wow, I thought as I settled myself on a sun lounger watching him, he has got a body to die for. A few days later I was doing exactly the same thing when I got the premonition that I was going to kiss Jonathan that evening. I think this is going to be it, I thought to myself. My psychic senses didn't let me down.

Later on that evening we did a few photos for *Hello!* The pics of me and Jonathan were quite striking because we looked like a perfect couple. We all went out for dinner and I just knew my premonition was going to come true. After a fabulous meal, Jonathan, me and Kim broke away and walked down to the beach. We were outside with the stars in the sky, it was absolutely glorious. Kim subtly gave me a little wink and said: 'I'm going to go back.' As far as she and Mum were concerned something was happening between Jonathan and me. 'I'll leave you guys to have a bit of time to yourselves,' she added as she walked towards the hotel.

Jonathan and I were still talking away by the beach when I noticed he was getting closer and closer to me on the sun lounger. The moment was nigh but I was still having last-minute doubts.

Then I panicked. 'Sorry, Jonathan, I've got to go and make sure everything's okay with Mum and LJ,' I gabbled, completely ruining my perfect moment. Before I got up to go I had one last lapse. 'You want to kiss me, don't you?' I said, the words coming out of my mouth at a rate of knots.

'Yeah, I do, Martine, but only if you want me to kiss you.'

'Oh, I want you to kiss me,' I replied, adding stupidly, 'tonight we'll have one kiss and that'll be it – I don't want this to carry on when we get home in case it spoils our friendship. OK?'

I leaned forward and puckered up my lips and off we went. My stomach got that lovely light feeling as Jonathan held his face to mine. When we finally broke our embrace I looked up at him adoringly. He suggested we give it another go but before I accepted I gave a final warning. 'One more? Fine. But only one more because we can't do this when we get home to London.'

We kissed again and began to walk back to the hotel. I was in a lovely apartment, sharing with Kim who must have gone out because she wasn't there when we got back. Jonathan came in with me, we sat down and looked at each other longingly. 'All right, we can have a kiss and a cuddle but that's it and nothing else,' I said. 'Tomorrow we go back to being friends. Oh, and Jonathan, I don't want anyone to know what we've been up to otherwise Mum and Alan will wind me up for the rest of the holiday about it.' Reservations out of the way, we jumped on to my bed, had a kiss and a cuddle then fell asleep.

Waking up the next day lying next to Jonathan, I was really pleased to find that I felt quite comfortable with the situation.

For some reason we moved into a bigger, almost palatial suite for some more pictures that afternoon. It was utterly gorgeous and came complete with its own plunge pool. I'd talked to him earlier about going skinny dipping, but didn't feel confident enough to do it under his gaze. He didn't seem to mind at all, and offered to leave me in my suite all alone for the afternoon while he looked after LJ. 'Look, Martine,' he said, 'it's your holiday. You've got to relax and do what you want to do.'

Once he'd gone, I got undressed and jumped into the pool starkers, only nipping out once to grab a bottle of champagne from the bar in my room. The phone kept going, which was almost certainly Mum wanting to know what time we were going to be ready for dinner, but I just let it ring.

When Jonathan came back I heard him before I saw him and shouted: 'Don't come out – I'm in the plunge-pool.' When I needed to get out he went and got me a towel and wrapped it round me while simultaneously averting his eyes. He was the perfect gentleman.

That night I had the suite to myself as Kim was staying elsewhere. I plucked up the courage to ask Jonathan to join me and so that night, after going out for dinner, we came back and got into bed together. I had little pyjama shorts on and a white cotton top. He jumped in with his little shorts on. It was an odd but beautiful moment. 'Look,' I said quietly, preparing to explain myself yet again, 'it's not that I don't think you're lovely, it's just that I don't want to lose you as my friend. If we put the condition on us being friends when we get home and nothing else, then this will just be a holiday thing, which is fine by me, but if you can't cope with that, you need to tell me now.' He told me he could cope, kissed me and that's when he stopped being a gentleman – which I was more than happy about, to be honest.

Every evening for the rest of the holiday was just perfect after that, apart from the fact it meant our departure date was growing closer. When the time came for us to pack up and go, Jonathan seemed desperately unhappy and I couldn't understand why. 'Because I know everything's going to go back to the way it was at home,' he said when I asked him why he looked so miserable. 'I accept that, Martine, but that doesn't mean I have to be happy about it. I would really like us to be the way we were on holiday forever.' I couldn't handle that and pleaded with him to stick to our bargain.

Looking back now I'm quite amazed that we did stick to the deal, if only for two or three weeks because it was obvious then that we were both crazy about each other. But I was determined not to be hurt again, as I was by Gareth, and that meant never risking losing Jonathan as a friend. But even the best laid plans go to pot and that's kind of what happened when we visited my friend Natalie Cooke at her house in the country one evening. The night wore on until it got so late there was no point trying to get home. Instead Natalie offered to put us both up in the spare room. Perhaps not surprisingly one thing led to another again. It was only then that I realised this staying friends business was over between me and Jonathan. We both wanted more from the relationship. We just talked about the pros and the cons for hours but ended up being with each other as lovers again, regardless of my daft insistence that things should remain innocent between us, which I even maintained the following morning.

I didn't see Jonathan for a couple of days after that night because I was busy promoting 'Perfect Moment'. I was working hard but missing him even more, so much so that one night I decided I couldn't be without him and drove round to his flat in Fulham. He was there with his cousin Sarah. I only popped in to say hello but ended up finally admitting to my true feelings. 'I've just really missed you,' I explained. 'I think we should carry on seeing each other as we have been recently, but I still don't want our friendship to pay the price. I'm not saying it'd ever be quite the same again but I don't ever want us to lose touch because of what's gone on between us. Would you be happy to just take it a day at a time and if we change our minds we change our minds?' He accepted those terms and pulled me towards him for a reassuring cuddle. Everything seemed to be falling in place nicely, I thought to myself.

Indeed it took a long time, more than two years, before I

could finally succumb to being fully in love with Jonathan. I suppose it took all that time for me to finally get over Gareth.

Jonathan is wonderful. He's never been in awe of the fame thing and doesn't seem to mind whether I'm fat or thin, tired or all glammed up. He was flattering about my appearance when I was at my biggest, all bloated by the glandular fever. And I know that wasn't just idle chat to win my heart. He has a way of looking at me like no other man has ever looked at me before, and it thrills me to the bone.

CHAPTER 18

Perfect Moment

A COUPLE OF weeks after returning from Barbados I gave 'Perfect Moment' its first public airing at a showcase gig in London's Café de Paris. The place was crammed – Innocent had done a good job promoting it, which did nothing to ease my nerves – and I spotted Mick Hucknall and a bunch of *EastEnders* people milling about the place as well as just about every pop journalist in the land. I even got a surprise visit from Paul Nicholls who I was chuffed to bits to see, as we had now become good friends and I needed all the support I could get.

I need not have worried as everything went like clockwork. My performance, introduced in the most glowing terms by Hugh, was filmed for a special Granada TV were making in conjunction with the record label. There wasn't a band, it was just me on that small stage, dressed in a gorgeous long black frock – black was very much the image for the 'Perfect Moment' single – singing to a DAT of the music. Everyone seemed to love the song and the showcase turned into a little party afterwards. Things seemed to be shaping up nicely, but I still didn't have a clue how the British public would react to the song or me not being Tiffany any more.

It had been a long time since I'd been involved with the whole chart and record industry during my Milan days, and I didn't have much of a clue about what was going on around me. Promoting singles is a massive operation, particularly for a new artist. But Innocent seemed to be completely on top of things and had a mind-boggling schedule of TV and radio performances set up for me. All I knew was that if I worked as hard as I could and it still didn't happen and 'Perfect Moment' flopped, then it wasn't going to be through any laziness on my part.

I was very confident with the song, but I knew that the biggest section of the record-buying public were teenagers, and 'Perfect Moment' was an emotional ballad. Hardly the younger generation's cup of tea. I don't know if they're going to want to buy a ballad – maybe they'd rather be dancing to Britney Spears, I kept thinking to myself. There were times during the last week of promo, the week when the single was actually in the shops, when I felt sure it was going to be a hit, but equally there were other times when I didn't. I mean, I was singing stuff that was very grown-up compared to a lot of other stuff in the charts, so I resolved to stick to my guns. After all, if I put my hair in bunches and dressed in a school uniform Britney-style, everyone would laugh their heads off.

As each day passed that week, I felt better and better about my song. I just knew it was going to chart, I sensed it. In my wilder moments I thought it may be even reach number one but only for a maximum of a week. I never imagined it would stay at the top for two consecutive weeks, especially these days when every record seems to go in and then out of the charts quicker than you can say *Top of the Pops*.

I spent the last few days before that Sunday's chart in a kind of limbo, wandering around my Chelsea flat, looking out at the river, praying to the skies and the clouds above. I'd done every promotional appearance there was to do. Virtually all that was left was to wait. I remember praying: Please God, I'll never ask for anything else, please let this go to number one! I kept praying because I knew I'd done all the work there was to do – bar the most prestigious gig of them all, BBC's *Top of the Pops*, every pop star's dream job.

The show is, of course, filmed at Elstree so I knew I would be back on familiar territory, which kept my nerves at bay. I got dressed up 'Perfect Moment' style in a dazzling Gucci outfit – all black with sequins – with my hair long and with a centre parting above dark smoky-looking eyes. The *TOTP* recording went well and gave me plenty of time to reflect on the enormous changes that had been going on in my professional and private life over the four months since Tiff's departure from Walford. I remember there was a time, not that long ago, when I was sitting in my *EastEnders* dressing room, devastated by Matthew Robinson's decision to kill Tiff and rob me of any chance of returning to the soap. I'd said to myself then, 'One day, Martine, you're going to come back here in your own right and shove two fingers up to everybody who said I wouldn't make it. Well, here I am, in my own dressing-room with make-up artists and assistants running around me, being treated like a proper pop star.' I was back in my own right and I hadn't had to record one bit of *EastEnders* while I was there. Magic!

A few familiar faces from Walford popped by. Leila Birch, who plays Teresa di Marco, said hello while Patsy, who was driving past, beeped me with her horn outside my dressing-room window and shouted 'Hello darling – well done, well done'. She couldn't pop in as she was on her way to do a

scene. Sid Owen came by later along with my dear friend
Barbara Windsor.

Top of the Pops is recorded the day before its Friday
transmission – which meant I got to see it go out on TV –
well just about. I always have trouble with TV aerials and that
Friday was no different. The communal aerial that serviced
the whole block of flats on the banks of the Thames in
Chelsea where I lived had broken, so all I had was the little
hoop one attached to the back of the telly which I had to keep
moving round and bending to get a decent picture. From
what I could see through the fuzz, I hadn't done half bad.

On the Saturday I got an anonymous message on my
answer-machine at home bearing good news. It must have
been someone from Innocent because the voice said that the
mid-week position, that's an unofficial chart based on sales at
certain record shops, put me at number one. The message
continued: 'By the sales figures we're seeing there's no way
you're not going to be number one on Sunday. Well done
and congratulations.' To this day I do not know who left that
message but I can tell you I was very grateful.

I actually got the message while I was in the back of Luke
Goss's jeep with one of my friends, Mack. I must have dialled
in to check my phone around 11 p.m., just after seeing Luke
on stage playing Danny in the musical *Grease*. We were on
our way to Covent Garden to get a bite to eat. I couldn't
quite hear the message first time around because of Luke's
stereo. 'Could you turn the music down a bit please?' I asked
him. 'I've got to hear that message again – I don't think I
heard it right.' I listened to it again and then started
whooping it up, screaming, 'Oh my God, I can't believe it
. . . I've got a message saying I'm going to be number one
tomorrow.' Exciting? I felt like I was the dog's bollocks.

We ended up eating at The Ivy, Luke's treat. There was

quite a crowd in the restaurant. I was there with Luke, his wife Shirley and Mack, while the tennis player Greg Rusedski was at the next table. It was a righteous celebration and even better, I didn't disgrace myself either! Thank you, Luke.

I got more and more excited the following day as I waited for the official chart to be broadcast over the radio. I had to keep waiting until just around seven for Capital DJ 'Dr' Neil Fox to confirm 'Perfect Moment's debut at number one. As soon as I heard I had to give a couple of quick interviews to Foxy and Radio One, and that was that. I had made it. I can assure you nothing beats being number one in the charts – there isn't a feeling in the world to compare. It's like you've made your own little piece of history as the achievement will get written into the Guinness Book of Hit Singles for ever.

I celebrated by taking family and friends to Browns restaurant in the West End. Jonathan was away working and the only other person I wanted there who couldn't make it was Mum. She wasn't feeling well, something I can now put down to her developing diabetes. She had been feeling under the weather for a few weeks, was getting the sweats and feeling devoid of energy. A few weeks after I got to number one the doctor diagnosed diabetes and put her on tablets – but things continued to deteriorate and she now has to inject herself with insulin every day, poor thing. After a slap-up meal at Browns I went back on my own to my flat in Chelsea. I was feeling really chuffed with myself and thought, what do I really want to do tonight? I put my favourite pyjamas on, climbed into bed even though it was before ten o'clock and decided to watch some telly while scoffing a big bag of Maltesers and some Häagen-Dazs ice-cream. I stuffed myself silly and was as happy as could be.

The next week it was business as usual, doing a few more promotions to ensure 'Perfect Moment' had a chance of a second week at number one. I was still on cloud nine all that week and most of the week after. I felt I had been vindicated in my decision to leave *EastEnders* behind and have a go at following my instincts and dreams.

It wasn't quite perfect. I had another unwelcome surprise in May when John, the man I had called my father, the man whom I had hoped would one day walk me down the aisle, decided to air his grievances with my Mum and me by giving a newspaper interview. I don't think his intention was necessarily to wound me – I was just the conduit he used to get at Mum. I presume, by then, he had caught wind of her romance with Alan. John was still having problems getting over the end of his relationship with Jenny, even after three years. I had been helping out financially after his accident but I found telephone conversations with him intolerable because they were never about the two of us. They were always rants against Mum. What he said in the newspaper wasn't the most hurtful thing I'd ever read about myself in print. But John knew how much I had wanted to be there for him, and how much I did not want their split to become public knowledge just because of me. I did not think that was fair on Mum, John, or my little brother, most importantly. But it happened. John knew full well how I had reacted in the past when men in my life had gone to the newspapers with untrue stories – I never forgave them.

With one number one behind me I felt increasingly confident in my new career and really started to enjoy myself. One episode that stands out in my mind was shooting the video for my third single, a double A-sided fund-raiser for the BBC's Children In Need charity – it seemed only right I should give something back having got my musical break from appearing on the telethon in 1997. The two songs were 'Love Me', which featured a bunch of normal kids in the video and was the main Children In Need song, and the classic Crystal Gayle song I used to sing with my Mum when we drove to Zayni Halil's Saturday dance and drama classes all those years ago – 'Talking In Your Sleep'.

Now the video for 'Talking' was shot in London's Savoy Hotel in September, and who do you think was staying there at the time? None other than Michael Douglas and his new girlfriend, as she was then, Catherine Zeta Jones. Catherine, whom I've met a couple of times, had seen her career go into orbit during the past five years with a string of Hollywood hit movies including *The Mask of Zorro*. The girl had done good, that's for sure. It was one of the video crew who told me the pair were staying at the hotel. I hadn't seen Michael since our couple of dates eighteen months earlier so I decided a bit of tact was called for, as I didn't want Catherine to think I was trying to hook up with her boyfriend. She might well have thought I was if she had read all the press that followed my drink with Michael at the Met Bar in February 1998. The Mirror ran that story on the front page, making out that I was on a serious date with Michael which was a bit of an exaggeration. So who knows what Catherine would imagine if I popped upstairs and knocked on their hotel room door. Instead I decided to send a note addressed to both of them.

'Dear Michael and Catherine,' I wrote. 'I'm so pleased that everything's working out so well for you both. I'm doing a video on the fourth floor here at the hotel. If you fancy popping down one floor and saying hi, I would love to see you both. Lots of love, Martine. PS. Catherine, well done, you showed them all.' I put that last bit in because, like me, Catherine had suffered cruelly at the hands of her detractors, many of whom claimed her career had died after she finished filming the ITV comedy drama series *The Darling Buds of May*. The critics, it struck me, didn't want to see Catherine make the leap from small screen TV in the UK to the far bigger screens of Hollywood movies, but she confounded them all.

I had the letter sent to their room by one of the runners and waited for a response. I could have waited a long time because I never heard anything back. Still, I'm not going to complain about that. A couple of people have mentioned to me how similar Catherine and I look, with our black hair and dark eyes. But I was never looking for romance with Michael; he turned out to be just a very sweet friend. I think Catherine is far more attractive than me anyway, and she completely suits Michael because she's got that terrific old-fashioned Hollywood look about her. I think they're great together.

After all the joy I experienced in 1999, the year ended rather bleakly. The biggest disappointment revolved around the collapse of a national concert tour that had been organised for me, due to the reappearance of my glandular fever. If that wasn't bad enough I also had to endure a series of piss-taking articles by 'critics' making out I had to cancel the tour because of poor ticket sales. They should have seen the box office receipts – ticket sales were no problem.

My health was a worry. I suppose I only had myself to blame but I was so determined to make my pop career work that I'd slogged my guts out day and night for more than nine months. By the time I was due to start touring in November, I had nothing left to give. More than just feeling unwell, I actually felt sick of going out, sick of meeting people. I needed a break, I didn't want to have to smile or say hello to anyone or make idle chit chat. My body gave way to a recurrence of glandular fever and then my mind followed suit.

Again, I felt I was losing the plot and sliding into another mini-nervous breakdown, as I had following my bust-up with Gareth. I didn't leave my flat for three weeks. Looking back I feel more sorry for Jonathan than myself, as he must have been so bored sitting around waiting for me to get out of bed. I didn't want the telly on because I didn't want any noise, so the poor boy had to sit in silence. Amazingly he only rarely left my side.

My doctor Peter Ryan came round to see me at the flat. I burst out crying as soon as I saw him and started sobbing about how everything was getting on top of me. 'I think it's all getting too much for me,' I babbled. 'I feel tired, my glands have come up a little bit and I don't seem to be able to shake it off. If anything it's getting worse. I don't feel I can cope . . .'

That, he said, was my weakness. My glands would keep coming up if I overdid it . . .

I interrupted him, 'But most of all I feel like my head is ram-packed and ready to explode, there's so much going around in there and I feel like people are expecting too much of me. I don't feel in control, I feel more like I'm some kind of nodding dog. I'm not allowed to say how I feel, I'm not allowed to say yes or no about anything in case I upset people . . .'

Dr Ryan agreed with my own diagnosis – that with my glands up and my mind down there was no point in going ahead with a tour where I could only give less than my best. That meant disappointing a lot of people, tens of thousands of fans, the tour promoters, everyone. But I had to be realistic. For the fans, I thought, it's only one night of their life that I would spoil by cancelling, but going ahead with it could have done me in big time.

I had booked on to ITV's *This Morning* with Richard Madeley and Judy Finnigan to promote the Children In Need single and the tour, of course. I felt I owed it to

Children In Need to drag myself on the show, but it didn't go at all well. A couple of fans faxed the studio while we were live on air, complaining about the cancelled tour. Their comments were quite harsh, especially as I felt in no fit state mentally to deal with them. They said things like, 'I booked tickets for the show and yes, all right, I've got my money back, but you look completely healthy to me, Martine.' Those faxes really got to me because I already felt bad enough for cancelling the tour without having my nose rubbed in it. Naturally it mattered to me enormously how the public felt towards me at any given time, I wanted them to follow me on my journey, but the public are not mind-readers. They don't know what goes on inside any performer's head when times are tough. It's not their fault they were miffed with me, but I didn't feel in any state to answer their complaints. I just felt like curling up in a ball and hiding from it all.

Ironically, even I didn't know the full extent of what was going on inside me. I found out a few days later when I dragged myself out of the flat for another Children In Need promotion, this time in Belfast. Almost as soon as I was upright I felt sick. Sick? In the morning? Oh Christ, I thought. Maybe I'm pregnant. I got through the show and headed home with Jonathan by my side. On the way back from the airport Jonathan stopped the car outside a chemist's and nipped in for a pregnancy test kit. We went back home and I did the urine test in the bathroom. I watched transfixed as the test immediately showed blue, the sign that you're pregnant. I told Jonathan who suggested we nip back out and get another kit. Jonathan did the honours in the chemist's again – if I'd gone in I'm sure the news would have been called straight into a newspaper. We went back home and did another test which also turned blue. 'Well,' Jonathan said, half smiling. 'I think you're pregnant!'

'Yup,' I replied, unsure of how I felt. 'I think I am.'

It was Jonathan who raised the next question. 'So how do you feel, Martine, and what do we do now?' I wasn't quite sure. I hadn't been taking the pill because I'm not a big fan of it. I know a lot of girls that have suffered side-effects and the idea of filling my body with a daily dose of chemicals never really appealed. Nevertheless it was still shocking to find out I was expecting and I wasn't at all sure how I felt. I didn't know whether to get excited and jump up and down and say 'I've always wanted to be a mum – this is really nice' or whether to say, 'Oh no, this can't happen now because I've got so much to do.'

Sadly, as it turned out, I miscarried, something that was in the newspapers and a lot of people will have read about. I was so heartbroken, but it obviously wasn't meant to be. At least I still had my Jonathan. It was a dreadfully upsetting time, and is still something I find difficult to talk about.

At this point, after all the changes that had been going on in my life, I decided to make it less like a roller-coaster and have some more foresight into what my future would be. I might have been a little doubtful of spiritual healers and psychics before, despite Mum's enthusiasm for them, but I went to see this guy out in Spain who didn't have a clue who I was which made me feel much better. Midway through the session, which was all taped so I could keep it with me, he said, 'I see that you've lost a baby. Do you know what sex it was?' I told him I thought it was a girl and he said I was right. 'You know you must stop feeling guilty about her, you must stop feeling that you have lost something because it wasn't meant to be.'

I trusted this guy because he seemed to know things that nobody else knew except me, even things that Mum and my nearest and dearest didn't know, just little things I think, feel and believe in. It was incredibly weird, but also quite uplifting.

'Everything is going to be OK,' he told me. 'Everything's going to be fine. You will get what you want quite easily from now on. Your health's going to get better, you're going to be feeling stronger, and if you work hard enough for it, you can make it to the top step of the ladder.'

I still do get upset about losing my baby, even now, almost a year later, but I've got no hesitation about having another try in the future. Certainly I intend to have plenty of fun in the process – whether I succeed or not is in the hands of God.

What a year 1999, the last of the millennium, was turning out to be. After the ecstasy of making to it to number one, the misery of the return of my glandular fever, the cancelled concert tour and then losing a baby, I'm glad I saw the year out with a bang at a special concert at Greenwich, part of the UK's millennium celebrations. I was invited to join the line-up through one of my agents. The brief was to come along, sing some songs and help make it a night to remember for the tens of thousands who were turning up. The line-up was impressive and included my short-haired friend, as he was now, Mick Hucknall and Simply Red, Annie Lennox and The Corrs. I really wanted to be a part of it, and having spent two months taking life easy, felt well enough to give it a crack.

Not surprisingly being Christmas it was time for me to pick up the annual flu bug and 1999 was to be no exception. I suppose I catch all these bugs because I come into contact with so many people and end up giving away kisses as if they were confetti. Mum got the flu first in early December but I didn't go down with it until just after Christmas with less than a week to go before the New Year's Eve concert. I was laid in up in bed for about three days but was still resolutely determined to make the gig. After all, I thought, there's going to be nothing better for me than to perform at the turn of the new millennium. I'll start the New Year as I mean to continue!

By the time the night of the concert came round I felt like I was suffering no more than a heavy cold, but the germs were still threatening to play havoc with my voice. Backstage, sitting in my Winnebago, I started to feel the pressure a little. Lots of my family were there, as well as Jonathan's. I just sat there quietly awaiting my turn, reflecting on my past and looking ahead, trying to imagine what the future might hold.

That night my hopes for the future were certainly running high. I hoped and prayed that my health was going to improve, that Mum was finally going to feel happy and have a bit of passion in her life. I looked at Jonathan, who was sitting there with me, and felt overwhelmingly happy that we had made the jump from friends to lovers. I thought about Keith, leaving Gareth, the pressures at work and John – who was now up and about following his accident, which was fantastic even if he wasn't a hundred per cent well. I got my news of him from LJ as we still weren't speaking. John's not the type to apologise and, while I had forgiven him in my heart for speaking to the press, I had no desire to have him back in my life. I resolved to make the year 2000 better than all the rest.

Stepping out on stage was one of the most magical feelings I have ever experienced. The atmosphere in Greenwich Park was sensational as you may imagine. Even better, my cold seemed to evaporate for the 30 minutes or so I performed. The crowd and the TV crews seemed to love my performance of 'Maybe This Time' from *Cabaret*. It was shown on loads of TV bulletins later. Everything came out loud and clear. I was over the moon. Even better, I got to watch the rest of the concert including Simply Red. Mick is such a superstar and seeing him sing 'My Way' brought tears not just to my eyes but just about everyone else's. His voice is pure magic, that's the only way I can describe it.

I joined up with all my relatives and friends for a drink or two a little later. My mind was buzzing. Year 2000, I thought, here I come . . .

CHAPTER 19

The Future

ONE OF MY prayers backstage at the millennium concert was answered very shortly indeed when Mum married Alan. He had been a rock for my Mum from the day they met on opposite sides of the bar at the Railway Tavern. The pub never quite worked out for Mum and she sold it not long after meeting Alan to come and work with me, running Angel Media Services and my fan club. Alan, who worked as dustman when he met Mum, but now works with a security company, was everything Mum was looking for. Tying the knot seemed only natural after almost four years as boyfriend and girlfriend.

It was my suggestion that we begin the New Year with a family holiday in Barbados that got the ball rolling. They had both enjoyed themselves so much the previous year, the year that Jonathan and I got together, and Alan had subsequently suggested that if he and Jenny were ever to say 'I do' that's the place they would like to do it.

Alan is a typical, genuine East Ender. He works hard and

seems a little rough and ready, but he has a heart of gold. Anyone who ever saw him playing with LJ recognised that straight away. So when I suggested going back to Barbados they both seized the opportunity to tie the knot there. After all, it would have taken forever for them to save up to do it themselves. I wanted this to be my treat, my little thank you for all the help they had given me. They began to make the necessary arrangements through our hotel, the Sandy Lane, for the service.

They got married on Friday 14 January 2000. I acted as bridesmaid, Jonathan as best man. In the end it was Mum, not any of the rest of us, who pulled the biggest stunt of the day. She arranged for 'Perfect Moment' to be played as she walked down the aisle – and she had never once let on to me that that was what she was planning. I would have died of embarrassment had I known, so maybe it was for the best. It was a fantastic no-frills marriage with a wild Caribbean-style buffet and music by the apartment swimming pool. Just as Mum had wanted. Fantastic.

So what of my future plans, then? Well, as I write this I'm busy working on my second album. I've got my own publishing deal now and spend a lot of my spare time writing lyrics and tunes. I've also had Ginette on the phone with a number of interesting projects, some of which have worked out well and one which fell by the wayside. But that's life, isn't it?

The first acting assignment I took on was a special guest role in the ITV customs and excise drama series *The Knock*, which I've always enjoyed. I wanted to try something very different from Tiffany. My character in the show is called Jenny, and is about as rotten as they come. She has the same name as my Mum, but the similarity ends there! She is a massive drug pusher with a string of clubs on Ibiza where the episode is set. There's a great tragic twist when I discover that my best friend dies as a result of the contaminated drugs I've peddled, while my screen brother accidentally gives me away to the Customs men.

I found her quite difficult to play because she was supposed to be bitter and hard as nails, never showing any emotion. She's also got a real mean streak and there's a fantastic scene where I end up clumping this guy across the head with the heel of one of my shoes. It brought back memories of Tiff and Grant, that bit did.

That was only a small job compared to the one offer I got that fell apart at the last hurdle, which was to play bare-knuckle boxer Lenny McLean's wife, in a movie based on Lenny's best-selling book *The Guv'nor*. I thought I was made for the part of his wife especially as I got a name-check and a picture in his book, which was published just before Lenny died. Lenny, known to the younger generation for his cameo role in the hit British movie *Lock, Stock and Two Smoking Barrels*, was close friends with Stuart Bilton, whom, as I mentioned earlier, I dated briefly. Stuart knew Lenny's son Jamie really well, and one evening as we were driving about town, he suggested we pop round and say hello. It turned out to be a fascinating night, as Lenny told me all about the book he was writing and his days hanging around with the Krays, who Mum knew, too. He even showed me some snippets which read really well.

It was weird reading about these fights and scrapes he got into while I was sitting next to him because he seemed such a sweet old man. I was quite flattered when he asked if he could have his picture taken with me for inclusion in the book. 'If the book gets published, darling, you won't mind if I put the picture in?' he asked. 'Not at all – and I'm sure the book will get published as it's really good,' I told him with genuine enthusiasm.

Tragically Lenny died not long after I was offered the part of his wife opposite *EastEnders* star Craig Fairbrass – who played evil Dan Sullivan in the soap – as Lenny. I was gutted for him, thinking he would never get to see the movie. As it turned out, none of us would . . .

The producers had turned to Sky for financial backing. Sky agreed but only on condition that the film would première on one of their satellite movie channels. Well, that wasn't what anyone really wanted and so the plug was pulled two days before we were to start filming. I'd already dyed my hair blonde for the role, ruining my barnet in the process! The film seemed to fall prey to all the usual pitfalls of the British film industry. It was just one of those things, it turned out, but hopefully it will happen one day. Lenny's life certainly deserves an airing on the big screen.

Only a couple of months ago I finished shooting another movie, *Kiss Kiss, Bang Bang* with Chris Penn. I played a girl called Mia, a real clubber. She's daft as a brush and loves wearing eccentric clothes which she runs up herself. Mia's not a druggy sort, just naturally high on life. She's got an innocence about her that I loved bringing out. She looks at things completely differently from most people. The clothes you see her wear make her look like she's from a different era like the thirties or forties. She loves to be different.

She meets a guy called Bubba, played by Chris Penn, who has been over-protected since he was born, to the point where he's never experienced the world as a grown-up. He's a little retarded. His Dad, who runs a nightclub, finds himself in a spot of bother and has to disappear for a while. He leaves Bubba in the hands of a former hitman. The film defies pigeon-holing as a movie, which was one of the things that appealed so much about it.

One night Bubba, who loves Barry White and Bruce Springsteen music, finds himself in a club for the first time. He loves what he hears and sees, and starts freaking out on the dance floor where Mia spots him. She's already having a bit of bother with her useless boyfriend and when the pair of them have a barney in the toilets, it's Bubba who comes to her rescue. Most people would classify Bubba as someone with special needs but Mia doesn't see him that way, she just thinks he's special, and falls madly in love with him. It's a very curious film which I hope gets the success it deserves. It's due for release in spring 2001. It was brilliant to work on and it was certainly very different from working at *EastEnders*. I had my own Winnebago and, it has to be said, lovely food. The experience has certainly whetted my appetite for more film work.

But by far the most exciting project on the go at the moment is the musical *My Fair Lady* at the National Theatre in London, which should also open in the spring of 2001. I am beyond excitement about it because it's an absolute dream come true for me. I grew up loving the film which starred one of my all time heroines, Audrey Hepburn, and is based on George Bernard Shaw's play *Pygmalion*. I must have watched that film hundreds of times as a little girl and I'm not afraid to admit I was gutted when I found out that Audrey hadn't actually sung any of the songs in the movie. It's a rags to riches story, of course, but so like my own I feel almost predestined to play the part of the flower girl Eliza Dolittle who is elocuted into becoming a lady.

'Wouldn't It Be Lovely?' is one of the best known songs from the film. I sang it years ago at junior school when we did an evening show called *A Night on Broadway*, arranged by my teacher Anne Smith. She told me that Elaine Page had also sung it. Whether or not that was true, I don't know, but when I was a little girl, the first female singer I ever saw was Elaine Page. Oh goodness, she really could sing live. She was truly inspiring, and sent shivers down my spine. After that, anything Elaine had sung was certainly good enough for me! She was a big part of me wanting to be a star.

Then, when I was at *EastEnders* and Children in Need approached us, the cast did an East End medley and my song again was 'Wouldn't It Be Lovely?' It was that song that led to me being called back the following year to perform 'Don't Rain On My Parade' which in turn led to my Royal Albert Hall concert with the Royal Philharmonic and ultimately to my album deal. The chance to do *My Fair Lady* was like coming full circle.

The circumstances that led to me getting the part almost put paid to it, though. Just before Christmas 1999 Ginette rang to tell me about a charity event going on at St Luke's Church in Chelsea, saying she really thought I should do a turn. She caught me on a bad day, as it happened, as I was still battling to get my health back. I declined, explaining how I had already worked myself ragged doing various things for charity over the past year. I couldn't understand why she was making so much fuss about it, so I knew there was something going on. Ginette only repeated, 'I'm just saying I really believe it's something you should do, I think it's something that will be good for you. Robbie Williams did it last year so it's a very good thing to do. Just *do* it, Martine. Make sure you get yourself a lovely frock and then sing like you've never sung before.'

Ginette was up to something, for sure. Anyway, a few weeks later, the day of the charity concert arrived. I went along to the church for a rehearsal and everything seemed fine although the acoustics were a bit weird. The sound was delayed because of the cavernous interior and everything seemed to reach my ears long after the words had left my lips. I'd left my dress, make-up and everything else back at my flat which was only twenty minutes or so from the church. After rehearsals I told the organisers I was just popping home to get changed and that I would be back shortly. Oh, Martine!

You see I'd been having a bit of trouble with the front door of my apartment. The door handle on the inside kept dropping off but the porter at the block had checked it out and everything was supposed to be fine. As I left the church I checked my watch and saw that I had an hour and a half before I was due to perform.

I rushed back to the flat determined not to be late, only for disaster to strike. I tried to unlock the door but it wouldn't open. This is very bizarre, I thought, wiggling the key about. Now, Martine, you're not doing what you do when you get pissed, are you? You're not on the wrong floor trying to break into the wrong flat? Yes, I'd done that before, I admit it. No, this was definitely my flat but the bloody door would not open. I dashed down to the porter and explained my situation. He said he'd call a locksmith to get me in. Great. Meanwhile Mum, Jonathan and Jonathan's aunt and cousin turned up and each took it in turns having a go at opening my door, to no avail. It would have made a great TV comedy but time was ticking on. I didn't have long enough to hang around for the locksmith otherwise I would risk missing the show. I decided I'd wasted enough time and headed back to the church.

When I got back to St Luke's one of the organisers smiled at me as I arrived all hot and sweaty from dashing here, there and everywhere. 'Hi, Martine, if you want to take your outfit and stuff downstairs to get changed . . .' I must have looked terrible. When I caught myself in the mirror I saw the black baggy tracksuit bottoms, a puffa-type jacket and a black polo neck. I didn't have a scrap of make-up on, either. By now everyone who had bought a ticket to the show was taking their seats and I'd not even warmed up. As if worrying about what I'd wear wasn't enough, I kept trying to figure out what Ginette had been setting me up for.

I asked Jonathan to try and blag some make-up from his aunt or my Mum and off he scuttled. It was hilarious – I watched him as he whispered my request to his aunt, who then whispered the same request to his cousin, who passed the message on to Mum who told Jonathan that all she could offer was a lipstick. That got a few others in the congregation involved and a few minutes later I peeped and saw this pink floral make-up bag being passed from one person to another while some poor bugger was trying to read poetry to the restless audience as part of the show.

Jonathan passed the bag on to me. I checked my watch. I had about five minutes to show time, tops. Well, I tore the bag open only to find a whole bunch of pink and blue eye shadows, blushers and so forth that wouldn't have looked out of place in Aunt Sally's collection. You know Aunt Sally? Wurzel Gummidge's friend, played by Una Stubbs? This bag was just stuffed with every shade of pink and blue you could imagine. Still, it had to be better than nothing, I reasoned to myself.

I went on stage with pink cheeks, pink lips, blue eye shadow and some mascara, giving Una Stubbs a real run for her money in the Aunt Sally stakes. I was only trying to give myself a bit of colour but I think, in retrospect, I went a bit overboard. I had nothing to change in to, so I kept on what I was wearing, minus the puffa jacket. Then I heard the compere, impressionist Rory Bremner make my introduction.

'It's my pleasure to welcome Martine McCutcheon here this evening,' he said, as I took a deep breath. 'She's going to sing "Perfect Moment" for you ... And here she is, Martine McCutcheon, everyone!'

I did my best to hold my head up as I walked on stage. Then, peering over the microphone – which was echoing like crazy – I felt I had to explain my appearance. 'Er, Hello everybody . . . as you can see I'm not my usual glamorous self tonight – but I just wanted to say thank you very much to the lady who lent me her make-up bag because you've really saved my life. I'm sorry about my clothes but I did have a really beautiful dress at home I was going to wear this evening, but unfortunately the handle on my front door has fallen off and I'm afraid I couldn't get in. However I'm trying to speak standard English, because as I'm in church I feel I ought to. Anyway, hopefully you'll like the song and you'll forget about what I'm wearing . . .'

Then the music started. I don't know what happened to the speakers but something must have done because I caught sight of Jonathan on one of the pews with his head in his hands trying not to laugh. I mean what else *could* go wrong? Mum, I noticed, had got her hands clasped together, praying no doubt for God to help me get through it. Maybe He was listening that evening because it all worked out fine in the end and I got a massive round of applause – I'd pulled it off, it seemed, despite all the trouble.

I didn't know that the actor Jonathan Pryce was watching the whole fiasco. Nor did I know then that he was to play Professor Higgins, the part immortalised by Rex Harrison, in the new stage version of *My Fair Lady*. He saw the whole thing and thought it all hilarious. Apparently he loved my voice and the good humour I'd employed to excuse my appearance.

He later saw the theatrical impresario Cameron Macintosh who was producing the show, and National Theatre boss Trevor Nunn, who was directing it, and said that they had to see me. It was only then that I realised why Ginette had been so keen for me to be there. She knew Jonathan Pryce was going to be in the audience and she also knew he was lined up for *My Fair Lady*. Her plan worked a treat, because a couple of weeks later she called me to say I had a meeting with Cameron and Trevor. 'You had better get those old soprano lessons in quickly because you've really got to be able to sing this,' she added. As it turned out I had no time to get any lessons in. I turned up at the National Theatre in late January wearing nothing more glam than my jeans and kicked off with 'Wouldn't It Be Lovely?'

It was the weirdest audition I'd ever been to. The two men started singing along with me. I could feel the excitement, the buzz they were getting. Then they asked me to sing 'I Could Have Danced All Night'. Oh no, I thought, here we go – this is the hard one. There's a bit at the end which is ever so high. As I was singing it I thought: Please God, let me hit this note, come on do it for me, do it for me. Again, maybe He was listening because I hit it perfectly. I could see Trevor and Cameron smile as if they were thinking that they had no idea I had this range. Nice one.

When I heard they wanted me for the part of Eliza Dolittle I was overjoyed. I couldn't believe it at first because it felt like one of my wildest dreams had come true, especially as I know they had considered some fantastic international stars for the part. The show will open in March 2001 for a guaranteed nine-month minimum run, first at the National and then on to the West End. After that there is already talk of taking it to America, but I don't want to tempt fate by thinking too much about that now.

My health, too, seems vastly improved. I've spent a lot of time reading various books and talking to experts to try and find the right diet because it strikes me that some people's body systems are more sensitive than others. One book in particular seems to have worked wonders. Called *Eat Right For Your Type*, it states that there are certain foods which react badly with some people's bodies, depending on what blood type they are. I followed some of its recommendations and found that I can eat some vegetables with no ill effects, but not all. If I eat the wrong foods for my blood type they can make me tired and bloated. I'm not that brilliant at following all the instructions but I've tried my best and I'm certainly very happy – not just with the effects it has had on my weight but also on my energy levels. I feel great. I met the opera singer Lesley Garrett at a tribute concert to the wonderful Dame Elizabeth Taylor in May. We got talking and it turned out she was following the same kind of diet. She looked full of health.

Just to let you readers know, I am not on a secret campaign to sell *Eat Right For Your Type*, it's just something that made me feel so much better. I must stress that I didn't follow this diet to lose weight, I did it because I wanted to live happily with myself and I knew something was wrong with the way I had been living, otherwise I don't think I would have been so prone to debilitating illness.

I'm very happy in my private life with Jonathan. Everything we do, whether it's intimate, sexual, or whatever, is still firmly based on the fact that we're friends first and foremost. I'm not saying that if we were to split up one day we'd find it easy, but we're too good for each other not to remain mates. We haven't got kids, we're not married, so it's not like we have to stick with each other like proper grown-ups, but at the same time we share loyalties and responsibilities. I wake up every day feeling so in love with Jonathan, it's wonderful. I'm the happiest I've ever been.

There were people, critics in the press, who mocked me for starting work on my autobiography at the tender age of twenty-four. I hope this book proves how shallow and twisted those cynics turned out to be. I wanted not just to entertain you, dear reader, but also to explain myself. No one has ever heard about my childhood until now. I hope my experiences prove that it doesn't matter how poor a start you get in life, you can still make it, that you can still be happy. No matter how successful you become, you will always have obstacles, but only you have the power to push them away.

I'm still hugely ambitious. I want to have a wonderful family and I will do so when the time is right. Of course, I would like to have a go at cracking Hollywood. I'm not saying I'd want to be there forever: I'm no fool and can recognise what a shallow existence it can often be. After all, despite all the glamorous faces I show the public, in private I like nothing more than running around in little Adidas trainers and big baggy tracksuit bottoms. Can you imagine what Hollywood would make of that?

Making it in show business is never easy, but if it's in your blood, you've got to give it a go. It is hard work. Dealing with the press alone is like riding a massive, uncontrollable machine. You buy your ticket and then you have to hang on for dear life. If it chucks you off, you must dust yourself down and jump back on again. It can be a thrilling ride at times and very frightening at others. If you never give it a go, you'll never know. This has been my story, but it isn't over yet. And remember, the great words of Barbra Streisand as Yentl: 'Nothing is impossible.' This has been my motto throughout my life.